Sandeep Chennakeshu

YOUR COMPANY IS YOUR CASTLE

Proven Methods for Building
a Resilient Business

SANDEEP CHENNAKESHU

Fedd Books
P.O. Box 341973
Austin, TX 78734
www.thefeddagency.com

Published in association with The Fedd Agency, Inc., a literary agency.

Cover Design by Deryn Pieterse

ISBN: 978-1-957616-04-9

eISBN: 978-1-957616-05-6

Library of Congress Number: 2022906629

Printed in the United States of America

First Edition 22 23 24 25 /6 5 4 3 2

To Sabitha and all the wonderful people
I have worked with over the past thirty years.

Table of Contents

CHAPTER SEVEN

The South Tower—Sales Channels Are Your Pipes of Sustenance 195

CHAPTER EIGHT

The North Tower—Execution Builds the Discipline of Success 229

Introduction

Most companies are not built to last. Is yours?

Companies experience constant disruption and change. New trends, technologies, business models, and operational models regularly emerge to produce new market leaders.

Mobile phones—the industry in which I spent the bulk of my career—reflect that constant disruption. The first mobile phones arrived around 1983.[1] They weighed nearly two pounds, were more than one foot long, and would run out of juice in thirty minutes. Despite being brick-sized, they could only make voice calls, and they were not secure. Almost four decades later, the modern mobile phone weighs six or seven ounces (about 20 percent of the original phone's weight) and fits into your pocket. Modern phones are used to talk, exchange email, text, browse the web, interact via social media, pay bills, navigate, take pictures, provide entertainment, and even remotely control your house and appliances. These phones last a whole day (and longer) on a relatively small battery.

As mobile phones have become more powerful and sophisticated, numerous companies have emerged as industry leaders. In the early 1990s, Ericsson and Motorola were the leaders outside of Japan. By the end of the 1990s, Nokia emerged as the undisputed leader. A decade later, Samsung and Apple took the lead.

Why do companies shoot to the top and then fall back to earth? Could this loss of leadership be due to complacency caused by the comfort of success, bad habits, dogmas, and bad decisions? In an excellent *Harvard Business Review* article titled, "Why Good Companies Go Bad," Donald Sull described these aspects as *active inertia*, "an organization's tendency to follow established patterns of behavior—even in response to dramatic environmental shifts."[2]

"In trying to dig themselves out of a hole, they just deepen it," Sull wrote.

Companies can fail if they do not take necessary action. They can get stuck in a mode known as "analysis paralysis,"[3] where they are incapable of making a move, frozen like a deer caught in a vehicle's headlights. And they can also fail if they take the wrong action.

Such was the case with the newspaper industry. Publications continued to soldier on without solutions to address the rise of online classified ads such as Craigslist and declining print circulation.[4] Facing continual cutbacks and reduced revenues, many publications remained committed to continuing to do the same thing and hoping against hope for a different outcome.

I do not know of a formula for leadership immortality, but I believe there is a method to building a company to be successful over long periods. You only have to look at great companies that have been around for more than one hundred years across a swath of industries—Boeing (aerospace), Coca-Cola (beverages), Colgate (dental hygiene), Ericsson (telecom), Ford (automobiles), Harper (books), Harley-Davidson (motorcycles), Johnson & Johnson (pharmaceuticals and medical), John Deere (farm equipment), Lloyds (insurance), Siemens (industrial), UPS (shipping and receiving), and Whirlpool (home appliances), to name just a few. How have these and other companies survived two world wars, depressions, recessions, and a host of other disruptions?

Yet for every enduring company, there is a slew of companies that fail and disappear. The U.S. Bureau of Labor Statistics states that approximately 20 percent of new businesses fail in their first two years, 45 percent in five years, and 65 percent in their first 10 years.[5]

Through my research, experiences, and lessons from mentors, I have developed a framework with which companies can fortify themselves to withstand storms and attacks—those visible far in the distance and those that arrive by surprise, both internal and external.

But it is not enough for companies to simply guard against threats. Companies need to be proactive and vigilant, looking ahead and staying one step in front of competitors and disruptive trends. They need to be constantly considering threats and opportunities, strengths, and weaknesses. Running a successful company means being in a state of continual evolution, construction, and repair.

In the ensuing chapters, I describe my framework of eight elements that contribute to the growth, evolution, and resilience of a business. Whenever my teams and I have implemented this framework, we have realized amazing results in far shorter periods of time than anyone predicted.

A Framework That Builds a Company

My team needed to achieve the ultimate turnaround, and fast.

It was 2003, and I was in Sweden, tasked with reversing the fortunes at Ericsson Mobile Platforms (EMP), a business division of Ericsson that built semiconductor chips and software for mobile phones.

EMP was bleeding cash and had microscopic market share; it had fallen to the rear of the supplier pack. Its most formidable competitor was investing ten times EMP's operating budget. Customers were nervously anticipating that EMP would fail. The company owners were contemplating strategic options, while EMP tried to subsist from one quarter to the next and stem waves of negative publicity.

It was a great opportunity to put my framework to the test.

When the head of EMP's board met me and offered me the position to run the business, I took it because EMP had incredible talent and technology, and I felt confident we could turn things around. The board wanted to know what I would do to save the business. I got the feeling that they had mixed emotions about me. I was known as a technologist and not a general manager. I understood products—but did I understand finance, strategy, sales, and building stakeholder value? I also had to relocate from the United States to Sweden, and there was the question of whether I would be a cultural fit. I got the job thanks in part to strong endorsements from EMP's largest customer and the chairman of its board.

I was ready for the challenge. It had taken twelve years of watching and learning on the job, aided by excellent mentors, before I had a framework for how to manage a business, but by the time EMP needed me, I had the experience to tackle the problem.

At EMP, the challenges—and thus, opportunities—were clear.

The second-generation, or 2G, cellular technology had stalled out, and the world was anxiously awaiting the launch of 3G cellular technology. If EMP could be the first to launch 3G cellular technology, the payoffs would be immense.

The challenges were to launch our 3G cellular technology in cellphones, make the business grow profitably, and reverse the negative sentiment held by customers and investors. The board did not set a specific timeline for the turnaround, but I felt we had less than a year before it would be too late. With this ominous, self-imposed deadline, I laid out a simple plan to turn EMP around.

My plan had three goals:

- Establish viability: turn profitable in one year.
- Get noticed: be the first in the world to launch 3G cellular technology (platform).
- Build momentum: sell one hundred million platforms, which would translate to a six-fold increase in sales, in three years.

The board and my team accepted this plan. The next step was to deploy my framework to achieve these goals.

My framework began with creating a vision for the company based on a comprehensive view of the market and its trends. This vision led to the formulation of a winning *strategy*.

The strategy drove the creation of winning products for our addressable market (*product creation*). Next, these products had to be delivered to the market on time, at the right cost and right quality (*product delivery*).

Even the best products do not just sell themselves and must be marketed and distributed through *sales channels*.

Furthermore, *execution* of the strategy required operational excellence across the company, which is achieved through rigor and discipline. Additionally, the *culture* of the organization had to be aligned—if culture and strategy clash, culture invariably wins. If you cannot align the culture with the strategy, you will not win.

Stakeholders—investors, customers, and employees—must have confidence in the company. That *stakeholder confidence* is reflected in their commitment to the company. Waning stakeholder confidence is the fire alarm that something is amiss.

Finally, the company must have a sound business model that can keep generating cash, which lays the foundation and creates the *financial fitness* to realize and pay for the above elements and fund evolution, as none of the elements are static.

The terms highlighted in italics above comprise eight essential elements of building a sustainable business. I like to visualize them in the form of an impenetrable castle, symbolized in Figure 1.

Rich and successful kingdoms built magnificent castles and forts. While castles and forts are strictly different, I will treat them as one and the same in this book. Castles were built to be resilient to attacks. Castles represented power. Many of these structures have been around for hundreds of years, weathering many attacks and the assault of nature.

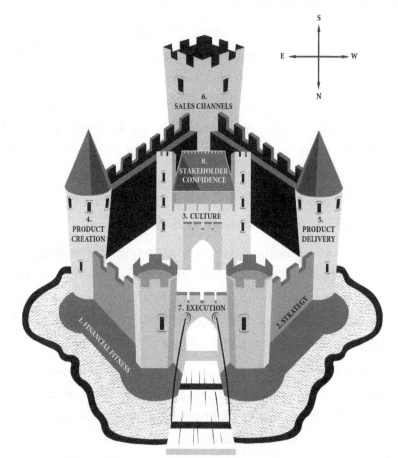

Figure 1: Framework of the Elements of Your Castle

Castles, which served as homes to the nobility and their citizens, have varying sizes, shapes, and appearances—each castle, like each business, is unique. But they all have similar, interlinked elements that must work together to maintain the integrity of the structure if the castle is to stand the test of time.

In Figure 1, I have used the following castle structures to symbolize different elements of a company.

Foundation

1. Financial Fitness: the business model of the company and the cash it generates, upon which the company is built.

Perimeter or Curtain Wall

2. Strategy: this frames the entire company and determines how it is built and armed with advantages.

Keep or Donjon

3. Culture: the heart of a company; it is the core structure within the castle that serves as the last line of defense.

Towers

These four towers are connected by the perimeter wall; together, they help protect the business:

4. Product Creation

5. Product Delivery

6. Sales Channels

7. Execution

Roof

8. Stakeholder Confidence: this protective cover results from the trust and belief that a company builds with its investors, customers, and employees, and is essential for a company's longevity.

The castle's construction begins with the foundation upon which the rest of the castle is built. It can take a long time to build a castle or company, and renovations and improvements are a constant process. Without a strong foundation, it is unlikely that a castle or company can reach true magnificence. The work you do to ensure that your company's financial foundation is sturdy—which I explain in the first two chapters of this book—may seem tedious, dry, and even banal, and while it largely remains hidden from view, it is vital to ensuring your company's success and should not be overlooked.

Before building the castle, we need to assess if the foundation can bear the weight of the grand structure we plan to build upon it. The outline of this structure is the perimeter wall—the strategy that frames the company's direction and progress. At the center of this structure is the keep—the culture and beating heart of the company. Enclosing the whole, the towers—product creation, product delivery, sales channels, and execution—are connected by the perimeter wall and protect the castle against enemy attacks.

The roof, which takes the form of stakeholder confidence, provides shelter against nature's elements. Stakeholder confidence occurs when investors drive up the company's market capitalization through demand for shares, customers buy a company's products and fill its sales pipeline, and current and prospective employees want to work for the company and give it their best.

It is important to make sure all eight elements work to reinforce each other to contribute to a balanced and successful business. When one or more elements of the castle are weak or stressed, they are more likely to collapse, allowing attackers to infiltrate the castle. Imagine a company with great products but weak sales channels, or one that is a market-segment leader but disconnected from its customers, or one with brilliantly designed products that are not delivered on time or with acceptable cost and quality. Such companies are likely to lose share to a competitor. When each of the elements is equally strong, the castle has a higher chance of withstanding the winds of change and attack.

The castle's location should be chosen, and its structure built to see any approaching threats well in advance, so the company can proactively prepare for an attack. Furthermore, for a castle to thrive, it must innovate and evolve. If a castle was eternally occupied defending itself, putting out fires, and rebuilding damaged walls, it would have little time or money to innovate, evolve, and stay ahead of potential invasions. If, on the other hand, the castle was prosperous, it could strengthen its defenses, build new weapons, grow its armies, increase its trade, and thereby bolster its ability to expand its domain and wealth.

While castles are essentially defensive structures, they represent a home base. The castle's armies might launch attacks and capture other territories. In doing so, it is important to build new castles to guard that new land. Defensive tactics need to align with offensive tactics.

Context and Design of This Book

My personal journey began in India. After receiving my bachelor's degree in engineering and a management diploma, I went to Canada on a fellowship to pursue a master's degree. During the 1980s, while studying for my MS in Canada, I read about mobile phones and the work at Bell Laboratories. I was captivated and came to the U.S. to pursue a PhD in this area.

After my PhD, I joined General Electric Corporate Research and Development, where I built a research team that worked on emerging mobile radio systems. Ericsson funded our research work for a few years and ultimately bought out my group. Seven years later, I became the chief technology officer (CTO) of Ericsson Mobile Phones, then the CTO of Sony-Ericsson, then president of Ericsson Mobile Platforms. I held executive roles at a few well-known semiconductor and software businesses before turning to management consulting and helping exciting start-ups grow.

During this fulfilling career, I was privileged to lead innovation; build products; and run wireless, semiconductor, and software businesses. My teams pioneered and built many amazing products, including three generations of cellular phones and technology (2G, 3G, and 4G); Bluetooth; semiconductor chips for consumer and medical electronics; and safety-critical software used in cars, nuclear power plants, high-speed rail, and medical appliances. I could not have wished for a richer experience.

Along this journey, I kept getting picked by management to fix difficult business problems and was fortunate to repeatedly deliver results, thanks to my incredible teams. Maybe this is why a journalist at the *Economic Times* gave me the moniker, "Dr. Fix."

Companies I've worked with experienced the highest of highs—as well as some disappointing lows. Analyzing what they did right to rise and what went wrong to lead them to fall was an experience itself. On this journey, I've found that reflection on failure is as valuable as celebration of success.

As a management consultant for multinationals, start-ups, and investment firms, I've gained a wider view on the problems companies face and an *outside-in* look at company operations. This perspective has been useful—when you are too close to the trees, you cannot see the forest.

Vision alone does not build a successful company. Many of the facets and details in building and running a successful company are ignored when companies opt for speed over steady and systematic construction of business elements—failure rates, hence, are alarmingly high. A Forbes article from 2018 cites a statistic from the Small Business Administration (SBA) that only one in three businesses survive ten years.[6] In this same article, the author cites that CB Insights did post-mortems of one hundred businesses on why they failed, and the top five reasons were: 1) no market needs for the product, 2) the business ran out of money, 3) the business did not have the right team to get the job done, 4) competition, and 5) pricing without market knowledge. Many of these pitfalls can be avoided if one builds a company systematically, with structure and prudent processes, to deliver on the vision. This is the focus of my book.

My book does not rely on any patterns or magic formulas—just solid principles and proven recipes that, if taken to heart by readers, will help them build strong businesses and in turn build themselves into strong leaders.

I have written this book primarily for those who aspire to be business leaders and are in the process of learning to build and run different elements of a business. Business students pursuing BBA and MBA degrees, including those who want to get an executive MBA, will find the book useful, as it ties business theory to business practice. Investment professionals looking at companies to back can gain an *inside-out look* into the various facets of a company that drive long-term growth and profitability. I liken assessing a company from just its financial statements, models, and management commentary to the assessment of an iceberg without sonar. It is hard to verify something that is not visible to the naked eye. It is my hope that the information in this book will serve as the sonar. Consulting companies will also be able to use the outlined principles and models to analyze companies and assist their clients.

The principles presented are applicable to small businesses as well as larger established businesses, which are more likely to experience *active inertia* when faced with new technologies, challengers, and radically new business models. Furthermore, this book is about principles and does not attempt to provide solutions, as each solution must pertain to a company's unique situation. However, the principles and recipes I describe can help you formulate the right solution for your company.

This book also focuses on for-profit companies. Non-profit companies, which provide many needed and valuable contributions to our world, operate differently and often rely on donations and government funding instead of maximizing cash flow.

Throughout this book, I interchangeably use the words "firm," "business," and "company." Treat them as the same. I share stories from my career as illustrations. In these stories, I have masked names and some aspects to protect privacy and confidentiality.

Many of the examples I offer pull from my experiences in the technology industry—primarily with cellphones, electronic devices, semiconductors, and software. It is what I know and can relate to and speak to with authenticity. While this is a limited lens through which to address a very broad variety of businesses, the lessons from these experiences in technology are applicable to other business fields.

I hope my framework will inspire you to build successful business structures, just as I was fortunate enough to do. More importantly, I hope it will guide you to build your company like a sturdy castle, to stand tall, and to be magnificent.

1

The Castle's Foundation
Financial Fitness Is What Matters Most

Chapters one and two are intimately connected. In this chapter, I will describe *what* is critical to establish a company's foundation, and in the next chapter, I will go into steps on *how* you can build that foundation to be strong.

Motte-and-bailey castles probably originated around 950 A.D. and could be built relatively quickly using earth and wood.[7] The motte was a large mound of piled earth upon which a fortified residence, the keep, was built. These structures were mainly defensive in nature. The bailey was an adjoining protected courtyard, where people lived and worked. It contained homes, chapels, stores, kitchens, barracks, stables, and workshops such as a forge.

The motte was the foundation. It was hard to haul large stones up the tall mound. Furthermore, due to their weight, heavy stones would sink in the earth that made up the motte. So, these castles were built with timber, which was readily available from nearby forests. Timber rots with time and can catch fire during an enemy attack. Therefore, not many of these castles survived, except for those that were later rebuilt at a significant expense using stones. A motte was relatively small, and so the castles built on them were also small.

In contrast, many magnificent castles were built high on hills that provided both a solid rock base to lay a foundation on and could also serve as a strategic vantage point against enemies—high ground. Thus, location was key. Take the Amber Fort, Mehrangarh Fort, and Chittor Fort in Rajasthan, India.[8] They were all built on hills upon a solid rock base. My favorite is the Amber Fort, built about 1,500 feet high on the Aravali Hills close to Jaipur in India.[9] This large, stunning structure occupies an area of one kilometer by three kilometers and was built in 1592 with sandstone and marble. The Amber fort has survived multiple generations of invaders largely due to its location.

A strong foundation is an often-overlooked aspect of a business, but it is also the most important. A castle built on a sturdy foundation can rise taller and taller, looming over its surroundings like the Amber Fort. But build a castle on an unsteady foundation or with poor materials, and it is liable to lean, sink, or collapse in on itself.

Likewise, a company that excels at generating ample free cash with a sticky business model has a higher chance for expansion and growth. Stickiness is akin to a castle's unassailable location, while generating ample free cash is the strength of the castle's foundation. Conversely, when a business has a displaceable business model and is unable to reliably generate free cash, it is more susceptible to disruptions from competitors, changing industry trends, and global macroeconomic impacts.

The following personal examples remind me of the value of cash and stickiness.

When it comes to my household, I know what I earn, my bank balance, and my credit-card limit. These are the sources of cash to cover my family's needs. If my wife and I did not have enough cash, we would not be able to fund our children's education, our retirement, and our daily living needs. Thus, cash has always been a necessity and priority.

I have been a customer of Bank of America for thirty years. To switch to another bank, I would have the inconvenience of opening new accounts, transferring money, changing my PIN number, my online bill payments, and the direct deposit of my paychecks. Furthermore, I have a rapport with the bank's customer service team, who help me with transactions such as international wire transfers, loans, and handling discrepancies in bill payments. Over time the bank has sold me mortgages and life insurance. Their investment arm manages some of my investments and gives me estate planning advice. They have given me credit cards with nice cash-back benefits. It would be very hard for me to switch to another bank, and there's really no reason to do so. This is stickiness.

These two criteria, ample free cash generation and stickiness, have also helped me in complex transactions.

Several years ago, an investor group was interested in buying a publicly listed company for billions of dollars and taking it private. They hired three consultants through our consulting firm to provide an analysis of the company—to protect confidentiality, I won't describe the products this company sold.

Their original plan was to buy the company by borrowing a lot of money (and taking on debt). Upon analysis of the company's financial outlook, products, and market position, however, it became clear to me that the company would not generate enough cash to pay the interest on its debt, let alone keep the business alive. This company would instead hemorrhage cash. I also concluded that the company's business model was not sustainable due to the power and momentum of its competitors' products. I was sure that if the investors proceeded with their original plan, they would fail.

We made two suggestions.

First, we suggested that the investors should not take on heavy debt to buy the company and take it private. Second, we suggested that they consider a change in the business model. To make this change, the company had to switch from selling their core products (devices), which generated high revenue but low profit margins, to selling non-core products (software and services) in their portfolio that generated lower revenue but far higher profit margins. The switch in model was motivated by the fact that the core products with high revenue were losing share, and the competition was gaining on them. Meanwhile, as this happened, the non-core products with high profit margins were growing in revenue. This switch in business model was a big decision and, frankly, radical.

These two suggestions followed my core tenet. The viability of any company must be based on embracing a sustainable business model that generates ample free cash. The investors took our advice and decided to keep the company public. The company, to its credit, also changed its business model and became profitable.

Free Cash Flow

Free cash flow determines a company's health and financial fitness. If one thinks of a company (or a castle) as though it functioned like the human body, then cash flow would be the company's lifeblood. Blood flows through the human body, carrying oxygen and nutrients to organs that help maintain bodily functions. When the body is starved of blood, bad things happen. The same is true with cash and a company. When a business is starved of healthy cash flow, it is difficult to invest in the company's growth.

In the Appendix, I describe how free cash flows in a company. For now, the important thing to remember is that free cash flow depends on several business parameters, such as revenue, gross margin, operating expenses (OPEX), capital expenses (CAPEX), working capital, debt repayments, interest payments, and taxes.

A general manager's goal is to optimize these different parameters to maximize the resultant free cash flow. Since free cash flow is dependent on these parameters, it is a diagnostic indicator of how a business is managed. This is the reason I use it as my key indicator of the health and strength of a company.

In summary, free cash flow is a measure of financial fitness because it funds day-to-day operations, gives investors the confidence to lend the company money, enables the company to pay interest on money borrowed, helps the company to weather periods of uncertainty, and allows for investments that help the company grow.

Golden Rule

If free cash flow is a key indicator of business health and fitness, then how much of it should a business generate? Is there a metric or rule that one can use as a guideline? There is. I will provide a simple guideline here that serves as my Golden Rule.

Tina, an entrepreneur, had dreamed of having her own toy and game store since she was a young girl. She founded Tina's Toy Shop, a small business, by borrowing $1 million from a bank at an annual interest rate of 5 percent, with the obligation to pay back the principal after ten years. The interest rate is the cost of borrowing money for this small business. The bank expects to get $50,000 in interest payments every year. Let us say Tina's Toy Shop makes a profit from its operations of $60,000, after taxes. This profit can be used to pay the interest on the loan, leaving $10,000 left over. Let us call this the toy shop's *retained earnings* or savings. On the other hand, what happens if, due to an economic downturn, the toy shop makes a profit of $30,000 in one year? This profit is less than $50,000, and the toy shop cannot make its full interest payments unless the owner dips into the company's retained earnings or savings. If this imbalance continues for more than a year, the bank is going to get worried because the small business may not be able to meet its interest payments or repay the money lent and may default. To be solvent, the small business must generate more than $50,000 in profit each year to pay the bank and have money left over to run its operations. If it generates significantly more than $50,000, the bank would be happy and might even lend it more money to grow.

This is the *Golden Rule*—generate enough cash to meet all your financial obligations and bolster investor confidence to invest in your business. Next, let us quantify this rule.

Tina is very enterprising and has grown her business significantly by migrating to electronic and educational toys and games and building sales outlets in different countries. Her growing toy shop needs a lot more investment. Tina's Toy Shop raises money by issuing shares (equity) and using debt (bonds). The total value of Tina's Toy Shop, assessed by the investors, is called the *enterprise value* (EV). Investors in Tina's Toy Shop want a return on their investment just like the bank-charged interest. It makes sense that the return expected ought to be proportional to the enterprise value, because if Tina's Toy Shop grew in enterprise value, the investors would like a proportional share or return. The proportional return is expressed by a term called the *weighted average cost of capital* (W). This is the cost to Tina's Toy Shop of borrowing money. This cost is a weighted sum of the return rate expected by equity shareholders and interest payments to debt holders, respectively. Following this logic, the return expected by investors is the enterprise value multiplied by the weighted average cost of capital, denoted as EV x W. This is similar in form to the interest the bank charged on the loan it gave Tina's Toy Shop to get it started.

Free cash flow to the firm (FCFF) is the cash generated in a period from all the sales of toys at Tina's Toy Shop after subtracting the cost to make the toys, operating expenses (employee salaries, shop rents, utility bills, advertisements, etc.), taxes, and relevant investments (buying equipment for its toy-making factory). This resultant free cash flow is available to the company to pay interest on its debt, pay dividends to shareholders, and add to its cash balance, which can be used to invest in new initiatives. Thus, the FCFF represents the net return on investment by the toy shop.

In this example, EV x W is the *expected return* investors want for their investment in the toy shop, and FCFF is the *actual return* the toy shop generates, which is a measure of its financial performance.

Therefore, the Golden Rule, which offers a key standard to a business leader, is to make sure that the free cash flow to the firm, or FCFF, *exceeds* EV x W. Simply put, a company must generate more free cash than the return investors expect on their investment. This is a well-known formula in finance, and the one I use to assess if my business is financially fit.

This rule applies to most companies in the market. There are exceptions to this rule, such as numerous start-ups whose valuation and success have not depended on free cash flow but on eventual value creation. But at some point, these companies must meet the Golden Rule to continue to be valuable, unless they get acquired.

This Golden Rule has been on the top of my mind ever since an executive of the Ericsson Mobile Platforms (EMP) board asked me point blank, "Why should I continue to invest in EMP?" He continued by saying, "If I invest the same money in corporate bonds, I will get a 7 percent return on my money each year rather than losing money every year, as I do by investing in your business. Please tell me you are sitting on a diamond mine and that it is just a matter of time before you will justify my investment and patience."

I heard his message loud and clear. I needed to be able to tell him what was in it for him—and the answer needed to be at least 7 percent annually on what he invested in my business.

Such wake-up calls are unnerving, but needed. If necessity is the mother of invention, survival is the father of rapidly aligned priorities.

First, I struck an opportunistic deal with my largest customer. They traditionally paid a per-unit fee (royalty) for using EMP's technology in their products. I offered them a lump-sum fee for one year to use EMP's technology in an unlimited number of their products during this period. This model was like an all-you-can-eat lunch buffet for a fixed payment. The customer accepted the offer happily because if they sold more products, they would pay a lot less in royalties, which in turn would help their profitability. This model, however, gave me guaranteed and predictable revenue for that year. Hence, it was a win-win deal.

Next, I cut our operating costs to match our affordability based on the revenue. To do this, I had to let a third of our employees go. This was a difficult decision, as many of those employees were my friends and had worked with me for years. The powerful labor unions in European nations where we had operations were unhappy. However, after a rational discussion, they supported me because they realized that if the company failed, everyone would lose their job.

With fewer employees, I cut the number of projects we were working on and focused on one product. This was not a popular decision at the time. But in my view, if we did not launch our 3G product in one year, we were surely done.

Finally, my team and I scrubbed every cost in the company and reduced it to what was essential for day-to-day operations. Nine months later, we showed a profit and a positive free cash flow. We had built our foundation.

The turnaround in company profitability was morale-boosting, and we built on the momentum to grow our revenue and profits with a singular focus on positive cash generation.

Business Model

The business model determines how the company generates and grows its cash flow and whether that will be sustainable. I look at a business model via three factors:

- Stickiness: the ability of the business to attract and keep its customers.

- Operating leverage: the efficiency of the business to scale free cash faster than the growth of its revenue.

- Capability readiness: the critical functions of the company needed to sustain the business model.

Businesses that are successful enjoy product stickiness, generate high free cash flow, understand what capabilities improve their operating leverage or efficiency, and excel at those capabilities by having a solid foundation on which they can build success. Let us dive into these factors with some examples.

Sticky or Not

Stickiness is crucial to the sustainability of a company's business model, and a great example is the iPhone. Many users who are accustomed to the iPhone's user interface and have their applications and content available on it are loath to switch to another phone, learn a new user interface, and transfer their content and applications to a different device. The same can be said for Samsung Galaxy phones and the Android ecosystem they support, or for Xiaomi (also Android) and their ecosystem in China. The stickiness comes from having user interfaces, applications, content, and ecosystem that customers like and are used to.

A second example illustrating stickiness is the model used by large data-center operators (cloud computing) such as Amazon Web

Services (AWS), Google Cloud Platform (GCP), or Microsoft Azure. These large data-center companies offer platforms upon which companies can build interesting software applications and services. For example, several insurance companies offer their clients rebates for driving safely. The clients are asked to install a small dongle in their cars that can measure acceleration, harsh braking, time of day, and other data. The measured data is sent from the dongle via the client's cellphone to a data center, where clever algorithms profile the client's driving. Based on a set of rules, the insurance company can give clients discounts for good driving. This is an application of a relatively new rage—Internet of Things (IoT). IoT companies use these data-center platforms to build many such useful applications and solutions. In return, they pay the data centers a monthly usage fee for use of these platforms. Once an IoT company has built its solution on, say, Amazon Web Services, and has developed many applications on top of this platform and deployed them to thousands of customers, that company is very unlikely to transplant everything they have built and move to a rival platform. It is too disruptive to do this. This, then, is a sticky business model for the data-center operator.

I like to bake, and for years, I always purchased a brand of flour that my aunt, who taught me to bake, enjoyed using. One day, my preferred brand of flour wasn't available at the local grocery store, and I bought flour from a rival brand. To my surprise, the cake I baked was just as good. There went my loyalty. The switching cost to the new brand of flour was very low, despite the years of brand loyalty.

Stickiness determines the relative power of a company's products and business model to retain its customers in the face of competition. The higher the stickiness, the higher the reluctance of customers to leave the company's products, even if there are compelling alternatives, as the switching cost for the customer is just not worth it.

Note that stickiness does not necessarily refer to whether customers like the business model; it refers to the cost or pain of leaving the company's product or service. Making products and services sticky and evolving them to continue to meet customer needs raises the threshold for switching to a competitor.

In summary, products and business models that bring higher value to customers and are difficult to replicate or replace are stickier. Figure 2 illustrates a simple model I developed to assess the stickiness of my company's products.

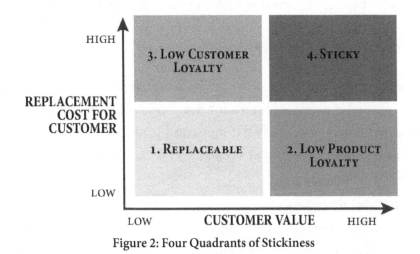

Figure 2: Four Quadrants of Stickiness

Quadrant 1 is where a product is easily replaceable because the cost for a customer to replace the product is low and the customer does not see much value in the product. These products are typically commodities that are widely available. Being in this quadrant is very risky.

Quadrant 2 is where the customer values the product highly, but the cost to switch is not high. For instance, the replacement product gives the customer what they value at a far better price. Two different pairs of branded shoes could be an example of a product and its replacement.

Quadrant 3 is where the customer does not love the product but finds it hard to replace. An example is a software application used by employees in a company for business-expense reporting. This application, though hard to use, is one that the company has rolled out extensively across their organization. Every employee hates the application, but the company sticks with it because the replacement cost to buy a new application and retrain all the employees is high. These non-user-friendly products often get dropped at the next refresh cycle.

Quadrant 4 is where you want to be. In Quadrant 4, the customer loves the product/business model, and the cost of replacement is high.

Operating Leverage – Business Efficiency

Operating leverage is a term used to measure the proportion by which your business profit increases for every incremental dollar of revenue earned. If revenue is the input and profit is the output, then operating leverage is output divided by input, which is nothing but business efficiency.

General managers need to understand the operating leverage of their business model. Otherwise, they may not understand the risks they need to manage to sustain profitable growth. When the business's capabilities are aligned to manage the risk, the model can thrive. If the business model and business capabilities are disjointed, the model often fails.

Let us say I am a small business owner, and last year, my business generated an annual revenue of $100,000 and a profit of $10,000. Let us look at two different outcomes for this year.

Outcome 1: My business revenue this year increased from $100,000 to $150,000, and the profits increased from $10,000 to $50,000, a gain of $40,000.

This case would represent *high operating leverage* because $40,000 out of the $50,000 increase in revenue was realized as profit. That is, 80 percent of the revenue increase was realized as profit.

Outcome 2: My business revenue this year increased from $100,000 to $150,000, and the profits increased from $10,000 to $15,000, a gain of $5,000.

This case would represent *low operating leverage*, because only $5,000 out of the $50,000 increase in revenue was realized as profit. In this case, only 10 percent of the revenue increase was realized as profit.

What is the reason for such differences between the two cases? The answer is fixed and variable costs.

Profit is revenue minus costs—fixed costs and variable costs.

Fixed costs do not depend on the number of goods sold. For example, operating expenses (OPEX) like employee salaries, benefits, and rent for office space are fixed costs.

Variable costs, on the other hand, vary with the number of products sold and resulting profits. Cost of goods sold (COGS) and taxes are variable costs. Consider a business that builds and sells decorative wood frames for artwork. Each piece of the decorative frame is made from wood on a machine. The frame is assembled from the pieces using nails and glue. It is then painted. The raw materials are wood, nails, glue, and paint. The cost of the raw materials, the manufacturing of the frame using the machine, and the painting of the frames are collectively called cost of goods sold. As more of these decorative art frames are purchased, the cost of goods sold increases proportionally. Similarly, as the business's profit increases, it pays more in tax.

Next, let us evaluate two different businesses to understand the relationship between operating leverage and associated risks.

Business One: Smartphones

Our first business builds and sells smartphones.

- This business sells its smartphone for $600.

- The cost of goods sold for each smartphone is $420.

- Hence, the gross margin is $180 ($600 minus $420) or 30 percent ($180 divided by $600).

- The business sells ten million phones for a revenue of $6 billion.

- The operating expenses (OPEX) of this business are $1 billion.

- To make our calculation easy, let us assume that the tax on profits is an artificial 10 percent.

The profit of this business is calculated as follows.

Parameter	Value in Millions
Revenue	$6,000
Cost of Goods Sold	-$4,200
Gross Margin	$1,800
OPEX	-$1,000
Operating Income	$800
Profit after Tax (10 percent)	$720

Now assume this business builds and sells an additional five million phones at the same price of $600. Typically, cost of goods sold per phone will go down with higher volume of units due to purchasing power, but in our example, let us assume it remains the same. To accomplish selling the extra five million phones, the business invests in its sales channels and salespeople and spends more marketing dollars. Let this additional OPEX be $200 million. The new profit would be calculated as follows.

Parameter	Value in Millions
Revenue	$9,000
Cost of Goods Sold	-$6,300
Gross Margin	$2,700
OPEX	-$1,200
Operating Income	$1,500
Profit after Tax (10 percent)	$1,350

In this example, the revenue grew by 50 percent, from $6 billion to $9 billion, and the profit grew from 12 percent ($720 million) to 15 percent ($1,350 million) of the revenue. I would classify this as a low operating leverage business.

This is still a very profitable business, and as the volume of smartphones sold grows, so does the profit. However, as its volume grows, so does its costs. As a result, the risk in the business grows due to two factors:

- The business has increased its OPEX (fixed costs) from $1 billion to $1.2 billion) to invest in sales channels and salespeople. Therefore, the volume of smartphones sold must grow to bring in more revenue to offset the $200 million growth in fixed costs—otherwise the profit will drop.

- Every negative deviation in cost of goods sold is amplified by the additional volume of smartphones sold. That is, if you have a $1 increase in the cost of goods sold, you stand to lose fifteen million phones times $1, which is $15 million. A smartphone has several hundred components that need to be purchased and requires complex manufacturing. Therefore, a $1 deviation per phone on a $420 cost of goods sold is not uncommon. Thus, this smartphone business requires very good management of its supply chain and manufacturing processes to control its cost of goods sold (variable cost).

Semiconductor chip and electronic device companies (e.g., televisions, smartwatches, cameras, tablets) operate similarly to this smartphone business. Many service businesses, like restaurants, also fall into this category because as their revenue grows, so does their variable cost (cost to provide the service).

Business Two: Intellectual Property Licensing

Our second business licenses patents in return for fees (monetary payments). Clever people invent things that could be of use to others. These inventions are protected by patents. When others want to legally use these inventions, they take a license to the patent that protects the invention. The license gives the licensee the right to make, use, and sell products that include the invention. In return for this benefit, the licensee pays the patent owner (licensor) a license fee. This can be a lumpsum amount or a royalty, which is a payment for every unit of the product they sell.

Patent licensing is a very complex business with many factors to consider. However, for illustrative purposes I will simplify how we calculate the operating leverage for this business.

This business invested in research and development for years to come up with novel inventions and then patented the same. It has 10,000 patents in its portfolio. The cost of obtaining and maintaining a patent over its life (20 years) is in the range of $20,000 to $60,000.[10] This number goes up if the patent is enforceable globally. So, it is only fair that if others want to use the invention protected by these patents, they should pay a fee to the patent owner.

The business licenses its patent portfolio for an annual fee of $10 million. It has 25 customers and therefore it earns an annual revenue of $250 million (25 customers times $10 million each). Let us assume these patents are valid worldwide and the average cost of maintaining a patent is $1,000 per year. Therefore, the annual maintenance fee for the portfolio is $10 million (10,000 patents times $1,000 per patent). This maintenance cost is part of operating expenses (accountants treat this as an amortized expense).[11]

The business incurs an additional OPEX of $40 million a year for research and development, patent attorneys, their tools (computer systems), licensing activities, and administration expenses. Finally, for simplicity we will assume that in this patent licensing business there is no cost of goods sold.

In summary:

- This business has an annual revenue of $250 million.

- The annual cost of goods sold is zero.

- The business has operating expenses (OPEX) of $50 million per year ($10 million for patent maintenance and $40 million for additional operating expenses).

- Again, to simplify our calculations we assume that the tax on profits is an artificial 10 percent.

The profit of this business would look like this.

Parameter	Value in Millions
Revenue	$250
Cost of Goods Sold	-$0
Gross Margin	$250
OPEX	-$50
Operating Income	$200
Profit after Tax (10 percent)	$180

This business doubles its revenue by adding new customers, and making its patent portfolio even more attractive. However, in doing so it gets rid of some patents that are uninteresting and replaces them with new patents that clients find very valuable. In doing so it keeps its patent maintenance cost the same. However, it increases its OPEX by $10 million to $60 million by investing in additional research and development. The business profit now looks like this.

Parameter	Value in Millions
Revenue	$500
Cost of Goods Sold	-$0
Gross Margin	$500
OPEX	-$60
Operating Income	$440
Profit after Tax (10 percent)	$396

In this case, the revenue grew by 100 percent ($250 million to $500 million), and the profits grew by 120 percent (from $180 million to $396 million). This is because there is no cost of goods sold (variable cost), and the additional OPEX (fixed cost) did not increase linearly with the additional revenue. This means most of the extra revenue earned from patent licensing flowed to profit. Such a business has high operating leverage.

Businesses with high operating leverage provide a higher return or profit with incremental revenue. This company's revenue and profits will grow as its licensee (customer) base grows. Therefore, to increase its profitability, it is essential for this company to grow its licensee base every year. This means it must invest in making its patent portfolio attractive to customers, and it must excel in closing patent deals by signing licensing contracts. However, in doing so, the company must manage the growth of its operating expenses to ensure these costs do not dilute the profits.

Many software and content-generation companies have a similar high operating leverage model.

So, which model is better? Both models are fine if you understand

and manage the risks in sustaining achievable efficiency in each. This risk management depends on the critical capabilities the company needs to have to make their model work and thrive.

Capability Readiness – Lions, Leopards, and Cheetahs

The capability of your company must match the needs of its business model. If it does not, you are in trouble.

Let us take a closer look at our lower operating leverage smartphone business in the previous section. To manage this business model, the company must be disciplined and capable of:

- Managing large and often rapidly changing variable costs and
- Ensuring sales targets are always met to keep the company profitable.

If revenues fall or there are supply chain disruptions that cause variable costs to increase, then the company can see serious drops in profits, especially if it has high fixed costs. Therefore, these businesses must be adept at managing costs and excel in operations and execution.

On the other hand, for our high operating leverage intellectual property licensing (patent) business to continue to grow profitably, it must constantly find ways to

- grow the attractiveness of its patent portfolio to drive larger licensing revenue opportunities; and
- be very efficient in controlling fixed operating costs, so that its larger revenue numbers are offset by only small increases in cost, meaning it can continue to generate the high growth in profits.

Thus, each model relies on critical capabilities and skills within the company to maintain or improve its operating leverage. In business one (smartphones), it was the capability to grow revenue and manage variable costs (cost of goods sold). In business two (intellectual property licensing), it was the capability to grow licensing revenue and manage fixed operating costs.

The following analogy, while stark, explains the relationship between business model and capability. Lions, leopards, and cheetahs are all big cats, but they hunt differently because their physical attributes are very different. The way they hunt prey (their business model) is based on their capabilities.

Cheetahs are lithe and hunt smaller antelope like the Thomson's gazelle. To eat, cheetahs must be faster and more agile than their prey. In India, cheetahs used to prey on the Indian gazelle (chinkara). When this antelope vanished from their hunting grounds, the cheetah vanished as well.

Lions live in prides and need a lot of meat to feed the members. So, they hunt larger animals like zebras, buffalo, and wildebeests. Hunting large and strong animals requires both power and teamwork.

Leopards are not as strong as lions or as fast as cheetahs. They use stealth to hunt. Their enormous forebody strength also allows them to carry their prey into the canopies of trees, keeping their food source out of the reach of lions, wild dogs, and hyenas. If challenged by these other animals on the ground, leopards would have to give up what they caught.

Cheetahs and leopards cannot go after buffalo. They would not survive a close encounter with a one-ton animal with horns and hooves. In some sense, each of these big cats has honed its capability to make its business model—its survival—work.

Similarly, in the corporate world, when a company has a business model without the capability to manage that model, its financial fitness invariably weakens over time.

At EMP, we designed and sold platforms comprised of semiconductor chips and software. We were very strong in designing chips, software, and system engineering. However, we lacked the ability to manage the complex operations of semiconductor manufacturing and packaging and logistics for customers around the world. We did not have the capacity or the money to invest heavily in these capabilities—and if we had invested, it would have increased our fixed costs dramatically and reduced our profits.

Therefore, we decided to partner with companies that excelled in semiconductor manufacturing and supply chain management. Since our partners built and supplied chips (designed by us) to our customers, they kept a larger share of the profits. So, we had to change our business model. We decided to increase the value of our software and charge for it. In effect, we went from selling razors (semiconductor chips) to razor blades (software) at excellent margins.

Our software added tremendous value to our customers. It reduced their development cost and allowed them to get to market faster with their products. It also allowed them to spend their engineering efforts in areas where they could differentiate, such as with applications. So, they were willing to pay for our software platforms. This also made our platform sticky, as our customers invested considerably in building their applications on our platform. Since software has little to no cost of goods sold (variable cost), this new model dramatically improved our operating leverage and helped us grow profitably for a few years.

It is essential that each business assesses and evolves its business model based on its capability or adapts its capability to match its business model.

Summary: Financial Fitness
The Castle's Foundation

The foundation for your company, its financial fitness, is determined by the following:

- Having a sticky business model that can withstand potential dilution and disruption from the competition.

- Its ability to generate ample free cash flow to the firm (FCFF).

- Understanding what elements affect your company's operating leverage (efficiency) and how these elements must be managed to maximize this efficiency,

- Building and honing those capabilities that enhance your company's business model efficiency in order to drive higher profits and free cash flow.

This chapter focused on the location for your foundation—a sticky business model that generates cash. In the next chapter, I will teach you how to build this foundation, stone by stone, to be very strong. Each stone is a parameter that can be optimized to improve cash flow generation. We will explore how to do this via the Game of Taps.

2

Strengthen the Castle Foundation

Tune Your Business to Grow Cash

A lot of forethought and planning went into the construction of the foundation—it determined the shape, fortification, and size of the castle.

It was advantageous to find a strategic spot that featured shallow bedrock or rocky terrain. Hence, many castles were constructed on a solid vantage point, such as a hillside, or a key transport route, such as on the banks of a waterway, a bridge, or a mountain pass. Take the sixteenth century Lindisfarne Castle, which is located on Holy Island, just off the North Sea coast near Northumberland, England. The castle is built on a high outcrop of basalt and looks like it grew out of the rock itself.[12]

Similarly, the Nakhal Fort in Oman appears to have burst through a rocky outcrop of boulders some six hundred and fifty-six feet high.[13] This castle, said to have been built to protect an oasis and nearby trade routes, is irregular in shape because of its terrain.

Another example is the imposing Krak des Chevaliers located at

Tallah, Homs, Syria. This magnificent castle was built on a six hundred and fifty-meter-high natural citadel (hilltop) by the Knights of the Hospitaller Order of Saint John of Jerusalem between 1142 and 1271 A.D. as a stronghold in the defense of the Holy Land.[14] It was built to withstand a siege of up to five years.[15]

In the absence of a rock base, builders would dig deep and wide trenches. A typical practice was to remove as much earth from the ground as the size of the structure to be built upon the foundation. Some trenches were even flared at their bases to make the foundation broader, distributing the weight it would carry over a wider surface area. These trenches would be filled with stone, bricks, rubble, and gravel, and then mixed with lime mortar to form a solid foundation. There are claims that as metals like iron and lead became available, they were used in constructing stronger foundations.[16]

The bases of the perimeter walls above the foundation were often thickened and sloped. These structures were called batters or taluses. This architectural requirement meant that the foundation had to be appropriately sized in these areas. The taluses made it harder for enemies to use scaling ladders and movable siege engines (covered towers) to scale the walls. Enemies would use these covered towers to get close to the wall and then use a gangplank to get onto a castle parapet. The broad base of the talus ensured siege engines had to stop farther away from the main perimeter wall, where their gang planks wouldn't be long enough to reach the parapet.[17]

In Japan, a technique called burdock piling was used to construct the foundation, such as in the Osaka Castle.[18] The foundation was an artificial platform, several meters high with sloping walls, built with carefully cut and fitted large stones. No mortar was used. The cracks between the large stones were filled with smaller, chestnut-sized stones. This ingenious technique allowed the foundation to move during earthquakes.

Castle building was not always welcomed by locals, as the structures would one day be used to launch attacks. Therefore, building the castle in hostile territory required protection of the construction site from attack. One way of doing this was to enclose the construction area with a low wall that later served as an outer wall. Such was the case for the Beaumaris Castle at Anglesey, Wales, constructed in 1295 A.D. with local limestone, sandstone, and green schists.[19] Similar caution and protection had to be exercised along the supply route for stone and timber to be delivered from nearby quarries and forests to the castle.

Thus, building the castle foundation took a good deal of planning. A mistake in planning and execution could mean supply shortages or work delays due to an enemy attack, a collapsed wall, or other structural failures due to a weak or hastily built foundation. Any of these could result in a significant loss of time and money. Even worse, mistakes in planning could result in lost territory.

Tuning your business to generate more cash is no different. There are many parameters to consider and optimize.

When I begin assessing cash flow, I adopt a detective mindset. I want to understand what is behind every number.

You need to be invested in knowing what could go wrong, or what has gone wrong already, so you pursue leads; follow the paper trail; and ask the right people focused, diagnostic questions. If you get fluffy or indirect answers, you must find someone else who can help you uncover the facts and truth. The answers are always there. You just need to keep digging. It is important to get the answers firsthand. Seeing and hearing things for yourself removes the translation bias that can crop up when information passes from person to person.

This gumshoe detective work is especially crucial in situations like the one I faced when I took over EMP. How do you generate cash flow when you are not bringing in enough money through sales, and few are willing to lend you money? It is a tough spot for a company, the ultimate catch-22 situation.

Companies often find themselves in trouble because they do not know what to do. Once you have completed your investigation and an implementation plan has emerged, it is time to proceed with your plan without hesitation. There is no time for reflection or uncertainty and no space for the *active inertia* so common in companies that lose their way.

At EMP, I asked myself two simple questions to solve the problem of returning to profitability in one year: First, how much revenue and gross margin could the business generate? And second, what operating expenses could it afford? The equation was simple, and my focus was to balance revenue, gross margin, and operating expenses to get profitable.

When you need urgent and creative solutions, concentrate only on those parameters that directly influence your immediate objective. This mindset reminds me of Paul "Red" Adair, the famed oil-well firefighter who used explosives to extinguish long-burning fires—the blasts suffocated the flames by depleting oxygen from the air.[20] When Adair went to fight a raging fire, his energy and focus were devoted to one singular task, and he put his plans into action. He and his teams did not have time to be tentative or to worry about extraneous issues like the blame game around who caused the fires.

While putting out oil-well fires involves nature's elements, like water and air, the process of improving a company's cash flow centers on seven parameters that influence your company's foundation:

- Revenue
- Gross margin
- Operating expenses (OPEX)
- Working capital
- Capital expenses (CAPEX)

- Debt and unfunded liabilities

- Risk

It is interesting that 82 percent of small-business failures within the first five years of their existence are in part due to poor cash-flow management.[21] This affliction is equally applicable to larger businesses, just with a different failure statistic.

Game of Taps

Maximizing cash flow is all about tuning the above seven parameters optimally. To learn how to do this, let us play a game with a made-up medieval structure—The Game of Taps, which is illustrated in Figure 3.

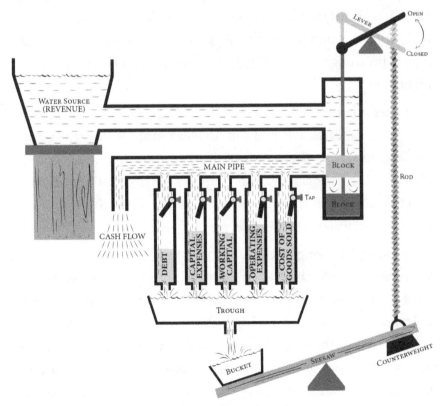

Figure 3: Game of Taps

This structure comprises a water source (large tub or tank) whose flow of water into the main pipe is controlled by a lever connected to a block. When the lever is in the closed position, no water flows into the main pipe, as the block covers the mouth of the main pipe. When the lever is gradually raised to the open position, the block moves downwards, uncovering the mouth of the main pipe and proportionally more water flows into the main pipe. The other end of the lever is connected to a rod that is fastened at one end to a seesaw. The seesaw has a bucket at one end and counterweight at the other end to balance the empty bucket in the equilibrium state.

The main pipe has a series of outlets, spaced along its length. Each can be opened or closed by a tap. If an outlet tap is opened (flap dropped), water flows from the main pipe via that outlet into a trough, and if it is closed (flap raised), no water flows from the main pipe into the trough through that outlet. As more water flows from the main pipe to the trough via the outlets, there is less water flowing out of the main pipe.

Water flows from the trough into a bucket. As this bucket fills up, its weight pushes the seesaw down, and the rod at the other end pushes the lever upwards. This increases the water flow into the main pipe. However, the lever can be pushed up to a maximum limit, at which point no additional water flows into the main pipe—this is the maximum flow of water into the main pipe.

The water flowing through this system of pipes represents cash. Water flowing into the main pipe is cash from sales (revenue). We want this flow to be as high as possible. Each outlet and its associated tap represent an element in a business that consumes and drains cash. This drainage is the water flowing into the bucket. As the bucket fills up, its weight increases, which in turn causes the seesaw to push the lever upwards, via the rod, and thus increase water flowing into the main pipe. This action signifies how cash spent (drained) helps increase revenue. The water that overflows from the bucket is wasted cash. The water that exits the main pipe is our much-needed free cash flow that we want to optimize.

The goal of our game is to adjust the outlet taps to maximize the water flowing out of the main pipe.

At one extreme, if you shut off the outlet taps, no water flows through them, ensuring nothing trickles down to the trough or bucket. Since there is no water in the bucket, the seesaw does not tilt downwards, and the lever remains in its closed position. This does not allow water from the water source to enter the main pipe, however. The result: no revenue (cash from sales) flow, and the main pipe is dry.

At the other extreme, if you open all the outlet taps fully, water flows directly to the trough and into the bucket, whose weight causes the seesaw to push the lever, via the rod, to its maximum open position. This allows the maximum amount of water to flow into the main pipe from the water source. However, in this case, most of the water from the main pipe flows via the outlets into the trough and bucket (which overflows), and very little water exits the main pipe. Therefore, neither of these extreme cases is optimal.

The challenge then is to find the *ideal setting* for each outlet tap to maximize the flow of water out of the main pipe. *This is what free-cash-flow management is all about.*

Companies that fail have invariably closed too many outlet taps (low spending) or opened them too much (exorbitant spending). Companies that thrive have found the perfect settings for the outlet taps.

Within this chapter, I am going to share how you can master the Game of Taps by increasing the inflow (revenue) and managing each outlet tap (parameter) to increase the water exiting the main pipe (free cash flow).

Three Cs of Revenue

Companies need revenue, and the more the better—just like the inflow of water into the main pipe in our example above. Revenue is generated by selling your company's products and services. This revenue generation is influenced by investing in three Cs (representing the control of the lever and attached block that allows water to flow into the main pipe):

- Coverage: refers to the ability of the company's products to address as many segments, shelves, and geographies of the available market as practical.
- Competitiveness: refers to having compelling products in each segment, shelf, and geography that can take market share.
- Conversion: refers to the ability of the sales team and partners to sell the company's products through the various channels to maximize revenue.

All addressable markets can be divided into two dimensions: geographies and segments. A geography is a defined area where you sell your product. Segments represent how you have mapped your products to customer preferences or categories. It is impractical to have one product that everyone will like or want. So, companies divide their products into categories based on user preferences or buying choices. Each of these categories is a segment. The company may further divide the segment into sub-segments. A sub-segment may be a sub-category such as a price shelf—a price range at which a product competes with similarly priced products.

The total available market, also known as the total addressable market, is the total of all products sold in every geography across every segment and sub-segment. The potential share that a product can take in a geography, segment, or sub-segment is dependent on its competitiveness and the effectiveness of your sales channels and sales team.

Consider laptop sales as an example. Laptops are sold to consumers and businesses. Within the consumer segment, there are sub-segments such as enthusiast laptops (high performance), mainstream laptops, fan-less laptops, and opening-price-point (or entry) laptops. Each sub-segment may have one or more price shelves.

Similarly, the business segment comprises two sub-segments: enterprises and small and medium business (SMB). Each of these sub-segments have different price shelves, depending on the specifications and capabilities of laptops sold into these sub-segments.

To visualize your business revenue and growth potential, create a map of every geography, segment, and sub-segment where you are selling your product. Next, assess how your products are doing in these geographies, segments, and sub-segments relative to the three Cs (coverage, competitiveness, and conversion). The results should diagnose your current revenue and highlight gaps to be addressed for revenue growth.

Let us consider a very simple example shown in Table 1. Our company sells its product in only one geography, the U.S.. The market comprises two segments, namely businesses and consumers. Each of these segments is further broken into two sub-segments, as shown in Table 1.

The percentage sales of products in each sub-segment relative to the total addressable market (100 percent) are shown in Table 1 as sub-segment share. For example, the enterprise sub-segment is 10 percent of the total addressable market, and the entry sub-segment is 50 percent of the total addressable market. The next two columns in Table 1 show the percentage sales within each sub-segment in the U.S. and the rest of the world. The dark-gray shaded region represents where our company sells its products—restricted to the consumer segment in the U.S.

Table 1: The Three Cs Diagnostic Map				
Segment	Sub-Segment	Sub-Segment Share	U.S. Share	Rest of the World Share
Business	Enterprise	10%	4%	6%
Business	SMB	20%	6%	14%
Consumer	Performance	20%	5% (40%)	15%
Consumer	Entry	50%	10% (20%)	40%

We begin our diagnosis by entering the adoption rate of our company's product in those cells in Table 1 where we sell our products. Let the white numerals in each cell in Table 1 represent the adoption rate for our company's product. Our company's product has an adoption rate of 40 percent in the performance sub-segment in the U.S. This means customers buy our company's product 40 percent of the time in that market. This generates a share of 2 percent (5 percent U.S. share times 40 percent adoption rate) in the performance sub-segment out of an available 20 percent.

If we repeat this calculation for the entry segment, where our company also sells products, it gives us a potential share of 2 percent (10 percent U.S. share times 20 percent adoption rate) of the entry sub-segment out of an available 50 percent. Adding up all our share numbers, we arrive at a measly share of 4 percent of the total addressable market (100 percent).

There are several observations one can make from this simple diagnosis.

We could grow our company's market share with the following options (increasing coverage):

- Expand sales in the U.S. for the consumer segment because we have only 4 percent out of an available 15 percent.
- Introduce new products that can be sold in the U.S. to the business segment, which is 10 percent of the market.

- Expand sales of our products to the rest of the world, which represents 75 percent of the market.

Next, our company needs to determine which option it should pick, build the right products, and market and sell these products to capture market share and grow its revenue.

Another observation from Table 1 is that our company has a 40 percent adoption rate in the performance segment in the U.S. but only half this adoption rate (20 percent) in the entry segment. A likely reason for this difference in adoption rate is that our company's products in the performance sub-segment are strong, but in the entry sub-segment they are weaker than competitors' products. This points to weaker competitiveness that should be analyzed and addressed. It could also mean the sales channels selling these cheaper entry sub-segment products are not as effective (conversion issue).

Such a diagnosis, while overly simplified, can help you drill down into each of the potential issues inhibiting share gain in the three Cs, highlighting what you must do to improve your revenue.

In subsequent chapters, I will explain how to create a methodical process with actions to systematically close the gaps via strategy, product creation, sales channels, and execution. During this investigative phase, you are uncovering the core issues to be fixed to improve cash flow, not seeking to implement changes or corrections.

Quality of Revenue

Not all revenue is created equal. Revenue generated by natural demand for the company's products and services suggests the company is doing well. Sometimes, companies can fill revenue shortfalls with certain undesirable tactics. When revenue is adulterated by these tactics, the quality of revenue drops. This is a warning sign that the company has issues.

Let me provide some examples of how revenue can be adulterated.

- Channel stuffing
- Buy-outs and buy-ins
- Prepaid project fees
- Factoring

Channel stuffing [22] means selling products into sales and distribution channels even when there is no natural demand. This has two negative effects: first, it means that the accommodating buyers (e.g., distributors) may require discounts and additional payments (for advertising or sales incentives) to move the products they are carrying; and second, it may reduce demand and revenue in future financial quarters. Further, if distributors can and do return the product, the revenue then must be reversed by the company (assuming the company uses sell-in accounting, which I will explain in chapter seven).

Buy-outs come into play when customers pay for software or intellectual property (IP) via per-unit royalties. To secure immediate revenue, the company offers the customer a buy-out, which is a lump-sum payment at a discounted price; thereafter, the customer stops paying ongoing royalties for use of the IP. This tactic dilutes true revenue due to the discounts and can affect future revenue streams, especially if the prepayment is recognized as revenue all at once. *Buy-ins* are another form of lump-sum pre-payment for using the company's software or IP across *a fixed number of units* sold by the customer. Buy-ins also carry discounts and are lumpy, impacting future revenue streams. Buy-outs and buy-ins differ in the number of units that are prepaid.

Some companies get upfront payments, or *prepaid project fees*, for projects they may execute for their customers. The companies usually amortize these payments based on work completed and delivered to the customer. These deals can be restrictive when it comes to how or where the company can use or sell the resulting work product. If a company uses these pre-payments to fill shortfalls in its revenue, it signals that the demand for the company's major products is not meeting expectations.

A company may sell its accounts receivable to a bank to get cash quickly. This is called *factoring*.[23] Accounts receivable refers to products sold for which the company has not received payment. The company must typically wait thirty to ninety days after the product sale to collect cash from customers. As such, some companies in need of cash sell the accounts receivable to a bank that will then collect money from the customer. In the meantime, the bank pays the company somewhere between 80 to 95 percent of the value the customer would have paid the company. That is, the bank charges a commission fee between 5 and 20 percent to provide immediate cash to the company. This commission fee dilutes the company's true revenue and cash flow by 5 to 20 percent. Companies that use factoring either have long payment terms given to their customers or are short on cash to run their operation.

Bottom line: Focus on improving the three Cs, and whenever possible, avoid the dilution of future revenue or cash flow. While such revenue-adulteration tactics are used when companies desire meeting quarterly targets, it is a dangerous game and should not become a habit. When a company regularly relies on these tactics, it means something is fundamentally broken.

Gross Margin – Product Mix and Cost

Gross margin is revenue minus the cost of goods sold (COGS). In businesses that sell tangible goods like television sets, COGS is made up of component and manufacturing costs. For service businesses like house painting, it is the cost of materials and providing the service. Pure software businesses that create and sell software have little to no COGS—if they have any, it is engineering services to support software sales. Hence, optimizing cost of goods sold is probably most impactful to those businesses selling tangible goods (devices), where COGS is a major determinant of the gross margin.

Cost of goods sold is an expense and the first outlet on our main pipe. You want to adjust the tap on this outlet such that the water flowing out is as low as practical. The water (cash) that flows past the first outlet down the main pipe is called *gross margin*. A healthy gross margin allows you to spend more on product creation, product delivery, and sales to improve your revenue and profits.

Most semiconductor companies operate with a gross margin of 50–60 percent, some even higher. This level of gross margin is necessary to invest in engineering, sales, and marketing if they want to compete and grow their revenues. These operating expenses are around 30 percent, leading to 20–30 percent operating income. This healthy operating income allows the companies to invest further, building and acquiring new technology to strengthen their product leadership. In 2006, I was recruited to lead one such business at Freescale. The gross margin was a tad under 35 percent. If we were to spend 30 percent on engineering, sales, and marketing, our operating income would have been below 5 percent, leaving little for investment.

I made a simple calculation to determine the impact of COGS reduction on our gross margin. I realized, using my calculation, that at 35 percent gross margin, my COGS was 65 percent, and every 1 percent improvement in the COGS resulted in a 1.85 percent improvement in gross margin. The business I ran at Freescale had an annual revenue of $2 billion; therefore, if we improved our COGS by 1 percent, we would generate $37 million ($2 billion times 1.85 percent) in additional gross margin.

To understand whether your company's gross margin is healthy and acceptable, compare it to that of your competitors. You can determine this from their financial statements or by performing cost-breakdown analyses of their products. There are many consulting companies that provide detailed breakdowns of such costs, called *tear-down analyses.*

If your gross margin is lower than your competitors, then you must dig to uncover why.

- Do you have a price or product-mix issue?
- Are your products costly to build?
- Do you have hidden inefficiencies in your operations?

In businesses I have run, common issues that impacted gross margin related to price and product mix were:

- Features being added during development of the product that increased the cost.
- Features being dropped to meet timelines, meaning the product could not command the projected sales price.
- Poor product-portfolio management, where we introduced high-volume, low-gross-margin products that weighed down the gross margin of the entire portfolio.

When there are price- and product-mix issues, I go into detective mode—I want to understand whether these are systemic or one-off events. To get this insight, I ask the following questions:

- What is the company's record of achieving the projected gross margin for approved products? That is, what did we say we would do, and what did we deliver?
- What caused us to miss projections?

Any trends that emerge from this analysis point to a systemic issue—a critical problem holding your company back from maximizing its profits.

Next let us consider COGS again. In competitive markets, the leader sets the price of products in a price shelf. To compete, your products must be competitive at this price shelf. If your products are not competitive, you will be forced to sell your products at discounts, hurting your gross margin. Therefore, if you cannot control price, you must focus on reducing COGS to optimize your gross margin. This logic led me to remind my teams with a favorite slogan: "The market sets the price, and we control cost."

I use a systematic way to reduce COGS. I identify every department that influences product cost, called cost-control centers. For example, in businesses I ran these cost-control centers were typically:

- Product management
- Research and development (R&D) or engineering
- Purchasing
- Manufacturing
- Quality (warranty and returns)
- Repair services (including labor)
- Finance (operational adjustments)

Next, I determined the following for each cost-control center:

- Is it cost-focused?
- Does it have clear cost achievement targets for each product?
- Does it have a roadmap with milestones for continuous cost reduction?
- Does it have dedicated people working on cost reduction, and are these people measured by how well they achieve those targets?

Ensuring that this framework is harmonized across all cost-control centers can transform a company's mindset and behavior when it comes to cost management.

Having my answers to these questions and determining what needed to be fixed, I resorted to four very powerful techniques to reduce cost:

- Bring awareness and understanding to each cost-control center on the value of cost reduction and set clear metrics for each center to achieve in each increment of time (typically one month).

- Coach the employees in each cost-control center on how to achieve cost reduction through *value-based engineering.*

- Have monthly progress review meetings and highlight the achievement of each group toward the common goal. Make sure targets and achievements are highly visible to the entire team. This creates healthy competition amongst the cost-control centers.

- Celebrate success by making cost reduction as valuable and visible as other achievements such as a product launches, customer wins, innovation, or filing a patent.

Value-based engineering, as its name implies, involves changing the way something is done to get larger savings. It means investing time and even money to improve your products and/or efficiency to get higher savings.

My first example of value-based engineering is from the late 1990s, when my group was building cellphones. Each phone had a printed circuit board. These circuit boards had screw holes drilled on their periphery to attach them to a metal frame. The manufacturing team found we could save fifteen cents for each circuit board if we stacked them four high instead of three high while drilling. The cost saving came from being more productive. Drilling four boards versus three resulted in a 33 percent increase in productivity for that step.

But this change required us to make the drill bit wider to drill through four boards. Our design team was okay with this change, as there were no drawbacks to the integrity of the product. This small change on fifteen million boards meant $2.25 million in savings.

A second example of value-based engineering involves software products. Our company's software was built from the ground up using many interworking modules. The company's design team found that many software modules, if modified, could be reused among products. I liken this to the LEGO™ model. LEGO bricks come in standard sizes, but they can be used to build a variety of amazing structures. The modification added a one-time cost but secured much larger savings since we could reuse modules between software products.

Finally, inefficiencies in business operations hurt your gross margin. To diagnose this issue, I enlisted the help of my finance team to scrub every financial line item that contributed to gross margin to uncover such inefficiencies.

These efforts helped me uncover something called *Operational Adjustments*, essentially a catch-all bucket of cost-adders such as warranty-reserve variations, inventory-reevaluation variances, yields not being achieved to target, scrap, and obsolescence. These items can get a bit technical—for instance, inventory reevaluation occurs when a business has a lot of inventory of material, and the purchasing department does a great job at reducing the price of material. Inventory that has not been converted into a product and sold is now reevaluated at the new lower prices. The difference in value, which is a loss, goes into this Operational Adjustment bucket. Scrap and obsolescence occur when one has inventory that cannot be used or resold back into the market.

Shockingly, these adjustments can account for hundreds of millions of dollars. Having identified this bucket, we can focus on improving it. In one business, we reduced these adjustments from $400 million to $25 million by improving our operational focus.

If a business is not run tightly, then this Operational Adjustment bucket grows and dilutes gross margin. This is one of those line items that never has a champion. It grows from an amalgamation of deviations from the plan by several departments in the business.

Cost reduction and gross margin improvement are a matter of focus and how much effort you want to spend on them. When you focus on them, the results will surprise you.

Optimize Your Organization

Every company has operating expenses. This is the second outlet on our main pipe. If the tap on this outlet is opened wide, there is less water flowing further down the main pipe, as much of the water flows into the trough via this outlet. However, if this tap is shut to maximize the flow of water down the main pipe, then less water flows into the trough and bucket. Recall from Figure 3 (Game of Taps) that our mechanism is such that if the bucket remains light, with little or no water, it does not push the seesaw down, and subsequently the lever is not opened to allow water flow (revenue and hence cash) from the water source into and out of the main pipe. Hence, there is a delicate balance.

In businesses I ran, operating expenses (OPEX) were categorized into three big buckets:

Operations (Ops)
- Product management
- Research and development or engineering
- Program management
- Purchasing
- Supply chain
- Manufacturing

- Quality
- Service and repair

Sales & Marketing (S&M)
- Sales
- Marketing

General and Administration (G&A)
- Finance
- Human resources
- Legal
- IT (Information Technology)
- Administration

These operating expenses include salaries and benefits for employees, rent for buildings, utilities, furniture, equipment in labs and on desks, telephones and cellphones, travel, coffee, food if subsidized, and material consumed by the various functions.

One way to reduce operating expenses is to reduce headcount and cut perks. This should be a last resort because it is people who create value in a company. I generally focus on efficiency before resorting to headcount reduction unless it is unavoidable. The following three principles helped me assess the efficiency of an organization.

- **Principle One:** Determine what a reasonable allocation of operating expenses is as a percentage of revenue for comparable companies and assess if you are spending more or less than they are. Determine where and why you are over- or under-spending to assess if adjustments are needed.

  One should never allow optimistic revenue projections to justify overspending. Rosy revenue estimates may lure one into allowing higher operating expenses to be budgeted. This is dangerous because if one does not hit upcoming revenue targets, the extra spending can dilute profits and lead to a loss. Costs should grow with realizable revenue and gross margin expansion. This may be a chicken-and-egg problem. One solution is to invest prudently and see if you are achieving the projected return. If not, be prepared to trim expenses. You can use efficiency ratios or metrics from well-run companies that are in your space to provide benchmark spending levels. These ratios can be calculated from financial statements reported by these companies. Alternatively, one can use published benchmarks from studies and reports.[24]

- **Principle Two:** Assess the organization by its *span, depth,* and *employee-experience* profiles.

Span refers to how many people report to each management layer. The optimal span depends on the type of business and functions within the business. Metrics from studies and reports by consulting organizations are useful guidelines for assessing if your organization has an efficient span. Span should not be about increasing one's power and exercising control in an organization. It should be designed to exert the maximum awareness and influence on your organization to improve the efficiency of working.

Depth refers to the number of management layers in the company, from the individual contributor to the highest management level. Flatter organizations tend to be more efficient, especially if they are empowered.

Next, it is important to assess the profile of the employee population in each department by the level of experience. This distribution will vary with each business and its strategy, but a top-heavy (highly experienced)—or, at the other extreme, an inexperienced—workforce will usually be less effective.

A top-heavy resource distribution will cost more, and experienced members may leave or retire, creating major gaps in your resource pool. On the other hand, an inexperienced workforce may be cheaper but may not deliver the desired outcome, which is ultimately more costly as non-performance hurts revenue. Therefore, a healthy distribution in workforce experience needs to be maintained. I like a 30:40:30 distribution—30 percent very experienced, 40 percent in the mid-range of experience, and 30 percent relatively fresh recruits.

- **Principle Three:** Evaluate all the business's sites in terms of ownership and accountability.

As a business, it is advantageous to have global sites, which brings many benefits, such as better cost balance across the workforce, diversity of thought, proximity to customers, and time-zone productivity. However, it is critical that every site has a clear charter (something meaningful that they own and deliver) and grows to be a center of excellence. Each site needs to own and deliver something complete (a product, a module, or a sub-module) for which they are accountable. This creates focus, encourages ownership, and builds competence. When you have geographically distributed and sub-scale sites, each with partial or unclear responsibility, you will be forced to do a lot of extra planning and coordination between sites, which increases cost and reduces efficiency. The lack of meaningful work and ownership also leads to an inability to attract and retain talent. Proper site design can increase efficiency and reduce costs.

These three principles should be managed in tandem with human resources (HR) or talent-management partners to optimize the operating expenses as an affordable percentage of sales.

Working Capital – Recycling Cash

The third outlet on our main pipe in our medieval water structure is working capital. This is a pot of cash used to run the day-to-day operations of your business. If the working capital increases (more outflow from the main pipe via this outlet to the trough and bucket), it means more cash is being used, and if it decreases, less cash is being used. The more efficient a company is at using its cash, the better the free cash flow to the firm.

Charlie owns a business that sells fish at a local market. He rents a stall in the market and pays his workers each day to help. Charlie needs cash to buy fresh fish, which he does early in the morning to sell that day. By 5 p.m., all the fish has sold, and Charlie uses the cash from sales to pay for the day's expenses and buy more fish for the next day's operations. If this buying and selling cycle is regular and predictable, then Charlie needs enough cash to manage a one-day operation cycle to fulfill his working capital needs.

Likewise, a company buys raw materials from vendors, pays them, then uses these raw materials to build products. Next, these products are stored as inventory until sold. Expenses such as rent, utilities, employee wages, and taxes must be paid during this period. When products are sold, the company can collect cash from the buyers and reuse this cash for its operational expenses, just like Charlie's fish market. The less cash you need over a given period, the more efficient your operation is.

However, companies generally pay vendors (accounts payable or AP) in forty to sixty days, and customers may only pay for goods and services (accounts receivable or AR) after thirty to ninety days. The timing of this payment of cash and receipt of cash makes things a bit more complex when calculating working capital needs. Only after the company collects cash from customers can it replenish the pot that was depleted to pay for raw materials, manufacturing services, and other expenses like wages, rent, utilities, and taxes. Unless it replenishes its cash, replacing what it has spent, the company will not have cash for the next cycle of spending and may have to borrow more. An increase in working capital dilutes free cash flow, while a reduction in working capital improves free cash flow.

If a company is sloppy—buying a lot of material and holding a lot of inventory that does not sell, while having long payment terms afforded to customers—it is going to need lots of cash as working capital.

There is a well-known metric called *cash conversion cycle* (CCC)[25] that is useful to measure how efficiently your business is managing working capital—namely, how fast are you recycling your cash.

Simply put, CCC is the difference between the cash spent (out-of-pocket) and unspent (in-pocket) in running a business measured in days during a given period. You are out-of-pocket in cash when you build product, store products, and don't collect cash for sales. When you don't pay vendors, you have cash unspent and in-pocket. Let me introduce you to some specialized terminology used in calculating CCC.

Days of sales outstanding (DSO) represents how many days it takes to collect cash for products you have sold. DSO is calculated as the outstanding value of accounts receivable (AR) in a period divided by the average sales per day.

Days of inventory on hand (DIO) represents how many days cash is locked up by inventory that is not sold. DIO is calculated as the average inventory value in a period divided by the average cost of goods sold per day.

Days of payable outstanding (DPO) represents what your company has bought but not yet paid for. DPO is calculated as accounts payable (AP) outstanding in a period divided by the average cost of goods sold per day.

Therefore, CCC is calculated as DSO *plus* DIO *minus* DPO.

Assume, for example, a company has the following annual figures: sales of $1 billion ($1,000 million), COGS of $500 million, $250 million in average accounts receivable, $200 million in average inventory held, and $150 million in average accounts payable.

Therefore, the DSO is about ninety-one days ($250 million of accounts receivables divided by average sales per day, which is $1 billion divided by 365 days). Similarly, DIO is calculated as 146 days ($200 million of inventory divided by average COGS used per day, which is $500 million divided by 365 days) and DPO is about 108 days ($150 million of accounts payables divided by average COGS used per day, which is $500 million divided by 365 days). These numbers give us a cash conversion cycle of approximately 129 days.

This means the company turns its cash around in 129 days. This is relatively inefficient because it means the company needs enough cash to last 129 days. The lower the number, the better. As a rule, I tried to achieve forty-five days for DSO, thirty-five to fifty days for DIO, and forty-five days for DPO, leading to a CCC target of thirty-five to fifty days. Using this rule in the mobile-phone business and semiconductor businesses that I ran, a cash conversion cycle of fewer than fifty days reflected efficient cash management. A longer cash conversion cycle meant I needed more cash to fund my operations, and my free cash flow would drop.

Buy or Pay-As-You-Go

The next outlet on the main pipe is capital expenses (CAPEX), which covers where and how a company spends its cash and whether it is necessary. If a business spends large chunks of money periodically, it detracts from the company's cash reserves. During my career, I have made different choices to optimize the setting of the tap on this outlet.

One example involved an Internet of Things (IoT) business. We tracked cargo trailers. A small device was attached to the cargo trailer, and it measured and sent data (such as the position of the cargo trailers) wirelessly to a software platform hosted in a data center. The software platform analyzed the data sent and presented it to the user. The user could visually see where their assets (cargo trailers) were and determine how to efficiently schedule the availability of the trailers to be rented. When we built this system, we had two choices: build our own data center and cloud platform or use a Platform-as-a-Service (PaaS) offered by a major service provider like Amazon (AWS), Google (Google Cloud Platform), or Microsoft (Azure). These providers depreciate and amortize the cost of running their mega data centers, which host these platforms, over thousands of customers, and can offer attractive prices. If I had chosen to build my own mini data center to create an independent PaaS-like platform, it would have been far more expensive. This would have entailed high initial capital expenditure and periodic equipment and software upgrades, requiring more cash outlay. In contrast, by using a mega data center's PaaS offering, I would pay a fee every month for usage (cost of goods sold) and would not need to spend valuable cash (CAPEX) on equipment while incurring the associated upgrade and maintenance costs. In this case, a pay-as-you-go model versus the CAPEX model was far less expensive in terms of cash usage.

In a second business, as a device manufacturer, we had to conduct extensive tests on our products. We had to make the choice to either spend millions of dollars to buy equipment for our test labs or outsource the task to several competent third-party test labs. Again, this was a trade-off between capital expenses (CAPEX), which would be incurred buying the test equipment, and the fees needed to pay the third party. I was producing a large volume of devices each year, so I could depreciate and amortize the capital expenses of test equipment across this large volume of devices. It turned out to be cheaper for me to buy equipment for my own test labs versus outsourcing the job to a third party, whose costs to test each device were far higher because they had to make a profit as well. A secondary benefit of having my own equipment was that I could turn around test tasks a lot faster, as I did not have to wait for my turn at the third-party test lab.

The use of capital (cash) depends on the business and application. It is important to conduct an assessment to uncover whether the use of capital is efficient and which options provide the best savings in cash over the target period.

Debt and Unfunded Liabilities – Buoys and Sinkers

The last outlet and tap in our pipe system regulates the final drainage of water from the main pipe—that is, cash for debt repayment, interest and liability payments, and taxes. I will ignore tax, as that is a fixed setting (by the government), and focus on debt, interest, and liabilities.

Debt can be a great tool for financing a company, especially if it is cheap, acting like a buoy. It helps a company raise cash, which the company can use to invest, including buying other companies to grow.

However, expensive debt at higher interest rates reduces free cash flow to equity (FCFE) and retained earnings. Growth in retained earnings is critical to increase the cash reserves of the company to fund future investments in growth.

In one company, shortly after I was hired, we were bought out by a group of private equity firms. The transaction used our cash balance plus an additional infusion of cash from investors, and the rest, almost half the total cost, was raised as debt.

As a business, we generated a profit that was 25 percent of our revenue. However, 80 percent of this profit went to paying the interest on debt each year. So, we had little to invest in growing our business. Then, as luck would have it, a major recession hit, and our revenue and profit dropped. Paying the interest on debt became much harder, and we had to squeeze our operations to find every bit of cash. This further exacerbated the challenges we faced to invest in growth. It felt like cutting a tree while climbing it.

Each business has a different ability to afford debt based on its capability to pay interest and pay the borrowed money back to its lenders.

Sometimes, companies can secure cheaper debt using convertible bonds. These bonds are typically offered at lower interest rates because the bond owner can convert their bonds to shares (equity) in the company at a premium over the prevailing stock price, called the *conversion premium*. Convertible bonds are attractive to lenders who believe the company stock price will rise. However, these bonds may not be attractive to the company.

If a convertible bond is used, it is important for the company to consider a high enough conversion premium, and/or the potential dilution that existing shareholders may incur when the bonds are converted to shares (equity). With a higher conversion premium, there is a lower chance the stock will hit that value and for the bonds to be converted. If the bonds are not converted to stock, the company will not have to issue new shares (dilution) or pay out a lot of money to buy stock and transfer it to the bondholders (cash outflow).

The bottom line is that there really is no free lunch, and due care must be given to debt-based funding options.

Another major sinker to consider is unfunded liabilities, which are financial obligations that are not funded by the company. A common example of an unfunded liability is pension-contribution obligations that are not adequately funded. A second example is when a company buys another company and offers the acquired company a time-based *earn-out* payment if the acquired company can hit certain revenue targets, but the acquiring company is unable to meet this obligation with its cash position when the time comes to pay. In such a situation, the acquiring company may need to sell its assets or raise debt to pay up to avoid defaulting on the payment.

With each business I ran, one of the first things I did was analyze my debt and liabilities and create a plan to pay them off as soon as it was practical. Focusing on growth is far more rewarding than worrying about default and squeezing your business.

Managing Risk

Risk is not a tap but a potential break or leak in our system. If left unchecked, it can result in weak or no flow of water through the main pipe.

Risk is categorized as a combination of market factors (like macroeconomic events such as recessions) and company-specific problems. A major goal for you as a business leader is to demonstrate to investors that your company is well-run and has low risk. When your company excels in operations and its financial results are predictable, it is more likely to be assessed as less risky. The best you can do is mitigate risks as far as possible, planning and adapting when situations arise.

The approach I take to assessing the risks that could affect my castle's foundation—its cash flow and business model—is as follows:

- Categorize the risks my company or business faces.
- In each category, ask questions regularly to assess the risk.
- Address identified risks immediately with corrective actions.

- Follow up on the corrective actions every month until the risks are resolved.

The following are examples of categories and questions I use to assess risk. You can modify or expand on these for your own business.

Customer Revenue Risks

- Does the company have a concentration of a few customers who generate a high percentage (say above 30 percent) of the revenue?

- Are these major customers geographically dispersed or in one region (to assess how susceptible is the company to regional risks)?

- How resistant are the sales orders from these customers to macroeconomics or other factors?

- Do these customers have alternative sources of supply via competitors, and is your company's share dropping or rising when compared to these competitors?

- Does the company have a healthy sales pipeline to replace revenue from customers whose revenue is at risk?

- Does the company get paid for its products in one currency or several? If the latter, does it hedge for currency-fluctuation risk?

- Are the company's products still valued by customers? How sticky are these products to the customer?

Supply Chain Risks

- How resilient is the company's supply chain to disruption from its suppliers? In other words, does the company have geographic diversity of supply and alternative sources and alternative materials in its supply chain, to mitigate shortages, natural disasters, or regional or supplier-centric disruptions?

- Does the company buy all its products in one currency, and, if so, does it hedge for currency fluctuation risk?

Execution Risks

- How forward-looking is the company's roadmap? Could it be surprised by a competitor or disruptive trend?

- How reliable is the company's execution on *new product introductions* (NPIs)?

- How reliable are the company's sales-demand forecasts?

- How reliable is the company's fulfillment of forecasted demand?

- Does the company carry a lot of inventory for extended sales periods?

Capability Risks

- Does the company have all the skills and experiences needed to manage its business model? If not, how will the company rapidly address this?

- Is the company able to hire the best of the best for its business needs? If not, why not?

- What is the company's talent attrition for employees and executives, whether they leave voluntarily or are poached?

Legal Risks

- What are the pending litigations and claims made by other companies or third parties against the company?

- Does the company have good ethics and business practices, or does it often fall foul of the law?

Other risks, such as disruptions caused by natural disasters or changes in government regulation, also need to be considered and addressed. Unexpected events like the COVID-19 pandemic, which stunted businesses and disrupted our way of life when it spread across the world, need to be managed in unique ways. It is important to have processes in place to constantly assess risk so your company can shift and adjust its operating model when something like the pandemic happens. In response to COVID-19, many companies equipped and allowed people to work from home to avoid productivity loss.[26]

Managing risk is a science and an art—and it also helps you keep your detective skills sharp. It is best to review the company's risk-management plan every month to ensure all plans are in place to manage risk, with key executives responsible for each risk category.

Summary: Growing Cash Strengthening the Castle's Foundation

Building strong castle foundations involves many critical considerations and decisions. Likewise, there are seven parameters to optimize to strengthen a company's foundation (its cash flow):

- Grow revenue. Focus on improving the three Cs (coverage, competitiveness, and conversion) and the quality of your revenue.

- Improve gross margin. Review your gross margin against your competitors' and assess whether it is healthy. If it is lower, uncover why and work to improve it via the methods I laid out.

- Optimize operating expenses. Focus on organizational efficiency before reducing headcount and perks.

- Reduce working capital by optimizing your cash-conversion cycle.

- Spend judiciously on capital expenses. Assess the trade-off between a pay-as-you-go model and a buy model. Choose the option that improves long-term free cash flow.

- Avoid getting weighed down by debt and unfunded liabilities. Understand the impact on the company and create a plan to lower the dilutive effects that these parameters have on long-term free cash flow.

- Manage risk. Proactively assess risk categories that impact revenue, cash flow, and your business model. Set up mitigation plans and follow through every month, acting with urgency to close issues identified.

Having built our foundation, the next step is to build and fortify our castle perimeter wall in the form of strategy. The strategy wraps around all the elements of the castle and is based on critical choices. In the next chapter, I will share a practical way to build such a strategy.

3

The Perimeter Wall
Critical Choices Fortify Your Strategy

A castle's perimeter, enceinte, or curtain walls required forethought to ensure that the castle was built with protection in mind. Medieval builders used layer after layer of stone and mortar, sometimes more than twenty-feet thick, to ensure that the castle walls were able to withstand just about anything. The walls were typically constructed from limestone, sandstone (a composition mainly of quartz, some feldspar, and rock fragments), and granite, depending on the availability from nearby quarries.

Every measure in the construction was deliberate. Alcoves and arrow slits—also known as loopholes—provided guards an opportunity to fire down on invaders, as did battlements, in the form of protective merlons separated by rectangular gaps called crenels that lined the tops of walls. Soldiers could shelter behind the merlons and fire upon the enemy. There were also fortifications called machicolations, which were openings in the floor of a battlement or projecting parapet through which stones and burning objects could be rained on the enemy. The walls also had to be tall enough that they were not easily scalable.

A moat surrounding the walls further set the castle apart and made it even more impenetrable, while a drawbridge served as an access point used to welcome guests or, in case of an attack, to hinder or trap attackers.

The most intricate castles included a series of inner walls as protection, making them even more difficult to breach. Enemies could breach one wall and rush to the next wall only to be picked off by archers on top of these inner walls.

The size, scale, and scope of the castle walls meant they needed to be built directly on top of the foundation to ensure that they did not lean or collapse. Walls were also thickened near the base to provide stronger support.

Two of the most amazing protective walls ever built are the Great Wall of China and the one at the Kumbalgarh Fort in India. The Great Wall of China, stretching more than thirteen thousand miles, was built to protect China's northern border from invaders, and its average wall is around twenty-feet wide at the base and nineteen-feet wide at the top.[27] Passes, or strongholds, were built along the great wall at the intersection of key trade routes. The second amazing structure is the impregnable Kumbalgarh Fort, located about fifty miles from Udaipur in India. It is located at 3,600 feet above sea level on the Aravali hills with a perimeter wall that runs for twenty-three miles and is fifteen-feet wide.[28]

Your company's strategy, like a castle's perimeter wall, represents fortifications meant to protect against threats while serving as a structural bond between products, sales channels, and execution. Your castle is only as strong as its weakest point. Use cheap building materials, fail to plan ahead, or cut corners, and your strategic advantage is gone. Likewise, in business, strategy takes time to formulate and requires analysis and deliberation. Performing flimsy analyses, taking shortcuts, and failing to plan ahead destroy company strategies.

The goal in building a sustainable company is to grow profitably and increase cash flow. Strategy identifies which market opportunities you target, and it sets a framework for defining and building products and how they will be distributed and sold, all with the goal of generating revenue and cash flow. Cash flow is the end goal, but it is also the resource that will allow your company to innovate and do amazing things.

Castles often evolved and expanded. Take Windsor Castle, the oldest castle that is still a residence for the English royal family. It was initially constructed as a motte-and-bailey castle around 1070.[29] It was gradually replaced by a stone fortification. Henry III built a royal palace within the castle, and Edward III later rebuilt the palace to make it even more luxurious and grand. This palace evolved over time and has grown to occupy 448,000 square feet with more than one thousand rooms.[30] Another example is the Jaigarh Fort built high on the Aravali Hills. It was built in 1726 as a garrison to overlook and protect the existing beautiful Amber Fort, built earlier in 1592. The two forts, still standing and in good shape, are connected by a mile long subterranean tunnel and considered to be one complex.[31] Likewise, company strategies must constantly innovate, evolve, and expand to guard against current and future threats to extend the longevity of your business.

The first definition of strategy appears to have originated from military campaigns, epitomized by Sun Tzu's (circa 400 BC) famous book, *The Art of War*. Sun Tzu said, "All men can see these tactics whereby I conquer, but what none can see is the strategy out of which victory is evolved."[32]

If an army or company had infinite resources, namely money and people, it would not need strategy because it could try everything possible, and something would be bound to succeed. This is never the case. Every company has a finite amount of money to spend and a limited number of people to create, build, and sell products and manage the business. Hence, all strategies involve making critical choices.

Critical Choices – Open Spaces

When I moved to Sweden to run EMP in 2003, we were losing a lot of money, and I had about a year to convince our board and customers that we were a viable business. We were building third-generation (3G) mobile-phone technology that was going to be used by original equipment manufacturers (OEMs) such as Sony-Ericsson, LGE, Sharp, and others. Each of our customers gave us requirements that we had to meet. Their customers, who were cellular operators such as Vodafone, AT&T, Hutchinson, and T-Mobile, also gave us requirements. This meant that we received thousands of requirements.

Had we tried to address all the requirements, we would never have launched a product in time. We needed to strategize how would we make it within our one-year deadline. With little money, pressure to deliver, and stiff competition—our largest competitor was spending ten times more on research and development (R&D) than we were—how would we get there?

Our prospects looked dim.

But I was not ready to surrender, and neither was my team. Thankfully, we didn't have to.

My family and I used to drive to scenic Ystad, which was a short distance from Malmo, where we lived at the time. There, on a bluff overlooking the Baltic Sea, are fifty-nine large boulders, called *Ales stenar*, arranged in the shape of a boat. Each boulder weighs up to five tons. How the ancients raised those stones to such heights when there were no cranes remains a mystery. I marveled at this magnificent engineering feat. This was an inspiration to do something no one imagined could be done.

With *Ales stenar* as my inspiration, I formed a strategy based on answering three questions that ultimately identified our goals to win.

- How can we get global attention and engender the notion that we are not laggards but leaders?

- How can we beat our biggest competitor to the market, so they are caught off guard?

- How can we differentiate to win in a sustainable manner?

To get global attention, we needed to be first to market—without meeting that goal, we would not be able to achieve the other two. So, I focused on my most aggressive customer and one cellular operator in Asia who needed our technology the most. This operator was also closely aligned with our customer, both motivated to be first to market with our technology. This was the perfect match.

Next, to differentiate, I asked myself what my competitors would overlook? Most of the competitors were semiconductor-chip companies that did not have experience in building cellphones. My team and I had built cellphones and understood the pain points that had to be overcome.

The hardest problem to solve, for my customers, was how to integrate a variety of chips and software from different suppliers and make their phones work by testing these combinations across thousands of use-cases across dozens of network-equipment configurations deployed in the field. If we could unburden our customers from doing this monumental task, it would save their companies engineering expense as well as shorten their time-to-market. This was what we needed to do and was our *open space*—an uncontested area that, when addressed, brings enormous benefit to your customers. In some sense, the concept of open spaces is embodied in the words that ice hockey great Wayne Gretzky was told by his father: "Go to where the puck is gonna be, not where it was."[33] I would only add, "and get there first." The concept is symbolically illustrated in Figure 4 on the next page.

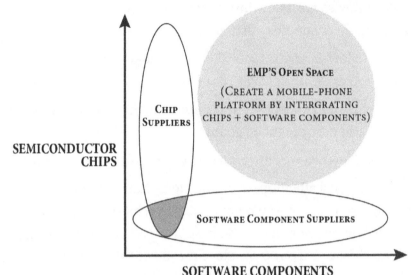

Figure 4: Open Space Illustration for What We Did at EMP

Our open space would be to create a platform for mobile phones that integrated all the required chips and software components. We would rigorously test this platform and make it work across the thousands of use-cases and cellular network-configurations in the field.

The final question I had to answer was, how would we create sufficient differentiation in our product that would act as our moat? Our differentiation had to create a more difficult entry into our castle.

The challenge with our open-space approach was that every customer needed a different software configuration. They all would use the same four chips we built, but the software for each customer was a bit different. This meant that every hardware and software combination had to be retested across our fifty thousand test cases before we qualified the platform to be shipped. This would be our moat. Our competitors were excellent at building semiconductor chips, but not at building software. So, we would build a software factory that could churn out a customized platform for a customer once per day, something only we could do because my team was very skilled in this area. So, our capability matched our model.

And then we had to convince our customers of our model and ask them to pay for software, which they were not used to doing. They paid for chips, and the cost of software was embedded in the chips. We chose to use a *total-cost-of-ownership* (TCO) argument. We convinced our customers that if they used our platform, they would save a lot of engineering costs and shorten their time-to-market, a major advantage in securing market share.

Fortunately, our strategy was successful, and we executed it perfectly, even though it was not easy. We launched our product, and it revived our company.

Other customers soon realized that if they adopted our platform, they would be selling phones in stores six months after we delivered our tested platform to them. Our product would shorten their development time by a year. This was the transformation they valued. We grew as more customers bought our solution. At our peak, we had 30 percent global market share, something we had never imagined a few years earlier.

Almost a decade later, I got the chance to implement the open spaces strategy again at BlackBerry in its division called QNX.

QNX

Many modern cars have more computer code than an F-22 fighter jet or Boeing 787 commercial airplane.[34] Some of these cars include as many as one hundred computers—from simple microprocessors that operate the automatic windows, to complex systems that control functions such as the transmission and engine—and feature more than one hundred million lines of code.[35]

QNX, owned by BlackBerry, is a premium supplier of operating systems and embedded software components sold into the automotive and other industrial markets.[36] QNX has long held a commanding lead in infotainment systems, the display in your car that shows you maps, directions, climate control, and radio functions. The infotainment market, however, was highly penetrated and growing at less than 3 percent per year at the time I was working at BlackBerry. Furthermore, the competition was entering this segment with alternative operating systems bundled with applications such as navigation maps. These competitors were bound to take share. As a team, we had to think of a new strategy to grow.

Talking to our customers, we realized that the evolving electronic architecture of the car would replace the many small, functional micro-processors with a single, more powerful processor that would control an entire domain comprising multiple functions.

As an example, the infotainment system and instrument cluster (which reveals mileage, odometer, fuel level, cruise control, and other information to the driver) are two functions in a car. Typically, each function has its own microprocessors and associated hardware. The instrument cluster must be accurate and can never fail because, if it did, it would be a safety hazard for the driver and occupants of the car. If these two separate functions could be made to run on one micro-processor and one piece of hardware, a car manufacturer would secure attractive cost savings.

This combination unit would be an example of what is called a domain controller. Thus, the evolving electronic architecture of the car comprising domain controllers created an open-space opportu-nity that would create a much larger addressable market than just infotainment for us.

However, for such a domain controller to work well, we had to solve a safety issue. Each function had to be isolated so that if a single function crashed, it did not affect the other functions supported by the same microprocessor. An infotainment system can crash and be restarted, but the instrument cluster just cannot crash. Imagine driv-ing without your fuel gauge or speedometer working.

Some of the finest software engineers and safety experts in the world were members of the QNX team, and they solved this problem elegantly. They received the most stringent safety certifications. This allowed us to evolve our business from one area to another, and this opened three times as many opportunities. Had we stayed in our comfort zone of infotainment only, our market share would have gradually whittled away.

These successful strategies did not happen by chance. They were carefully planned via a structured method called the ORCa model.

The ORCa Model

ORCa is my framework for creating a strategy and is illustrated in Figure 5. It uses three elements—Opportunity, Relevance, and Capability—to formulate a strategy based on answering the following questions:

- Does your strategy address a market *opportunity* that provides a good return on your investment?
- Are your products, based on your strategy, *relevant* to the market? That is,
  - Does the market *need* your products?
  - Can your company *differentiate* itself from the *competition*?
- Does your company's *capability* match your strategy?

Answers to these three questions provide the insights you need to create a strategy with a higher chance of success.

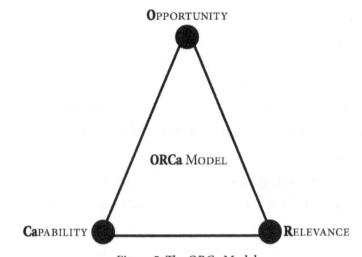

Figure 5: The ORCa Model

Opportunity Assessment – Casting Your Net

Assessing opportunity is a lot like finding the perfect fishing spot.

The ideal location is stocked with lots of fish, and there are not many others fishing there—you have the chance to explore different areas of the waterway and experiment with various types of bait and tackle.

But once you find the ideal spot and have the right equipment, you would not expect to spend your time fishing for minnows along the shoreline—no, you are seeking the best possible return on investment, a trophy bass.

You should be trying to catch something big. Otherwise, why bother scouting the location and buying the bait and tackle and waiting patiently for a nibble?

In business, opportunity lakes with a lot of fish are those created by:

- New trends
- Technology disruptions

- Unaddressed needs

- Business-model disruptions

New Trends

New trends provide opportunities in places where they did not previously exist. For example, in recent years there has been a massive migration of business data from private enterprises to public cloud storage. This data contains sensitive business and personal information that needs to be protected. This opportunity has given rise to a new category of companies called content-access service brokers (CASB, pronounced Kas-Bee).[37] These companies build software products that enforce strong security policies between consumers who want to access this data and the public-cloud-storage providers.

Another example is the opportunity for sensors and high-performance computers when it comes to autonomous driving. Humans use their eyes, ears, intelligence, and motor skills to drive cars. An autonomous car must mimic these human senses and skills. Companies are attempting to do this with sensors such as radar, cameras, lidar, and ultrasonics that sense and classify objects around the car. Then, powerful computers running artificial-intelligence software analyze the objects in relation to the scene and the car and send commands to drive the car via actuators. This object recognition happens in milliseconds. The human brain has the recognition power of performing around fifty million billion operations (yes, fifty followed by fifteen zeroes) per second while consuming very low power.[38] Imagine mimicking this with a computer. Such innovation has created a massive market for sensors, powerful computers, and intelligent software. This area will create a wide moat for those who find solutions.

The earliest online food delivery service for restaurant food appears to have started in 1922 by a Los Angeles-based Chinese restaurant called Kin-Chu—you placed an order via telephone and the restaurant would deliver as late as 1 a.m.[39] Yet, it is only recently that online food orders and delivery has exploded. Global online food delivery, which accounts for 40 percent of restaurant sales[40], is growing with a compounded annual growth rate of 11.5 percent and is projected to hit $154 billion in revenues by 2023.[41] This hyper-growth may have been triggered by lockdowns caused by COVID-19, but it is a trend that will grow due to its convenience, our changing lifestyles, easy-to-use apps on smartphones, and technology-equipped driver networks for delivery. Popular food delivery services include Uber Eats, Door-Dash, Grubhub, and Seamless in the U.S.; Zomato and Swiggy in India; Ele.me in China; FoodPanda, Just Eat, Deliveroo, and Hungryhouse in Europe; Shuttle Delivery in South Korea; Menulog in Australia; Demae-can in Japan; and Mr D Food in South Africa. This list has been growing steadily since 2014.

Anticipating new trends and intersecting them in a timely manner brings giant opportunities. It is like finding your ideal fishing spot. Once you begin to catch a lot of fish, you get noticed, and others join you at your spot. The likelihood of you catching the same number of fish rapidly diminishes.

Technology Disruptions

Technology disruptions change the status quo. A well-cited example is the emergence of the quartz crystal in the 1970s and its impact on the watch industry, which had previously relied on the hand-wound clockwork mechanism. Hundreds of suppliers in the watch industry were disrupted, and new leaders emerged.[42]

Today, quartz crystals are used in 95 percent of all electronic circuits, serving to provide a reliable heartbeat called a clock.[43] This clock signal is essential for smartphones, computers, and all electronic devices. Interestingly, this essential quartz crystal is now being challenged by small, silicon-based micro-electro-mechanical machines, or MEMs. This cycle of disruption is perpetual.

Mobile phones have been around for more than thirty years, and every decade a new leader has emerged. This is because every decade has brought a new generation of technology (called a standard), new customer preferences, and new use-cases. We are now in the fifth generation (or 5G) of mobile-phone evolution. New leaders emerge because they anticipate and adapt to leverage the changes faster than the incumbents.

For decades, the television industry used cathode-ray-tube displays (CRTs) that relied on electrons streamed to hit phosphors that produced red, green, and blue.[44] When the TV industry migrated from CRT displays to liquid-crystal displays (LCDs), the leadership changed. Companies like Philips made way for Samsung and LG.

More recently, artificial intelligence (AI) has gone from textbooks to real applications thanks to powerful computers that can run sophisticated algorithms. Take smart speakers (Amazon Echo, Google Nest, Bose, Sonos, etc.) that act on your spoken commands to implement "Skills or Actions" such as: place orders to purchase things; answer questions; control your home appliances, lights, and doors; and even tell jokes. AI is used in medicine to identify target molecules for new drug discovery shortening the time from years to months, and in computers that scan pathology samples via cameras and diagnose disease such as cancers. Your web browsers use AI for automated language translation. Companies use AI for automated voice response for reservations and other queries. It is even being used to identify fake paintings. The applications are numerous.

Those that have the foresight and invest wisely reap the benefits of leadership.

Unaddressed Needs

Unexplored and uncontested spaces, when addressed, bring great value to customers. They change the status quo and become a new norm. Those who capture these spaces become leaders. This strategy is described in a terrific book called *Blue Ocean Strategy* by Renee Mauborgne and W. Chan Kim published in 2004.[45] My open space implementation at EMP in 2003 was an early form of the Blue Ocean Strategy.

Facebook, LinkedIn, WhatsApp, ByteDance (TikTok), and YouTube are examples of companies that exploited this strategy. These companies created a social need for sharing information, connecting with others, and expanding their relationship networks. Each of these companies has experienced viral growth driven by a core human need to share. TikTok has one billion *monthly active users* (MAUs), and the average user spends fifty-two minutes per day on this platform.[46]

Facebook, LinkedIn, and YouTube were pioneers in their categories, while WhatsApp was one of a multitude of messaging applications. It competed in an era of BlackBerry Messenger (BBM), KakaoTalk, Line, WeChat, Skype, and more. It was free and worked on any phone. You could download it onto your phone and communicate across the world. People could share messages, pictures, and videos, and use it for international calls, and it offered a convenient way for families and friends to network. Nothing else mattered to those who adopted it, and it soon became sticky as connections grew virally. What the other messaging applications did not get was the value of the accessibility and truly global usage model that WhatsApp provided.

New Business Models

Business-model disruptions bring new opportunities. Here are five striking examples with which you may be familiar.

Peloton is more than an indoor bike with a twenty-two-inch screen.

The bike allows users to clip into their pedals and ride to different streaming programs via their screens. Users can select from a variety of spin classes. Riders can track their metrics, compare them to other riders, and interact with remote riders. In a sense, it is a socio-athletic exercise. It allows a form of vicarious participation with a wider set of people who share similar interests. The confinement imposed by COVID-19 has helped this business, and subscriptions rose as the need to exercise increased.[47] While Peloton addresses an unmet need of the customer, it has a novel business model. It does sell bikes—hardware— but also charges a monthly subscription. The subscription results in recurring revenue every month, which will eventually eclipse the sale of bikes.

Amazon pioneered online shopping and convenient delivery to your doorstep. Today, online shopping is a trillion-dollar industry that has disrupted conventional retail and luxury-goods stores. Farfetch, whose revenues exceeded $2 billion in 2021,[48] is an on-line luxury fashion platform that connects shoppers with over a thousand brands and retailers, equipping them with e-commerce tools and an eco-system to sell and purchase with global same-day delivery and returns.[49]

Uber, Lyft, and similar rideshare companies (e.g., DiDi, Ola Cabs, Grab, Careem, Gett, Easy Taxi) have disrupted the rental-car industry as well as taxi businesses around the world.

Streaming services like Netflix and Hulu have disrupted traditional cable and satellite TV subscriptions. Movie disc rentals have almost vanished.

Softbank backed OYO Rooms (on your own rooms) is disrupting the budget hotel business. OYO targets underperforming budget hotels, renovates, and rebrands them as OYO franchises (OYO Hotels & Homes) and takes a cut of monthly revenue.[50] They don't buy the properties. They drive reservations and bookings via their mobile app. They move incredibly fast. When they enter a country, they have hundreds of properties within months. They have expanded from their home base in India to China, Japan, and the U.S. and are in eighty countries and eight hundred cities. You will be surprised to hear that since their launch in 2013 they have become the third largest hotel chain, after Marriott and Wyndham,[51] and the fastest growing in the world, with forty-three thousand hotels, one million rooms, and one hundred and thirty thousand vacation homes.[52]

Some may argue that companies like Peloton, Uber, Swiggy, Farfetch, Netflix, and OYO would have never been successful if it were not for technology innovations such as tablet and smartphone apps and efficient, high-speed internet streaming.

New trends, customer behaviors, and technology all bring new business opportunities. Hence, one must look at opportunities from more than one dimension to create a strategy.

Return on Investment Analysis

Having found the right lake to fish in, you need to assess whether the opportunity being addressed by your strategy is worthwhile. That is, if I am going to invest a lot of money in my strategy, will it provide a good return on my investment?

A company based in Asia has decided to build and sell smartphones in its region. This company believes it can make attractively designed, affordable smartphones with excellent local applications and content and sell these devices via its well-established distribution network. The CEO has asked his team to prepare a business case for such an investment. They could go about this task as follows.

The *total addressable market* (TAM) for smartphone sales is around 1.5 billion phones per year, which grows at an annual rate of 2 percent. This is all the smartphones sold in the world in every price segment and every country in the world.

Let us assume this market is segmented, by price, into high-end, mid-end, and low-end phone tiers whose shares of the TAM are 25 percent, 35 percent, and 40 percent respectively. The company decides it will build and sell only mid- and low-end phones because its target market will not pay high prices. Therefore, this company's *serviceable addressable market*, or SAM, comprises the segments it will address, which is 75 percent (the sum of the 35 percent mid-end and 40 percent low-end shares of the TAM) of the total market.

Next, assume the company's distribution network can address a major part of Asia outside China and Japan, and this represents 40 percent of the total market. Therefore, the company's *serviceable obtainable market* (SOM)—the subset of the market where the company can sell its products —is 30 percent of the total market (i.e., 40 percent times 75 percent of TAM).

After assessing the competition, the company assumes it can capture 10 percent of this obtainable market. Its estimated market share is therefore 3 percent (i.e., 10 percent of the SOM or 3 percent of the TAM), or forty-five million phones, which would be a rather small share relative to the market leaders, who sell more than two hundred million phones per year.

To conduct its market-opportunity analysis, the company begins by modeling the TAM, SAM, SOM, and its expected share. In this top-down approach, it models the SAM as some percentage of the TAM, the SOM as some percentage of the SAM, and the company's share as some percentage of the SOM (all based on rational estimates). Next it translates this estimated unit share into revenue based on the calculated volume of units and the price of the product or products it will sell into this market.

The company should also use a bottom-up approach that identifies each sales channel (e.g., direct customers, wholesalers, retailers, distributors) in every geographic region that can be addressed and model the percentage of share the company can capture in each of these respective sales channels. It then adds up all the modeled sales from each channel to arrive at an estimate of the total share it can capture, from which it calculates its estimated revenue.

When the top-down and bottom-up models align independently (as opposed to being contrived to align), it adds credibility and strength to the market-opportunity analysis. A bad model leads to bad results. This modeling must be treated as a serious exercise—the cost of being wrong is expensive. The time and effort required for return-on-investment (ROI) analysis pales in comparison to the time and effort required to develop, market, and sell a product or service that customers don't want.

Once the company has an aligned model in terms of share that it can capture (typically over time), it needs to translate this model into a business case. This step involves the following:

- Calculate revenue, which is share (in unit volume) multiplied by product price.
- Calculate the corresponding cost of goods sold which includes smartphone components, manufacturing, warranty, intellectual property licensing, packing, and shipping costs.
- Calculate the company's gross margin from the revenue and cost of goods sold.
- Calculate the company's operating expenses for engineering, manufacturing, sales, marketing, general administration, and all functions it needs to run its business.
- Ascertain the company's operating income, which is gross margin minus the operating expenses.
- Calculate the company's free cash flow (please see the Appendix if you are unfamiliar with this calculation) using

operating income, tax rates, capital expenses, working capital, and interest payments.

- Finally, use standard financial models such as discounted cash flow (DCF) or internal rate of return (IRR) to assess the company's payoff based on its cash flow over several years.

A sophisticated model will include price erosion of products over time, improvements in cost of goods sold, effects of inflation on operating expenses, currency-hedging risks, capital-expense needs, taxes, and interest payments to render the business case as realistic as possible. The model should span five to seven years to capture meaningful trends.

Getting the model wrong can hurt in two ways:

- One could abandon a tremendous market opportunity. Two examples often cited to me came from early consulting reports that forecasted there was no market for cellphones and portable music players. Today, more than 1.5 billion cellphones/smartphones are sold each year.[53] The Sony Walkman sold more than four hundred million units over its lifetime, [54] and the iPod sold around four hundred million units. [55]

- At the other extreme, one can be over-optimistic and create a bad business case followed by high investment and poor returns. Would you be surprised to learn that almost two-thirds of start-up companies do not provide a positive return?[56]

Product Relevance – The Market Factor

The second criterion in my ORCa model for creating a strategy is to assess the relevance of the product to the market. This is measured by potential acceptance of the product in the market, which in turn is determined by:

- Customer need
- Power of the competition
- Differentiation to win

These three criteria are illustrated in Figure 6.

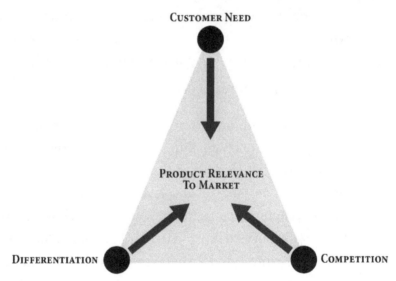

Figure 6: Three Criteria for Determining Product Relevance to Markets

Customer Need

There are numerous reasons why products fail and why innovations fall short, but some of the most epic and memorable center on similar themes:

- The product addresses a need that is already addressed by other products on the market.

  Jibo, an advanced social robot launched in 2016, struggled to gain a foothold against popular smart speakers like Amazon Echo, Amazon Echo Dot, Google Home, and Bose's Home Speaker and was discontinued in 2019.[57]

- The timing is not right. Sometimes, a product is just way before its time.

  The Newton launched by Apple in 1993 was a personal digital assistant on which one used a stylus to take notes and that could sync with one's computer.[58] Great idea, but its utility was not compelling. The iPad, on the other hand, launched seventeen years later in 2010, became a huge success.[59]

- Customers do not like the product, or its use-case is limited or unappealing.

  In 1985, the Coca-Cola company launched New Coke, and it failed because loyal customers did not like the taste of the new formula.[60]

- There is simply no demand.

  Aibo was a robotic dog and a technical marvel of its era launched by Sony in 1995. But there was no demand or business case for such a pet.[61] Meanwhile, Tamagotchi, a handheld digital pet launched by Bandai Corporation one year later in 1996, sold more than eighty million units because of the value it created for customers.[62]

If a product creates demand and satisfies an unfulfilled need or behavior, it is likely to be successful. Examples include the PlayStation and Xbox. Who would have thought at their inception that console gaming would become such a large industry? These products addressed a largely untapped market, were very usable, created stickiness (loyalty), and evolved over time from disc-based games to network games, offering other content as well. They became major revenue generators for their companies. But initially, these consoles were not profitable. Both Sony and Microsoft invested with persistence to make their franchises dominant because they smartly recognized that there was money to be made from the content rather than the hardware.

Competition

Competitors influence the dynamics of the market. It is useful to understand your competitors and their current market share, their relative strengths, their weaknesses, and how they may evolve, since they will not stand still. Assuming your competitors will fail is a bad bet for your company's strategy.

I often use this analogy from the Wild West. If you challenge a gunslinger, you better be fast on the draw, have a loaded pistol, and be an accurate shot. There may not be a second chance.

I try to assess my competition with two questions:

- Power: What share of the market does my competitor have and why?
- Reaction: How will they respond to a new threat?

To answer my questions, I revert to the well-known and well-used SWOT analysis. SWOT stands for *Strengths, Weaknesses, Opportunities, and Threats*. Normally, SWOT analysis is done on one's own company. I like to use this analysis also on my competitors and their stickiness in the market. I put down my SWOT analysis on PowerPoint slides and share it with my management team to raise awareness. Collective awareness brings more ideas and solutions.

Strengths and Weaknesses

Assess your competitor's strengths and weaknesses regarding their

- product portfolio breadth and depth;
- intellectual property;
- sales channels;
- customer confidence and loyalty;
- pricing and marketing tactics;

- culture when reacting to threats; and

- financial strength, which they can leverage to invest in fighting potential threats.

Each of these aspects needs to be assessed to understand what will stand in the way of your gaining share. To do this, you should map your company's products and positions in each of the above categories alongside those of the competition and determine relative strengths and weaknesses.

Financially strong competitors have deep pockets and can respond to a new product on the market with tactics such as increasing marketing, investing in more sales channels, and providing price subsidies. If they have multiple product lines, they may sandwich your product between two of theirs. They may even sue your company for patent infringement and drag out litigation for years, draining your company of valuable cash. In short, they can potentially disrupt your business model severely with their financial strength.

Finally, expect your competitor to do the unexpected, and be prepared to outflank them.

Opportunities and Threats

If your competitors are addressing a small portion of the available market, you have a big opportunity to enter and take share. Further, if the market is such that not every competitor has figured out how to gain or retain share and your strategy can disrupt the status quo, you should explore the opportunity. If your market is consolidating, with larger players driving out or absorbing smaller players, you must be extra cautious. Finally, if your competition has captured most of the addressable market it is hard but not impossible to enter and disrupt if you have discovered something vital that everyone else missed.

A good example is Apple entering a crowded mobile-phone market in mid-2007 and rising to be a leader. At the time, Nokia was selling more than four hundred million phones per year.[63] Apple entered the market with inferior technology, but they understood what customers wanted most: style, usability, and applications. They designed a phone that was desirable, most easy to use, and useful, supported by a large application store. Their competitors had fatefully ignored this—maybe it was *active inertia*. Apple disrupted the market and became a leader in a relatively short time.[64]

As a counterpoint to the above example, one can learn from Google's response. Google had been developing its own phone, and engineers admitted later that when they saw the unveiling of the iPhone, they scrapped what they had and went on to build a software platform with features the iPhone did not have.[65]

At that time, cellphone manufacturers had no response to the iPhone and were in a state of disruption. Google saw this as an opportunity for their software platform (Android) and the applications they could create and distribute on it. It was exactly what cellphone makers wanted. The rest is history, as Android took 85 percent of the smartphone market share in 2014.[66]

Incumbents and Customer Loyalty

Understand how long your competitors have been in the business and how entrenched and sticky their products are. If they have strong customer loyalty and their products are sticky, it is harder to displace them. On the other hand, as mentioned above, if your company's product and service can disrupt the status quo by addressing an unaddressed customer need, then you create a strong opportunity, just as Apple did when they entered the mobile-phone market, or as Tesla did in the car market, or as SpaceX has done in the spacecraft and rocket market.

Let's consider some more examples of products launched by leaders with a lot of cash.

- Zune was a portable music player launched in 2006 by Microsoft in the era of Apple's super successful iPod. It failed to disrupt the iPod.[67] And while Microsoft was pouring money and resources into the Zune, Apple was developing the iPhone, which did disrupt the market by combining a music player with phone and internet capabilities, leading to the Zune's demise.

- MeeGo was an operating system for mobile phones based on Linux, launched in 2010 by Nokia and Microsoft. Nokia sold huge volumes of mobile phones. MeeGo had the right architecture, comprising a common core platform and customizable user interfaces. This is what the industry needed. Yet MeeGo did not have the ecosystem to deliver consumer applications, nor did it capture an installed base—unlike the popular Android operating system from Google—so it failed.[68]

- Microsoft Office suite (now Office 365) is made up of Word, Excel, PowerPoint, Outlook, Teams, OneNote, and OneDrive. This suite has excellent features and a massive installed base.[69] These products are optimized for PCs and Macs. Users are familiar with these products. Microsoft Office suite engenders strong customer loyalty. It constantly evolves. As such, it is hard for the competition to displace this suite.

Differentiation

Our last factor in determining product relevance is differentiation.

Differentiation refers to the factors that compel customers to adopt or switch to your product. A company can differentiate its product in many ways, but the differentiation must be truly appreciated by your target customer base for them to want to switch—and that perceived value needs to be sustained for your company to retain and grow its customer base.

Differentiation is what makes your company's products and services unique. The following are some examples of how companies choose to differentiate.

Technology

For years, NVidia has offered high performance graphics processing units (GPUs) for video gaming cards, laptops, workstations, and data centers. They invested heavily in their GPU architecture, software platform (CUDA) and an eco-system of game developers. Their technology leadership has given them over 80 percent market share for these GPUs.[70] Technology differentiation is invaluable, especially if your company can afford the investments and execute to stay ahead of competitors.

Solution

At EMP, the solution we offered customers served as our differentiator. We sold a platform (chips plus software), all integrated to work as a solution. Our customers could take this platform and build a phone around this solution. When our customers used the EMP platform, they could build a phone in six months versus the eighteen months required by their previous approach. Our solution reduced the engineering costs for the customer and shortened their time-to-market dramatically.

Attribute

Jet fighter aircraft like the F-16 (Fighting Falcon) use avionics such as mission computers, weather radar, position and navigation systems, and early-warning systems.[71] These are mission-critical applications and must not fail. These avionics run special software that needs to be safety certified (the attribute) to a standard called DO-178B. When this software is deployed with the attribute holding (no failure) for multiple years, it builds immense confidence and trust in the software used.

Nike and Lululemon sell sports apparel. These companies rely on creating a positive association and appeal for their products through inspiring advertising and marketing. This positive association reinforces the perceived qualities of what the brand symbolizes.

Thus, an attribute, or attributes, can be both measurable and perceived. Both are effective differentiators.

Service

Credit card companies, banks, and manufacturing companies rely on service as a differentiator. Many of us have trusted our main credit card or bank for years. Ask yourself: why?

Taiwan Semiconductor Manufacturing Co. (TSMC) is the world's largest dedicated semiconductor foundry.[72] They make chips for many customers and has more than 50 percent market share.[73] TSMC provides their customers with a very reliable and cost-effective service, manufacturing and supplying semiconductor chips. They offer production of a variety of semiconductor technologies used by different customers with different needs. Their reliability, efficiency, and broad manufacturing options for customers are unmatched, which is why TSMC has been a leader for decades.

Business Model

Disruptive business models are differentiators. Take Uber's model versus the prevailing rental-car company model, or IKEA's modular-furniture model versus the standard furniture-store model, or Amazon Prime's model versus the retail-store model. Customers love the convenience that the new models offer.

Business models that create a compelling need, such as licensing intellectual property, that you must have to produce and sell your products are also sticky.

Multiple Factors

If one can differentiate with multiple factors, then the product stickiness increases significantly. An example of a business that has built a strategy to differentiate with attributes, price, and service is Costco. Their Kirkland Signature products have come to be recognized as affordable with high quality. They have a very wide range of offerings at very competitive prices, and they have unmatched return policies. It is no wonder that they have one of the highest customer-satisfaction ratings, measured as Net Promoter Score (NPS). Their 2021 revenue was $200 billion.[74]

Ultimately, your strategy must be based on being able to compete with *sustainable differentiation that customers value.*

Capability – Wood Behind the Arrow

The third criterion in my ORCa model for creating a strategy is to be able to execute the same by investing wholly in it, which I call "putting wood behind the arrow."

Companies often develop strategies and say they want to implement them, but then fail to put the right resources behind the strategy's success. I consulted for a company where a group of brilliant engineers developed a novel tool that could scan software for coding violations and security vulnerabilities. An expert friend told me that there are anywhere between fifteen and fifty bugs for every one thousand lines of software written. The company's product could scan large amounts of software and detect violations and security weaknesses in minutes, whereas a human expert would need weeks. This automated scanner would eliminate human error caused by fatigue. What an opportunity!

However, the company, took a tepid approach to investing in the product's roadmap, marketing, and sales channels. It was probably not a priority or possibly a lack of conviction in the product's success. The product did not gain traction with customers and ended up being used as an internal tool for software development. Had the company invested with conviction, I am sure the payoff would have been immense. It was a case of not putting enough wood behind the arrow.

In archery, a sharp arrowhead cannot go far by itself. It requires a shaft, fletching near the tail for stability, and force from a bowstring. Implementing a strategy to hit a target is no different.

In business, hitting your strategy target comes down to two elements:

- Investing in the capability to execute the strategy.
- Having the right timing.

Capability to Execute

First, the strategy must mirror the capability of the company.

At EMP, if we had not known how to build a software factory and deliver more than two hundred software releases per year with military precision, our promise to customers would have failed, and we would have failed.

For our competitors to catch up to us, they would have had to invest in software and build this capability over a few years. Had we failed on our promise to lower development cost and shorten time-to-market, our competitors would have taken our share. We would never have recovered.

Engineering prowess helped us deliver our strategy. However, in many companies, you need more than just engineering. You need skills such as market and customer research, product management, program management, supply chain, manufacturing, and sales and marketing.

Take the example of Lululemon—a powerhouse in the athleisure (athletic and leisure) clothing market. They are a relatively young company that was founded in 1998.[75] They have well-designed and well-made athletic and casual clothing, but more importantly, their branding is based on research into societal cultural shifts that emphasize wellness, health, self-worth, and personal achievement. Their in-store workouts, one-on-one and group workouts, and social media engagement are not just activity, but also educate and promote outcomes that their clients believe in. In short, they know what their clients want and value. Their product managers must be paying close attention to customer feedback to find ways to improve their products, or else it would be hard to secure such loyalty. Their strategy is to connect with their clientele personally, and they are clearly doing that, as reflected in their revenue and share-price growth. No wonder they can compete with the likes of Adidas, Nike, Under Armour, and Puma.

Companies must understand what capabilities are needed for their strategy to succeed, and they must invest to build these capabilities. This is not a one-time investment. It needs to be an ongoing commitment to constantly innovate and stay ahead of the competition. It gets increasingly difficult to differentiate with limited factors and win for long periods because the competition will catch up. Hence, the investment must be balanced across all functions that determine the success of the product in the market.

Companies must back their strategy with the right investments in all relevant functional areas, such as customer and market research, engineering, product management, program management, supply chain, sales channels, marketing, and customer support to build and bolster those capabilities that make the strategy thrive.

Timing Is Everything

Strategy is a perishable item that comes with a time frame. There are many clever people in the world who are also thinking like your company and have come up with similar ideas to address your identified market opportunity. A first-mover advantage is a gift that allows you to set the benchmark and create a wider moat between you and your competitors. If you are a late mover, you are playing catch-up.

This means that to succeed, you must deliver the proof of your strategy *on time* to intersect critical market windows.

Trends and market opportunities are like trains running on reliable schedules. You must be on the platform on time, or you will miss the train. And the next train might take a while to arrive.

Take the case of Kodak.[76] By 1976, the company had captured 85 percent of the market for photography and 90 percent of the market for film. Yet, it chose to ignore the rise of the digital still camera, even though one of its own engineers invented the device in 1975. Kodak had the brand, money, and distribution power to capitalize on the invention, but it did not launch a digital camera product until 1991. During this time Fuji Film, Sony, Panasonic, and other companies had made great strides and ran away with the market. Kodak never recovered and went into bankruptcy in 2012.

Summary: Strategy
The Castle Walls

Your perimeter walls surround and protect your castle. They must be built well and arm your company with advantages to repel invaders. The following elements help create a good strategy:

- Make critical choices about where to invest your company's money and resources.

- Pick opportunities in markets where you will get a good return on investment—new trends, technology disruptions, unmet needs, and new business models are rich with opportunity.

- Ensure that your products are based on what customers value and need.

- Carefully assess your competition and their stickiness in the market to understand their strengths and weaknesses and what opportunities and threats they may present.

- Create sustainable differentiation to continually evolve to build a wider moat between you and your competitors.

- Find an *open space* to differentiate in if you can—it is very powerful.

- Always match your company's execution capability to the strategy.

- Invest consistently in those company functions that influence the success of your strategy—putting wood behind the arrow.

- Execute to hit market windows and set the pace for the competition—strategy is a perishable item that loses value with time. Timing is everything.

Having created the strategy, we will next look inward at culture—an element that, if damaged, can erode your company from the inside. If upheld, it can make your company indestructible.

4

The Castle Keep
Culture Instills the Will to Win

Culture serves as a company's heart and soul.

Culture is not quantitative like finance, strategy, products, and sales. This may be why it is not always prioritized in companies. Yet, it is what defines the company.

Culture is a collection of ideas, values, beliefs, and behaviors exhibited by employees. To a large extent, culture is created by the company's leadership and how they reward and discourage certain behaviors. However, employees play a crucial role in creating culture because they need to embrace it, spread it, and own it. Hence, culture has a strong influence on execution. If strategy is what *needs* to get done, culture *determines* what gets done. You could come up with a winning strategy to transform your company, but without culture in alignment, your implementation and execution of that strategy is destined to fail.

In many ways, culture is like a medieval castle's keep, known in old French or Middle English as its *donjon*—a large tower within the castle's perimeter or curtain walls.[77] The keep was generally a castle's defining feature, the element that loomed the largest. For instance, the Chateau de Vincennes, built near Paris, France in the fourteenth century, stands out for its imposing fifty-two-meter-tall donjon.[78]

The keep gets its name from "that which keeps or protects—the strongest and most secure part of a castle".[79] The keep represented feudal authority, as aptly described by medieval Spanish writers who called it *torre del homenaje,* or the tower of homage.[80]

The keep could be several stories high and topped with battlements and turrets. It was constructed with extra thick walls and was the safest place in the castle in the case of a siege. These keeps housed the chapel, great hall where inhabitants gathered and ate, residential quarters, and food supplies. In the event of an attack, the keep needed to be protected. It was the last line of defense. For example, the Himeji Castle in the Hyogo Prefecture of Japan has a main keep that is five-stories high built on a thirty-six-foot tall foundation of hand-cut riverbed rock.[81] The castle complex has a very intricate maze of paths leading to the main keep—the gates, walls, and courtyards (baileys) were all arranged so an attacking force had to approach in a confusing spiral path.[82] If the keep fell, the castle fell. Likewise, culture is the central part of any company—it looms the largest and must be defended at all costs, because when it falls, the company also falls.

Just as a castle keep could take many different forms, such as square, quatrefoil, round (shell)—so can company culture. It is essential that you build a culture that is in concert with your strategy. This culture can raise your company to new heights—a monument to your company's successes. It can also serve as a refuge in tough times. But a weak company culture is liable to render all the other elements of your company ineffective.

I have chosen two dysfunctional cultures and one desired culture as illustrations.

Indifferent Culture

This organizational culture takes root when a leader or leaders hesitate to make decisions and do not communicate clearly with their organization. The broader organization does not understand or embrace the strategy. Work goes on every day, and while lower levels of management make decisions with all good intentions, but progress is not guided by market knowledge and strategy—meaning the outcome in the long run is suboptimal at best. In the absence of leadership, these organizations foster heroes and influencers, as well as the formation of loyalist groups around these influencers. Departments are unsynchronized and operating expenses go unchecked. Results are hit and miss unless the company is a virtual monopoly in the market, where mistakes often go unnoticed for a while. Since the leader or leaders are virtually absent, it is not clear how the organization is energized.

Controlled Culture

This organizational culture is the antithesis of the previous culture. The organization has a leader or leaders who make every decision and tend to micromanage. The over-reliance on these leaders causes other management levels to be unsure and indecisive because they are often overruled. They learn to be order-takers. Empowerment, if there is any, is ad hoc. There is a lot of busywork, a bit like running in place on a treadmill, and the organization is typically exhausted. These organizations demand strong loyalty and are typically structured so that all critical decision-making is routed via a small set of leaders. Such organizations can be successful, but usually not in the long run for two reasons: 1) the leaders suck the energy out of the organization, and 2) when a key leader or leaders leave or retire, the company begins to falter as the bench has little experience in making important decisions.

Departments and managers have clear roles, and their responsibilities are coupled with authority and accountability. Leaders drive the strategy, set clear goals, use metrics to track progress, and follow through on execution status. They encourage their managers to make decisions and empower them to get things done. Most of all, these leaders are not averse to having their managers challenge the status quo for improvement. Such organizations usually reinforce a meritocracy because they are results driven. It is no coincidence that they are well in tune with the market and execute steadily. Leaders in such cultures pump energy into the organization, and the organization's progress energizes the leader.

Management guru Peter Drucker is widely credited with the phrase, "Culture eats strategy for breakfast."[83] That is, when a company's culture clashes with a company's strategy, culture invariably wins. If strategy determines what you want, culture determines what you get.

Several years ago, a colleague recommended that I read a book titled *Execution: The Discipline of Getting Things Done* by Larry Bossidy, former chairman and CEO of AlliedSignal and Honeywell International, and Professor Ram Charan.[84] This book ties together strategy, culture, and execution. My colleague said it reinforced much of what I had been practicing. This book is a masterpiece and a must-read for every practicing manager.

In their book, Bossidy and Charan discuss seven leadership qualities that help form the right culture:

- Know your business and people
- Be rooted in realism
- Set achievable goals
- Follow through
- Reward doers

- Expand people's capabilities

- Know yourself

Curiously, Mr. Bossidy and I worked for GE at the same time. He was a top executive, and I was a junior team leader for a group of research scientists. Much of what I learned about culture and execution came from management training at GE in the early 1990s, when the company was in its heyday.

Every time a project or a business where I was involved failed, I took time to reflect on what my team and I could have done better and what we learned from the failure. I learned a lot about myself, my team, and our actions. This reflection over my career led me to formulate a two-pronged model to build a culture that supports strategy by fostering the right behavior and fostering the right leadership.

I found that when I implemented these two tenets (right behavior and right leadership) consistently, cultural transformation happened rather rapidly.

Foster the Right Behavior – Raise the Right Army

If your castle is under attack, everyone within its walls, not just the rampart guards, needs to be aware of the situation. Everyone needs to know what to do to help repel the attack. For everyone to act as one unit, each person must have a clear role and responsibilities. Everyone in the castle must be resourceful and act with a sense of urgency. This is not a time for dissension or power grabs by those trying to exploit the situation. Based on these principles, I have relied on the following seven actions to foster behaviors that build a productive culture:

- Raise awareness

- Know your numbers

- Assign playing positions

- Engender a sense of urgency
- Grow your capability cube
- Prune yellow leaves
- Validate and reinforce

Raise Awareness

Castles, just like companies, can be large. If there is a fire in one section, it is easy to ignore it until it spreads. By then, it may be too late. Likewise, in companies, the important issues must be escalated to the right levels to bring timely awareness. Awareness brings understanding. Understanding fosters action.

In two underperforming businesses I was appointed to run, I was surprised to learn that the employees were not more aware of the dire issues facing their organizations. It was not their fault—they were just not told.

At the first company, our largest customers were unhappy. I found this out the hard way by visiting our four largest customers in the first month after having come on board. Every customer hammered me about our product quality and delivery accuracy. We were on the verge of losing business with these customers.

In a second business, our product gross margin was 18 percent below the industry average. When we did not get paid a bonus that year —having missed this metric—the employees seemed surprised.

Clearly, these organizations did not understand the gravity of their situation. Why was this the case?

As a leader, you must invest significant time and talk to all levels of the organization to make them aware of the company's status and issues. How else can you enlist support to fix things?

You can bring such awareness via town halls (all-hands meetings), leadership calls, roundtables, and regular check-ins. Establishing a personal connection between the leader and employees breaks many barriers and shatters misconceptions and preconceived notions. Dialogue helps break myths.

I have used three communication tools to foster engagement and build awareness and alignment.

We called the first Ask-Me-Anything meetings. I began these meetings in 2003 at EMP. They were designed to build awareness widely across the organization. Every month, I would talk to two groups of employees, randomly selected by HR, for an hour-long dialogue. We would start the meetings with me providing a brief overview of the business status, and then it turned into a question-and-answer session. Employees could literally ask me anything. But they need to engage in a dialog. To do this I would tell a humorous business incident involving me to bring some levity to the meeting and then ask an icebreaker question like, "What is your favorite movie and why?" After a few people spoke, many more would. A key to a meaningful ask-me-anything dialogue is transparency. Transparency unveils issues, but it also builds trust.

About a year into my job, we had turned around the business. It was a demanding job and people had to work long hours and forgo vacation. I could not have been popular because I drove a tough-as-nails delivery culture. So, I was surprised when a senior employee told me he was worried that I would leave in a year, as I was an expat on a two-year contract. He asked me to tell everyone why I was committed to staying and taking the business further forward. A great question to tie my commitment to the company to my ask for employees to commit to hit the goals for the company. I ended up extending my stay, beyond my contract, for an extra year.

My HR business partner and I noted every rational concern and made sure we addressed each one. We shared the employee comments with my management team so that they were aware of employee feedback and could also help address issues. My management team, in turn, held similar meetings, and this cascaded throughout the organization, creating multiple touchpoints. When all our messages were aligned, it was powerful.

As a business leader, I spent a significant amount of time with customers to build rapport and to bring their input back to my teams. I mentioned earlier that at one company where I had just joined, our customers were very unhappy. They would voice their distrust of our delivery capability at every meeting. My team needed to hear this message, but it was hard for me to convey the gravity of our situation because I was new to the company and could be viewed as complaining about my predecessor just to enhance my position.

My communications team hit upon a brilliant idea, which became my second tool. They decided to record video interviews with our customers, asking them about our products and services. We then shared these video clips at our town halls or all-employee meetings. These videos were amazing because our customers were candid. In one such interview, the CTO of a major wireless carrier told us that we were an excellent supplier of technology, but he had lost his bonus for the year because we did not deliver on time. Nothing I could have said to the employees in a hundred town halls or Ask-Me-Anything meetings was as powerful as that one statement. The CTO had trusted us, and our actions had caused him personal loss. Everyone in our company had to hear this truth. We never had another delay. My teams would jump on planes and spend holidays, such as Christmas, away from home to ensure on-time launches.

Interviewing customers and capturing this to be replayed for employees via video may not always be possible. Worthwhile alternatives are to present customer surveys or invite customers to speak at all-employee meetings. When taking surveys, use tangible, quantitative metrics relative to competitors or customer expectations so that the team can act on the same.

The third tool we used was to write a monthly newsletter, co-authored by me and each member of my management team. In this newsletter, we shared the progress that the business had made in the previous month as well as our asks of the employees, so they could address what needed to get done. I wrote the first page, and each management-team member got one page to write about how their function was doing. Every employee received this newsletter, and it gave them an overview of what was happening in all parts of the business. The information shared in these newsletters led employees to raise questions at the Ask-Me-Anything meetings. Employees appreciated that management spent the time to put such a newsletter together every month to keep them informed.

My tools are a touch old-fashioned. In today's times, with work from home and hybrid models, one can use tools like Slack, Teams, Webex, Chime, Zoom, or any of the multitude of applications that allow virtual meetings where you can share the same information, have the same dialogues, get questions, and have employees exchange thoughts and questions via chat channels. You can even anonymize the questions for privacy so employees find it easier to ask the hardest questions that need to be answered.

Once employees are aware of issues, they can help you overcome those issues and achieve the company goals.

Know Your Numbers

Having raised awareness of the issues, you need to clearly identify what you want to achieve each year and what qualifies as progress. At each business I ran, I used five targets that were quantitative, measurable, and doable, even if they were a stretch. Unrealistic goals represent failure before the ink is dry. Invariably, my five preferred targets are revenue, gross margin, cash flow, delivery accuracy, and innovation. I chose these targets as they are outcomes of *what* and *how* we performed every day. These became the key metrics we, as an organization, would drive toward. Everything we did had to contribute to these metrics and targets. It was key for everyone in the organization to know these numbers without ambiguity.

Three of the five metrics are financial in nature (revenue, gross margin, and cash flow). They measure the financial fitness of a business. I used product-delivery accuracy as the fourth metric because that was what our customers cared about. We set the goal that over 90 percent of our product deliveries had to be made within five days of the committed date. Product quality was embedded in delivery accuracy, as delivering on time without quality has no value. Innovation is also important, as it protects the company's future. You can measure innovation in many concrete ways, including patents, trade secrets, or product ideas that can be realized into tangible revenue for the company.

These numbers are what I expect my organization to rally around to achieve. To create a common purpose, I tied the company's rewards, such as salary raises and bonuses, to achieving these targets. In turnaround situations, everyone got the same targets. The purpose was to ensure that everyone was rowing in the same direction.

The next step was for the leader and the management team to spend time explaining why these numbers matter to the organization and to get commitment. This process establishes *knowing your numbers*. Just throwing numbers over the fence and saying "get it done" does not work.

To truly *know your numbers*, one must thoroughly understand the business to be able to take actions that realize achievement. For example, if gross margin is a target number, then you know that it is impacted by product pricing, product mix, and cost of goods sold. Assuming price cannot be changed, if gross margin drops, the team must try to rebalance its product mix and/or reduce the cost of goods appropriately to recover as much of the lost gross margin as possible. Therefore, your numbers guide decision-making, planning, and prioritization.

Once the key numbers or targets are established, progress must be reviewed regularly, and people must be held accountable for results. Targets, regular reviews, and accountability are what mold culture.

Periodic reviews are essential to assess progress. Periodic reviews allow what I call *delta correction*—correction in small steps. If you wait too long, a problem grows with time, and it often requires people to move mountains to correct the issue.

Set the clear expectation that everyone will be held accountable for their targets. Therefore, it is critical to get alignment with and commitment to the targets. Once everyone has committed to the targets, there should be no excuses or debates.

Encourage your team to explain deviation from plans with timely solutions. Eliminate wishy-washy answers like, "I have to get back to you on your question," "We are working hard on the problem," or, "It is on my critical to-do list." Encourage answers like, "This is the problem and here is my analysis," "These are the issues, and this is how I will fix the problem," "I will share the result by this date."

If you implement this process consistently, you change behavior. And behavior molds culture.

If an organization does not know their numbers, that lack of knowledge will become evident in missed targets and a failed strategy. Consistent misses lead to mistrust and loss of confidence. Investors, customers, and employees do not trust management teams that miss targets. No one gives authority and money to someone who will fritter it away due to indifference, inexperience, incompetence, indolence, or inability.

Assign Playing Positions

The role and responsibility of every function in a business or company must be crystal clear. When roles and responsibilities in an organization are not clear, there is a duplication of effort, conflicts arise between functions, and there is an increasing probability of finger-pointing and blame games when things go badly. The result is low accountability.

An analogy that I have often used in employee meetings is to compare a professional soccer team with a kindergarten soccer team. In the professional soccer team, every player plays a position and has a role and responsibility. The players pass the ball up-field as they try to score goals. They collectively defend against the other team scoring. Players pass in an organized manner and play as a team to win, leveraging each other's strengths. Players do not listen to the spectators, who have lots of opinions on what to do. The players, not the spectators, are responsible for possession of the ball. In a kindergarten soccer team, players do not play positions for long. They hog the ball, pass inconsistently, and are likely to listen to their parents cheering them from the sidelines. While they may all have fun, the result is unpredictable.

To foster accountability, it is critical to assign clear roles and responsibilities to every function in the organization, so everyone understands who does what and what they need to deliver.

In every organization I have been appointed to run, I have made sure to clarify roles and responsibilities as follows:

- Create a list of major deliverables related to company operations.

- Assign each deliverable to *one owner* in the company.

This assignment of responsibility is based on the role the function serves in the company. The owner is responsible for delivering the results and making the decisions to secure those results. The owner is accountable for the deliverable. Each owner cooperates with other functions in the company that serve as *contributors*. The contributors assist the owner, but the owner calls the shots on this task. This distinction is critical.

When this distinction is clear, and when everyone knows who does what and what their responsibilities are, it leads to efficient parceling of work with clear accountability and little duplication. So, when things go wrong, one knows where to begin the discussion to quickly get to the *what* and *why*.

The following is an illustrative example of roles and responsibilities in a business I ran. The business had the following major functions (departments), listed in alphabetical order:

- Customer Support
- Finance
- Human Resources (HR)
- Legal
- Marketing
- Product Management
- Program Management
- Research and development (R&D)
- Sales
- Supply Chain (including manufacturing, purchasing, service and repair)

The management team was comprised of the president and the heads of each of the above functions.

Table 2 offers an example of the roles and responsibilities at this company. Every company is different, so you should make your own table relevant to your company. The major deliverables are the responsibilities. Each deliverable has one owner and several contributors who define the roles played to secure each deliverable. Owners are responsible for calling the play, running the play, and securing the results. Contributors need to be involved and assist the owner in securing the results. By being involved, the contributors cannot deny they were aware of what was happening unless they were absent by choice.

Table 2: Example of Roles and Responsibilities		
Major Deliverables (Responsibility)	Owner (Role)	Contributors
Profit and Loss	President	Management Team
Metrics & Price Setting	President	Head of Finance or the Chief Financial Officer (CFO), Sales, Marketing
Core Platform Roadmap	Head of Product Management	R&D, Customer Support, Sales, Marketing
Delivery of Core Platform	Head of Program Management	R&D, Supply Chain, Product Management
Supply Chain (Procurement, Capacity, Fulfillment, Quality)	Head of Supply Chain	Sales, R&D, Customer Support, Marketing
Hardware Design	Head of R&D	Product Management, Program Management
Software Design & Release Management	Head of R&D	Product Management, Program Management
System Design & Release Management	Head of R&D	Product Management, Program Management
Sales, Demand Forecasts & Inventory	Head of Sales	President, CFO, Marketing, Supply Chain, R&D
Marketing	Head of Marketing	President, CFO, Sales, Product Management
Customer & Field Application Support	Head of Customer Support	R&D, Sales, Supply Chain
Financial Reporting, IT & Systems	CFO	Management Team
Contracts	Head of Legal	Relevant Departments
Talent & Performance Management	Head of HR	Relevant Departments

Next, establish coordination between owners and contributors through a regular cadence of meetings, each focused on a specific deliverable. The owner calls the meeting, sets the agenda, and presents the status and issues. The contributors attend and participate by providing their input. The conclusions and actions are documented. By ensuring that there is a regular cadence of meetings and that each meeting is focused on solutions, the company can make much progress.

In the companies where I worked, we experienced three common conflicts in roles and responsibilities that we solved.

The first conflict was between demand forecasting and inventory disposition. When sales owned the demand forecast and supply chain owned inventory, it created a mismatch in accountability because sales could over-forecast, supply chain would build to the forecast, and the company would be stuck with high inventory. The rule we used was that supply chain would build to the demand forecast from sales after it was appropriately judged by the management team. Sales would own what was built and had to sell it. This created accountability not to overbuild. Accountability needs to drive the right results for the entire company, not each function.

A second area of conflict was between product management and R&D. R&D wanted to control the product roadmap, but they were execution-driven and did not have the time or expertise to rationalize customer requirements in business terms that impacted the product roadmap. As such, we assigned this responsibility to product management, where they had to create a roadmap that met customer requirements and simultaneously optimized the return on investment in the products. R&D assisted product management, as a contributor, to build the roadmap.

A third example of conflict was between R&D line managers and program managers and related to who managed the program. We followed the principle that program managers define *what* and *when*, while line managers define *who* and *how*.

It is important to note that the above roles and responsibilities table must be created at each level in the organization, so everyone understands what their role is and what they are responsible for delivering based on knowing the numbers. When this is clear throughout the organization, it leads to efficiency.

Engender a Sense of Urgency

At one of my businesses, we had a critical deadline to deliver a software drop for a customer. We were late, and it was nighttime when this customer called me from Asia. The customer read me the riot act for my organization's lack of urgency after missing the promised delivery. The customer was upset because our delay caused their own delays delivering to their customer. The next morning, a Friday, I went in early to meet with the department manager, who had failed to deliver the software to the customer. Having not bothered to confirm the delivery, going on mere assumption, the manager had given most of the engineers on this project the day off, and they planned to return after the weekend. This organization did not understand the sense of urgency, nor was it accountable.

The pulse of a company is hidden in its sense of urgency, which is not an attribute of a single individual but a collective one. There is no point in a few people working as if the deck they are standing on is on fire if others do not see the value in it. All efforts in a company are collective because the output is an amalgamation of individual outputs.

To address this issue, appoint managers who are willing to be held accountable for their commitments. These managers possess the following characteristics:

- Self-motivation to drive actions in their respective areas because they feel accountable for their deliverables and understand the impact of not hitting their goals.

- A very good understanding of their domain or subject matter, how to secure solutions, who to cooperate with, and what needs to be done.

- Ability to make timely decisions to keep the business moving forward every day.

When every group in a company works with such like-mindedness, failure is seldom seen.

I want to share a great lesson from a supplier about what a sense of urgency can mean. We were designing a new chipset at EMP that had to meet a strict cost budget. Our design, unfortunately, grew larger than planned—and so did the cost. I met with the senior vice president of our chip manufacturer, and I explained that our design had caused a problem. I either had to eat the added cost as a gross margin hit or reduce features or performance by reducing the size of our chip to get back to the cost target. He took some time to mull it over.

I had invited him to dinner at a local restaurant that evening. As we were sitting down to dinner, he pleasantly surprised me by saying he had a new design that would get us back on budget. He had relayed my concern from the afternoon to his team, and in six hours, they had found a solution. This sense of urgency showed me that this new supplier was invested in our success. It left a lasting impression.

Grow Your Capability Cube

In turnaround situations, you never have enough resources (people, money, equipment, etc.). You must make do with what you have. For this, you need to be resourceful.

Contrast the following answers when you give a very well-defined critical task to two people.

- Person A: Will I get additional resources to do what you want me to do?
- Person B: Let me study the problem and see if we can do

the task with existing resources. If we need more people or money or reprioritization of resources to secure the desired result, I will get back to you.

Essentially, Person B leaves you with the impression that they want to know *what* they are solving and *how* before they determine they do not have the wherewithal. Resourceful people typically know their organizations well. They know their business well and they know how to solve problems. They know their priorities and they can juggle things around to accommodate uncertainty and still provide results. They may cut a task or delay a less important task to do a more important one.

Resourcefulness is the ability to find timely solutions to overcome challenges with what you have.

Leaders and managers in organizations need to be resourceful, but it is equally important that they teach their organizations to be resourceful because it is only then that one sees the bigger impact of this trait.

Leaders can use a tool called the *capability cube* to grow and build resourcefulness. The capability cube, illustrated in Figure 7 (see the next page), comprises three dimensions: capacity, competence, and clarity of purpose.

- Capacity is the ability to handle incrementally more tasks with the same resources, through experience and efficiency.
- Competence is the ability to solve a broader array of problems and challenges.
- Clarity of purpose enables one to focus on what is important and what is not.

If this cube grows in each dimension every year, it naturally grows resourcefulness.

When department managers focus on growing their capability

cube, they are driven to hire top talent; they innovate in process, methods, and tools to drive efficiency; they manage performance; and most of all, they improve the definition of what needs to get done.

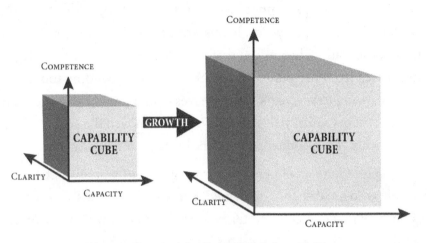

Figure 7: Growing the Capability Cube with Time

Competent leaders also know how to get their staff to be efficient through prudent task allocation, balanced priorities, and clear direction. They just do not throw tasks over the fence and say, "Deal with it." Leaders who throw tasks over the fence without any accountability are typically out of touch with their organizations and are usually incompetent.

Prune Yellow Leaves

When you are forming a culture, you do not have time for distractions. Imagine a raging fire that is burning in your castle. A group of guards is blocking the fire wagon because they have a set of demands that need to be met before the wagon is allowed to pass through or help. What would you do?

I learned an invaluable lesson about solving this problem from Professor Willie Pietersen of Columbia University in 2001. He was conducting a two-day seminar for the newly formed Sony-Ericsson.

At this meeting, he told us a story about how he and his wife bought two plants of the same species, one for each of them to tend. They kept them on their balcony in their apartment in New York. Both plants got about the same amount of water and sun, but with time, his plant continually developed yellow leaves while his wife's plant seemed lush. Upon observation, he noticed that his wife regularly removed the yellow leaves from her plant. Maybe his plant was spending too much energy trying to revive its yellow leaves—affecting other leaves and causing them to turn yellow, too. When he removed the yellow leaves, his plant also got healthier and became lush. There is a great lesson here.

Too often, management spends a significant amount of time on people who are difficult, unaligned, and passive-aggressive and who cannot be made to come to terms with the company strategy or cultural change. These are the yellow leaves, and they need to be pruned.

Someone once asked me, as the newly appointed leader of the company's largest business, how I was going to make myself accepted by a small gang of opinionated employees with a negative attitude, all of whom reported to me. He was taken aback when I told him the story of how Alexander III of Macedonia (also known as Alexander the Great) solved the riddle to unravel the Gordian Knot—he cut it.[85] Companies have no time for fiefdoms and influence centers, especially when they hinder progress. The faster you get rid of such blockages, the better. They are yellow leaves.

I have a low tolerance for yellow leaves because they harm the tree. After I set expectations, I wait three months, and if I do not see improvement, it is time to begin pruning.

Another problem that companies face is employee complaints—some of which are very legitimate. If left unresolved, the complaints spread virally and detract from productive work. Maurice Cohen, a management consultant who ran a two-day workshop at Ericsson around the year 2000, gave me priceless advice on this topic. He said that when employees complain, you should ask them to convert the complaint to a request, and then you may be able to help if it is within the scope of your authority.

For example, if a person says they are overworked and tired, you cannot do much other than empathize. You may suggest a solution, but it is better if the complainant brings this solution forward. If the same person says, "I am tired and need two days off," though, you can approve the request. The reverse is also true. Managers should not just complain. If they do not like something, they need to make an actionable request to address the issue. By making a reasonable request, the complainant becomes a partner in resolving the issue. It makes everyone who has an issue convert negative thinking to a positive outcome and be part of the solution.

Validate and Reinforce

As an engineer, I admire Linus Torvalds, the inventor of Linux. He was once quoted as saying, "Talk is cheap, show me the code."[86] Essentially, enough talk about how good the code is—let's see the source code that you have written. This is a great saying because one needs tangible proof that the product of one's efforts is paying off. If those efforts are not paying off, your organization will not follow you for long.

In essence, you need to validate and reinforce that the path you are on is right.

- Validation: Show proof of success compared to the targets you set. Results are the best form of validation of how the company is executing to meet targets (preferably customer-oriented or financial targets).

- Reinforcement: Recognize and celebrate success in a timely manner to encourage and thank employees.

Recall my previous example where our customers were upset with the quality and timeliness of our product deliveries. To fix this issue, we implemented a process to make a delivery to each customer every six weeks. The product would be hand-delivered, and we would stay at the customer site until it was implemented on their reference solution and shown to work and meet their metrics. We focused only on what was required for the next delivery and hit our goals consistently until the customer's product launched. The feedback every six weeks was a validation of what worked and what did not. Our customers appreciated the focus and improvement, which reinforced our approach. With this validation, the team began to make the process even better. The results were amazing.

In the second business, where I mentioned the gross margin was 18 percent below the industry average, we created a systematic plan to improve our gross margin by 1 percent every month using a value-based engineering approach—18 percent improvement in eighteen months.

To kickstart that turnaround, I gathered my management team and asked them to join me in an exercise. Our products, semiconductor chips, were fabricated in geographically dispersed factories, packaged at yet another set of factories, and then shipped off to be tested in different locations. These locations were scattered around the world, and each factory had different capabilities. Some factories were better than others at improving yield, minimizing defects to maximize output of good chips. The problem I asked my team to solve was to remap where we built our products with two goals in mind: maximize the yield of our products and minimize shipping costs.

We split ourselves into three teams and began the remapping exercise. After a few hours, I was amazed to find out that all three teams came up with the same answer. The experts knew what to do, as is so often the case in most companies, but no one had previously asked them for a solution.

This remapping of products to factories improved yield, which increased the gross margin by 10 percent. The yield improvement meant that we produced more good chips for the same cost. So, each chip cost less, hence improving the gross margin. My finance team identified an additional 2 percent improvement in gross margin reserved for operational sloppiness like inventory revaluations, scrap, and warranty reserves. We knew how to tighten things up operationally to eliminate this buffer. The remaining 6 percent came via a list of fifty-plus action items. These items included eliminating unnecessary quality checks that added cost and no value, improving the test time for our chips by seconds, and qualifying a new supplier that offered a more cost-efficient packaging process.

On a $2 billion business, the 18 percent improvement was $360 million of savings per year. The additional profitability every quarter was visible to every employee, who could take pride in what they had accomplished. The results also validated my focus that this was a problem that could be solved.

When results are made visible and recognized, it brings pride and reinforces what the company appreciates. However, make sure

- you correlate the reward to an outcome, so people know what it is they are being recognized for; and
- you reward or recognize at the appropriate time, as warm porridge tastes a lot better than cold porridge.

As you build your culture, try to promote people from within the organization. This tells the organization that if you contribute to the company's success, you also benefit by rising in your career. Recognizing your employees who deliver will keep them passionate and inspired to contribute to the team, and it gives them added incentive to stay at the company, when they may otherwise be looking for opportunities outside of the organization.

As you identify and develop leaders internally, experts suggest looking for those with a balance of IQ (intelligence quotient), EQ (emotional quotient), CQ (cultural quotient), PQ (perception quotient), and strong work ethic.[87] Per my interpretation, IQ helps us reason and solve problems, EQ and CQ help us connect with others, and PQ helps us perceive and anticipate. In plain words, look for people who are smart, know themselves, can relate to others, and work hard. Too often, I have seen people promoted up management ranks based on IQ, and they do not get the best out of their teams because they lack the other attributes.

Do not only rely on a hierarchical pipeline to promote. Look deeper in the organization and uncover hidden gems. You can only uncover these gems if you walk around and get to know your organization. In large organizations, this is hard to do, but encourage your management teams to do this. When they do, they will uncover talent. I have done this and promoted the unlikeliest people, who went on to amaze me and the business.

In this regard, I see the rags-to-success story of Sidney J. Weinberg as an inspiring lesson for any manager.[88] Sidney dropped out of school at the age of thirteen and started as a janitor's assistant at Goldman Sachs. Paul Sachs, one of the founders, was impressed with young Sidney's work ethic and saw much potential in him. Sachs sent Sidney to college, where he learned economics and finance. A few years passed, and Sydney rose in the organization. In 1930, right in the midst of the Great Depression, Sidney rescued Goldman Sachs from bankruptcy. He remained chairman of the venerated firm for the next thirty-nine years and earned the sobriquet "Mr. Wall Street." Sidney Weinberg was an amazing person, but spare a thought for Paul Sachs, who looked beyond titles to discover and groom this incredible talent.

When you spend the time to create awareness, inculcate knowing the numbers, establish roles and responsibilities, motivate a sense of urgency through your leaders, teach resourcefulness by growing your capability cube, prune yellow leaves that enervate the company, validate your effort with visible wins, and reinforce achievement with recognition, then you have a high chance of speeding up cultural transformation.

Change is hard and often not easily accepted, especially cultural change. I liken this change to the reaction your immune system has to a vaccine. You may develop a fever and your body may ache. You can have bad headaches, fatigue, and nausea. These are side effects of your body developing immunity. It is not rejection, but the normal process of building immunity. You need to take the entire dosage of vaccines to build full immunity, and you cannot stop just because you have a mild reaction. And when you get the full dose, your immunity gets stronger, just as productive change makes a company stronger. The lesson here is to be prepared for a hard haul and weather the side effects in bringing cultural change. Conviction, resilience, and perseverance will bring results.

Foster the Right Leadership – Leading the Army

The second part of building culture involves fostering the right leadership. Empowered organizations are created by leaders who build understanding across the company and reinforce positive behaviors. These leaders gain credibility through substance and are typically admired and respected by the organization. It is easier to follow someone you admire and respect. The leaders I admired and learned the most from had the following five qualities:

- Vision
- Leading by example
- Managerial courage

- Communication clarity
- Curiosity to evolve

Vision

Vision is the ability to see ahead and chart a path of success to the desired goal.

First and foremost, leaders need to have vision. Each of us has our favorites in this category. Henry Ford of Ford Motor Company, Jamsetji Tata of the Tata Group, Lars Magnus Ericsson of Ericsson, Masaru Ibuka and Akio Morita of Sony, Steve Jobs of Apple, Josephine Esther Mentzer (Estee Lauder) of the Estee Lauder Companies, Bill Gates of Microsoft, Larry Page and Sergey Brin of Google, Elon Musk of Tesla and SpaceX, Jeff Bezos of Amazon, and Morris Chang of TSMC top my personal list.

A vision is created by understanding where you are, where you want to go, and how to get there. Great leaders are never satisfied with where they are. They want more and develop their wanted state and plans to get there.

If the vision is significant in scope, the leader needs help, and for this, they need to convince people in the organization to follow them and help realize the vision. This is not an easy task—the leader is asking their team to trust them with something that does not exist and also trust their ability to lead them to the goal. This means the vision must be credible, realistic, create excitement, and be valued. An unrealizable vision is a fantasy. A vision that is driven by illusions of grandeur is a vivid imagination at work.

To create a vision, the leader must possess a deep understanding of the factors highlighted in the prior chapter on strategy:

- The market the company operates in

- The company and how it is placed in the market relative to competitors
- The company's competitors and how they may evolve
- The company's capabilities and gaps to realize the vision
- What it takes to win and what may trip the company up
- The history of how and why others have tried and failed or won with similar approaches

These factors raise hard questions that must be answered before one can pitch a vision and get buy-in.

The leader must possess deep conviction that their vision is right and that they will get there come hell or high water. This requires the leader to display courage and persevere, because there will be bad periods that will test their belief, abetted by the scores of skeptics. It is the leader's confidence, conviction, and focus that will get them through these times. I say "focus" because when people panic, they thrash about. When the chips are down, one needs to stop, take stock, and start fixing things step by step.

I met Neil Armstrong, the first person to step onto the moon, at a company event and was privileged to take a photo with him. I proudly display that photo in my home office. He was the most humble and respectful person I have ever met. He described himself as an engineer sent to place a mirror on the moon for the guys at Los Alamos. And he told us that when he and Buzz Aldrin were about to land on the moon, their spacecraft's guidance computer had a series of glitches.

They could have aborted the mission due to the possibility—and extreme danger—of not coming back. But he could see the moon just below. He had not come 238,000 miles to abort his mission. He landed the module and walked into history. Now that is courage and conviction.

As for perseverance, I am reminded of my time racing sailboats. We would occasionally lean so heavily off the boat to reduce the surface area on the water that the boat would capsize with a gust of wind. When that happens, you have a few options. You can hang around the boat hoping to be rescued and not finish the race. Or you can stand on the centerboard, causing the boat, still full of water, to flip over. Then you can climb into the boat and start bailing water with a can.

I typically chose the second option. As the water got to a very low level inside the boat, we tightened up the sail and let the boat start moving. When the boat gained momentum, we pulled the suction valve and released the remaining water in the boat. And this process speaks to wanting to persevere and not give up. When things go wrong, you need to right the boat and follow a process before you start moving again, and then you can drain the remaining water.

Most visionaries also think far and deep and are pragmatic. They do not try to scale a mountain all at once. They break their scaling into phases and plan each phase meticulously. They hire people with the right skills for each phase. They set what needs to be achieved by when and judiciously spend money along the way to the top of the mountain, because money is like oxygen—without it, you cannot reach the top.

Finally, realize that a vision is time dependent. One may be ahead of one's time. Maybe the market is not ready for the product, the technology is not there to make it usable or cost-effective, or there is just no compelling use-case. Sometimes, one falls behind because the product takes too much time to develop, and others get ahead.

All said and done, for a company, a leader without vision creates an uncertain future.

Leading by Example

The technology and business futurist Joel Arthur Barker wrote that the difference between a leader and a manager is that a manager manages within a paradigm while a leader manages between paradigms.[89]

Managing between paradigms requires the leader to convince their employees to buy into a vision and strategy and deliver to it. As we all know, it is easier to follow someone who walks the talk and leads by example. Such leaders are more aligned with their employees, avoiding the creation of a chasm of power and position.

Feudal lords of the Middle Ages ruled their serfs through dependence and deprivation. Serfs had no rights. Employees in modern society have more choices, and it is my experience that they work for people as much as for companies because it is easier to relate to people.

Leading by example is an attribute that drives culture via behavior. Such leaders exhibit behaviors to be mimicked to set the tone and the way they want their companies to act. This is no different from parents who want to bring up their children a certain way. If the parents do not behave properly and set a positive example, they should not expect that their children will. As the well-known adage goes, "The apple does not fall far from the tree." Parents set an example by teaching, coaching, mentoring, and inculcating a value system that will, with hope, last the child's entire life. A child watching his or her parents working long hours at work and home to ensure the family's comfort and safety gets this ethic etched into their system. Leadership in companies is not that different.

Leaders I admired worked as hard as their hardest-working employee, met their commitments and promises (just as they expected others to meet their commitments), had the highest integrity in everything they did, were accountable, and judged employees and results with facts and not opinion. Leading by example to them meant setting a higher bar for themselves versus their employees. These leaders subscribed to the Latin phrase *primus inter pares*, or first among equals.

I will end with a simple story to illustrate a powerful form of leadership. A few years ago, I watched a young coach training a pre-teen boys' basketball team for the Texas Special Olympics. Many of the players wore hoodies that hampered their game and shooting. The parents tried to coax them to take their hoodies off, but the players would not. The coach, who was also wearing a hoodie, took his off and began to shoot from a long range with precision. Then he began to dribble and dunk, as the jargon goes, with serious "hops and handles." Soon enough, the boys took off their hoodies and began to play. Is it possible that they wanted to play like their coach? Is it possible they felt he was one of them? Leading from within is leading from the front.

Managerial Courage

Have you ever worked in a company where you felt the boss had favorites—that there was a club, and you were outside that club? How did you feel?

Earlier in my career, I saw a lot of this, even though I was never affected by it. I saw clubs and fraternities formed, places where you were either in or out. We lost many exceptionally talented people who felt disenfranchised and did not accept how they had to fit in. The focus was "who you knew" and not "what you knew." This was one pattern that I decided I would never allow or compromise on.

Good leaders run their organizations via a meritocracy. Every day, when they walk into their businesses, they park their friendship badges at the door, and everyone is treated based on the merit of their actions and arguments. Consistency drives behavior, which drives culture. It builds organizations, where the rules and boundaries are clear.

When leaders show nepotism, favoritism, or bias toward certain people, others watch because the leader and their actions are very visible. In organizations where people emulate leaders, these actions are amplified, and very soon, you have a fragmented organization of those who are entitled and those who are not. This creates resentment, uncertainty, and resulting inefficiency.

The biggest driver of fairness is managerial courage. This does not mean insubordination or taking your own path. Managerial courage means doing what is right for the company irrespective of the consequences.

In the movie *Invictus*, directed by Clint Eastwood, there is one scene that remains etched in my memory. Nelson Mandela, played by Morgan Freeman, and his chief of staff, Brenda Mazibuko, played by Adjoa Andoh, are about to drive to stop a committee from abolishing the Springboks, the South African national rugby union team—viewed by some as a vestige of apartheid. Mazibuko tells Mandela not to sacrifice his political capital by intervening. Mandela responds that the reason he was elected leader was to make such decisions.[90]

Managerial courage, to me, means:

- When you see something amiss, even among your closest friends, you address it head-on and in the same way you would with any other person in the company.

- When you disagree with your manager or your colleagues, you discuss differences with them frankly. In the end, rank prevails and those above you call the shots. At that point, you have a choice to make—accept it or move on. What is not okay is to regress into passive-aggressive behavior. Rational dialogue creates understanding. Understanding may drive agreement.

- Never reward someone or fail to address an issue because of fear of a particular consequence. Mark Twain said, "Courage is resistance to fear, mastery of fear—not absence of fear."

- Have the same rules to assess, judge, address, and reward everyone's actions.

- Base every judgment and decision on the merits of the facts and not relationships. It is more *what* rather than *who*.

- Hold everyone accountable, and reward employees based on their actions and results, not merely for loyalty.

Communication Clarity

Communication has the force of nature's elements—it can shape ideas, values, beliefs, and behaviors, just like the elements have shaped our geographical landscape. Great leaders possess the ability to communicate and can shape organizations.

Leaders I learned the most from spoke succinctly, with facts, were engaging and engrossing, and most of all, made me think and reflect on what they said. I gleaned brilliant nuggets of wisdom and lifelong lessons through their communication. They were genuine and convincing. They energized their organization with clarity, encouragement, and hope. The most significant part for me, however, was the clarity of their communication.

As the newly appointed CTO of Ericsson Mobile Phones in the year 2000, I was preparing for my first meeting with the chairman of Ericsson's board. He was visiting our site to understand why our business was underperforming. We had lost over $500 million in the previous year. The presentation I prepared was horrible—long and rambling with every fact that I believed led to our misfortune—forgetting that my talk was only thirty minutes. Had I given this talk, I would have confused everyone and confidence in me would have dropped.

My former boss and mentor agreed to review my slides. He was a person of few words, used email sparingly, and preferred pen and paper. Yet he had the amazing ability to be crystal clear and impactful in as few words as possible. I realized with time that this ability comes from clarity of thought. He gave me the following advice: succinctly state the problem you are solving, then state how you will solve the problem, and finally state when your solution will show results, all in three slides, and avoid acronyms. Making three impactful slides is harder than making thirty. In essence, his advice was to think clearly and educate to foster understanding. His view was that clarity brings understanding, and understanding may bring agreement. I followed this advice and did not disappoint the chairman. This advice has been invaluable and has guided my presentations ever since.

While leaders can energize an organization, the way a company communicates reflects its culture. If every topic and issue is escalated up the management chain versus being solved at the right level in the organization, it means the organization is not empowered, or there is a lack of trust. At the other extreme, if most topics and issues are delegated, redirected, consistently delayed, or ignored, it may indicate a lack of accountability and engagement. Either way, it is a problem. Ideally, issues should be discussed by owners and contributors to find a solution, as explained in this chapter under Assign Playing Positions. If the solution needs a decision that is beyond the authority level of the owners and contributors discussing it, then it should be escalated to the next level for the decision.

Emails and other electronic information exchange tools like Slack and Teams are common forms of communication in many organizations. They are all useful tools but often hurt productivity and sap energy when overused. It is important to know which messages to send to whom, and how to make the messages succinct, with clarity of purpose. If this rule is not followed, inboxes get cluttered; tons of unread messages pile up in Outlook, Slack, or Teams; and people spend hours every day at work and at home going through messages and replying, creating even more messages. This is a stressful situation for many employees and detracts from productivity. Furthermore, when employees' inboxes or chat channels are bombarded with an overdose of messages, they might not feel a strong urge to read their messages—meaning they could miss a crucial message. Often, messaging via email or Slack or Teams is not the most expedient way to get quick decisions on complex topics; unless the request is clear with supporting data, it leads to multiple exchanges that take significant time. I prefer face-to-face meetings or conference calls when making quick decisions. Such calls, even when done long distance, are supported by these modern applications. On hard problems, I still prefer face-to-face meetings where we can draw on a whiteboard and brainstorm without time constraints to solve problems.

When I spent more than two hours a day on email or other information exchange tools, I had to ignore more important tasks, such as talking to investors, customers, suppliers, partners, and employees and working on strategy, administration, and problem-solving. As such, I informed my organization of my preferred methods of communication if they needed to get decisions from me, as well as when to involve me to avoid pulling me into things they could solve themselves. This process took a fair amount of time before it became efficient, partly because I was not disciplined enough.

Curiosity to Evolve

Many years ago, a friend of mine told me a great story, which turns out to be a well-known experiment on selective attention, described in *The Invisible Gorilla: How our Intuitions Deceive Us* by Christopher Chabris and Daniel Simons.[91] My friend and his management team were participating in a team-building exercise. They were situated in a gym and paired to pass a basketball to a partner without dropping the ball. Each pair began this exercise with intense focus on passing the ball. Midway through the exercise, a person dressed in a gorilla suit ran through the gym, and many participants missed it. Too often, leaders and their organizations get so engrossed in their work that they do not see the gorilla in the room.

The leaders I admired were curious. They spent time learning about trends, reflected on their research, anticipated, and thought about disruptions. The more they learned about their market, customers, technology, business models, competitors, and channels, the more prepared they were to anticipate and proactively thwart disruptions by creating these themselves.

Most disruptions, in hindsight, could have been predicted. The key is how to foretell, prepare, and generate the disruption instead of being upended by it. This reflects a need to constantly innovate in every element of your business.

One such disruption occurred during the summer of 1997, when I was heading technology at Ericsson Mobile Phones in the U.S. Our phones, like everyone else's in those days, had poor battery life. So, we developed the technology to radically improve our battery life. This technology involved putting all the circuits in the phone to sleep when the phone was not in use and waking the phone up periodically to check if there were messages for it—"sleep mode." Implementing sleep mode was tricky and required extra development effort in software. Our product-development team felt no urgency to implement this feature, as they thought the competition, Nokia, was two years behind.

But Nokia soon leapfrogged us by introducing phones with incredible battery life. They skipped an entire generation of technology to get ahead. They did what we least expected. We scrambled to respond, but it took us a year to catch up with Nokia's progress, during which time we lost market share. It was a hard lesson that we had to learn due to complacency and arrogance.

The second disruption was self-inflicted by not thinking ahead. Phone user interfaces in the late 1990s were not intuitive and were hard to use. A typical user interface required using a joystick to scroll through a tree of options to find a function. Motorola and Ericsson had the foresight to address this user-interface problem, and in 2001, they launched black-and-white, pen-based touchscreen phones called the Tai Chi (A6188) and P800, respectively. Shortly thereafter, Ericsson/ Sony-Ericsson launched what I consider the precursor to Apple's iconic iPhone, the P900. This phone had a full-color, icon-based touchscreen user interface based on the Symbian UIQ operating system. The main drawback with this screen was that it had to be used with a pen or sty-lus, due to available technology.

My boss—Katsumi Ihara, the CEO of Sony-Ericsson—and I met regularly to discuss new product visions. As the CTO, I tried to gather as much insight as possible to develop technology roadmaps. During one meeting in the fall of 2002 at a London restaurant, Ihara-san explained his vision of a slim touchscreen phone evolved from the P900 that would not use a pen but your fingers. Sony labs had created just such an intuitive interface called the "Feel Interface," which allowed you to drag and drop files, pinch and zoom, and scroll through menus with your finger. This vision would have been transformational had we executed on it. However, our business division, which made prod-uct-investment decisions, decided to discontinue the P900 product line, probably for budget reasons. As a business, we lacked conviction.

Four years passed, and in 2006, at the Freescale Technology Forum, I was on a panel hosted by Jeff Greenfield, a respected and notable talk-show host. He asked me what I thought the next killer app for phones was. I had not forgotten Ihara-san's vision and said it was the user inter-face. Six months later, Steve Jobs announced the iPhone, and the rest is history. Steve Jobs understood what the market really wanted and had the conviction to bet his business on it.

I found having periodic strategy sessions essential to promoting new thinking. At these strategy sessions, you should challenge the status quo. Dedicate different sessions to focus on how global trends are impacting every facet of your business—business models, technology, HR and talent, compensation, manufacturing, contracts, marketing, and so on. Ask managers to present how can they leverage global trends to grow their capability cube.

Every few sessions, you should try to invite a broader group of managers to attend so they, too, can participate and add to the conversation and thinking. It is important to stress at these meetings that you must always expect your competitors to do the unexpected.

In short, a healthy dose of paranoia in every element of your business will prepare each team to evolve and not get consumed by their daily work.

Summary: Culture
The Castle's Keep

Fostering the right behavior with the right leadership can transform cultures to realize strategies, as follows.

- Driving the right behavior involves creating awareness, instilling knowing the numbers, establishing roles and responsibilities, motivating a sense of urgency through your leaders, teaching resourcefulness by growing your capability cube, pruning yellow leaves, validating your transformation through visible successes, and reinforcing it through timely recognition of those who contribute to that success.

- Leadership is equally essential to molding culture. The leaders I admired had vision, led by example, were impartial and championed a meritocracy, communicated with clarity, ensured their organizations communicated efficiently, brought energy to their organizations, and were curious to evolve, so they invariably anticipated the gorilla in the room.

- You will need conviction and resilience to bring about cultural change. Be prepared for an adverse reaction and side effects but persevere to prevail.

Having focused on the company's culture, we will now move on to building the defensive towers, which are used to look outward to determine an approaching threat.

- Will the attack come from poorly defined products?
- Will the attack come from failed product delivery?
- Will the attack come from a weak sales channel?
- Will the attack come from poor execution?

If you are under constant bombardment and putting out fires, you will have no time to build your company's culture. Castle towers reinforce the perimeter wall and give it both defensive and offensive capabilities. In the following chapters we will go into details of building the various towers that protect the castle walls and the keep.

5

The East Tower
Winning Products Are
Your Most Effective Weapons

One key to defending a castle involved the ability to look outward—keeping an eye on the horizon and recognizing when a threat was incoming.

There were different types of castle towers that protected the castle perimeter or curtain wall. Each tower featured unique design flourishes. Sometimes, towers were built directly into or above the wall, sometimes beside it.

Watch towers gave guards a bird's-eye view of approaching enemies. Some castles had small turrets mounted on the outside of the perimeter wall, called bartizans. These turrets were also known as guerites or echaugettes. They could accommodate one or two guards and gave these watchmen a good view of the landscape. It also allowed guards to shoot down at enemies who came close to the base of the perimeter wall.

Defensive towers were strategically built along the castle's perimeter wall to house guards. These towers included features like those of the wall, such as alcoves, loopholes, and arrow slits to fire projectiles on the enemy. Some castles included secret compartments in the ceilings of entryways and passageways called "murder holes,"[92] which guards used to shoot down at or drop harmful items on attackers.

Corner towers were placed at the abutment of two sides of a perimeter wall. These towers housed guards armed with bows and crossbows who could fire at enemies who got close to and tried to scale or tunnel under the walls. When the perimeter wall got too long, archers and crossbowmen could not cover the entire length of the perimeter wall, leaving some of the wall exposed. To strengthen the defense, intermediate structures called flanking towers were constructed. These flanking towers strengthened the perimeter walls and shortened the distance to the next tower, allowing archers and crossbowmen to protect the entire perimeter.

Our castle has four such towers, which we will label north, south, east, and west after the cardinal directions. Each tower, representing a major function in your company, protects a section of the perimeter wall—your strategy. The towers and wall are interlinked via ramparts, symbolizing the interdependence between the strategy and the major functions. One cannot exist without the other.

Product creation is represented by the East Tower.

Products and services, which I will collectively refer to as products, are what a company sells to grow revenue and profit. Products build the company's brand. They are a company's most effective weapons.

The collection of all products that a company produces and sells is its product portfolio. This product portfolio should evolve from the business strategy, just as the shape of the perimeter wall determines the placement of the defensive towers. However, strategy and dynamics differ from company to company, which in turn defines their product portfolios.

Companies like Tesla have a few complex products (battery-powered electric vehicles), while publishers like HarperCollins have giant offerings of far simpler products (books).

The five most valuable companies in the world as of March 2022 (Apple, Microsoft, Saudi Aramco, Alphabet, and Amazon) all started off with one product and then diversified their portfolios as they grew. Apple started as a computer company and now offers a variety of devices from phones, tablets, laptops, watches, applications, content, and digital services. Microsoft started as an operating system company and now offers a wide variety of software and collaboration tools, devices (e.g., Surface, Xbox), and cloud computing. Saudi Aramco began producing crude oil and now produces a variety of hydrocarbons and chemicals, mainly derived from oil, such as gasoline, diesel, propane, ethane, butane, kerosene, fuel oil, jet-fuel, LPG, sulfur, and asphalt, used in homes, businesses, and farms. Amazon began selling books and moved into e-commerce and on-line marketplaces, cloud computing, digital streaming, devices, and artificial intelligence (smart speakers like Echo and Echo Dot). Alphabet (Google) started as a search engine on web browsers but now offers smartphone software and applications (Android), mapping, cloud computing, devices (e.g., Pixel, Nest), content via YouTube, and security services.

Without the ability to define and create compelling products that sell, your strategy is effectively doomed. There is no magic formula, but the following eight principles can help you increase the chances of success significantly:

- Intersect transformational trends through systematic research.
- Be a first mover, as often as possible.
- Define multi-year product roadmaps for offense and defense.
- Convert disruptive ideas to disruptive products.

- Define products using scientific methods.

- Prioritize what customers need.

- Build product stickiness through customer investment.

- Constantly assess your position via the quadrants of truth.

Intersect Transformational Trends Through Systematic Research

New trends in technology, business models, customer behavior, and unmet needs all bring big opportunities. They are giant ocean waves that sweep away everything in their way. If you intersect and leverage these waves to your advantage like a windsurfer, however, you can go far. Like a professional windsurfer, you must meticulously study your area, the currents, wave patterns, then paddle up to catch the right wave and ride it.

Likewise, uncovering transformational trends requires systematic, continuous, and thorough research. Use the ORCa model I described in chapter four as a guideline for this research and analysis and to catch the right wave. With this research and analysis, you can create scenarios and bet on the most promising option to pursue. This takes courage and conviction because you are about to make a big investment.

By late 2002, Nokia was the most dominant mobile-phone supplier in the market and a hard act to follow. The newly formed Sony-Ericsson, where I was CTO, was struggling and had lost 30 percent in revenue since its formation eighteen months earlier. We initially tried to copy Nokia, which was futile. Nokia had cost advantages due to scale and a superior supply chain, broader sales-channel coverage, and excellent execution. We had to do something different.

As a management team, we realized that none of our competitors were building true multimedia phones, which required a completely new chipset and software architecture. This endeavor would take major investments in innovation and time. It was a big bet, and we could not risk that it might fail. But if we succeeded, we would generate global buzz and interest. Consumers wanted phones with color displays, cameras, music, videos, and games. We were attempting to change the way people used their phones.

Market trends offered us a window of opportunity. First, the world was racing to launch 3G cellular systems, and no competitor had a technology lead. Second, 3G cellular systems offered high data rates over which users could download music and video files with low latency and even exchange pictures. If we could exploit these 3G capabilities with suitable applications, we would have our differentiation. Third, one of our parent companies, Ericsson, was a leader in 3G systems, and we could learn a lot from their feature roadmap. Lastly, our other parent, Sony, had multimedia content and a great consumer brand. Our plan was to leverage all these advantages to build winning products.

We proceeded to architect and build a new platform that would enable multimedia phones. These phones would have rich color displays, download and play music and videos, take high-quality pictures, and allow people to play games. This approach leveraged Sony's consumer brand and content assets as well as Ericsson's leadership in 3G wireless technology.

We successfully built our new platform via EMP, and Sony-Ericsson used this platform to launch exciting multimedia phones. Sony supplied great multimedia content. Sony-Ericsson's engineering, supply chain, marketing, and sales teams executed perfectly. The products wowed customers with many firsts, such as the T610 (the first sixty-five thousand-color display phone) and later the Walkman™ brand of phones. These hit products built the brand value, and over the next five years (2002–2007), the revenue tripled.[93]

As the CTO guiding the technology strategy, I learned firsthand that a recipe for defining winning products is to anticipate and intersect transformational market trends or consumer needs at the right time. But more importantly, this experience taught me that it takes all your advantages to differentiate in the marketplace.

Be a First Mover, as Often as Possible

As with so many things, product timing is crucial. The goal is to make your products create or intersect future market trends and to get there first. Be a *first mover* and not a *late mover* as often as possible. First movers can set the pace to gain an insurmountable lead. This happens when the first mover has not only great products but excellent sales channels to distribute their innovative product and capture large market share.

Of course, it is not always possible to anticipate every trend, and companies do react late when they miss a trend. When this happens, companies are typically forced to invest heavily and shift resources to catch up. Being a late mover works in large markets with unmet demand and where the leader has not addressed the demand, creating openings. In such situations, these late movers can also erode a leader's position if they close the product competitiveness gap and have the channel power necessary to capture a sizable customer base.

Coca-Cola was the leader in the soda industry, and Pepsi settled into the second spot.[94] Today Coca-Cola is the world's largest beverage company, and PepsiCo has evolved into the world's largest food processing company. Uber innovated and gave us rideshare, and Lyft emerged later. Amazon set the trend for online shopping, and many retailers have followed. Apple launched the iPad, and it was disruptive. From 2011 to 2021, Apple has led the tablet computer market. Its share, as of early 2021, had dropped from 55 percent to 32 percent as other tablets have emerged, but even with a reduced market share, the iPad still sets the bar and commands a brand premium.[95]

There are also many examples where late-mover products did not make a dent, such as Google Plus versus Facebook—or consider Keurig Kold, an expensive answer to SodaStream's home carbonation products, that failed to catch on and was discontinued within a year of its launch.[96] Another example is Apple Maps, which tried to match Google's mapping technology. However, Apple Maps had several glitches when it launched in 2012 and never caught up with Google's superior maps. Google still dominates mapping.[97]

If you are a late mover and entering a market with strong competition, you need to find a weakness in your biggest competitor's castle wall. Then focus your trebuchet at that weak spot and blast away until the wall falls. Such was the case when Apple entered the phone market in 2007 and toppled a leader who was selling more than four hundred million phones per year, taking the pole position. Apple has never been a late mover since.

Next, consider the case of Tesla. It entered a market dominated by car manufacturers whose vehicles were powered by internal combustion engines that run on petrol/gas or diesel. Tesla entered with battery-powered electric vehicles. There are three good reasons to drive an electric vehicle. First, the price per mile of driving an electric vehicle is well below 50 percent that of a gas/petrol powered car.[98] Second, electric vehicles have fewer moving parts than cars with internal combustion engines, which leads to lower lifetime maintenance. Third, it is eco-friendly.

However, to succeed, Tesla did several things differently from other automakers. They introduced a nationwide network of superchargers to charge their cars, aided by applications in their cars and smartphones to find these stations. Tesla sold directly to customers and not via dealer networks used by all other auto manufacturers. This allowed them to connect more intimately with their buyers, build loyalty, and get feedback to innovate faster. They built massive battery factories to control the innovation and cost of the most important part of their car: the battery.

Their strategy has worked. Many automakers have now announced that their line-ups will be fully electrified within five years.[99] As of October 2021, Tesla's valuation was one trillion U.S. dollars, which compares to the combined valuation of Toyota, Volkswagen, BYD, Daimler, GM, BMW, Ford, Stellantis, Honda, and SAIC, despite having a miniscule market share.[100] Was Tesla a late mover or first mover? I would say the latter.

Well-run companies do not consistently choose to be late movers—it happens when they miss trends, something that should not become a habit due to the risk factor. Moving late requires unplanned investments coupled with expedited and rigorous execution to close the product, sales channel, and execution gaps compared to the leaders so that your company's product can be an alternative. There is also the risk of intellectual-property infringement in copying what the leader has done. Furthermore, if the leader has compelling differentiation, it takes time to nullify this advantage, if catching up is even possible. Thus, the risks of achieving a good return on investment as a late mover only increase with time.

This is exactly why you must have multi-year product roadmaps, thinking well in advance of the battles you will fight to defend your castle and capture new castles down the road.

Define Multiyear Product Roadmaps – Defensive and Offensive Game Plans

Multiyear product roadmaps are an outgrowth of strategy and reflect the payoff of choosing the right landscape around your castle—from moats that are wide and deep and full of predatory creatures, to jagged rocks that are difficult to traverse. The goal is to make it as time-consuming and treacherous as possible for attackers to infiltrate your castle and to give your tower guards opportunities to neutralize threats and even launch counterattacks.

But defense alone is not enough. By capitalizing on strategic advantages, your company's product portfolio must aim to completely address market opportunities and be more competitive in order to launch attacks to capture larger market share. Do your innovative products positively surprise the market? Do you regularly check if your products cover all segments of the market, every relevant price shelf in each segment, and all geographies, and are they competitive to maximize your revenue and profits? Do you make sure you are not leaving openings for competitors to enter and erode your market share?

In most companies, product management is responsible for creating and maintaining these roadmaps. The better defined your product roadmaps are, the harder it is for competitors to successfully attack you, and the better your chance of attacking them to capture territory (market share). By having a roadmap of products launched with a cadence, you never stop the barrage on the enemy. They need to be scrambling and putting out fires constantly to minimize their time to innovate. And, by chance if you miss an important feature in one product, your next product can address the oversight.

To define a product roadmap, I recommend following the ORCa model, outlined earlier. Recall that this model considers the market opportunity, product relevance (customer need, competition, and trends), and the differentiation needed in your products to be successful.

Creating a good roadmap begins with defining what products you will produce and launch each year, over multiple years. This roadmap must be composed of the following elements:

- A definition of each product

- A detailed breakdown of all technologies necessary to realize each product
- All supporting material (collateral) and tools that are needed to make each product a commercial success
- A timeline of what is needed and when to secure each product's launch

Product definition is hard. You must get it right from the start. Don't fall into the "buzzword trap" and define too many features—or, at the other extreme, miss key features or forget the core value proposition for your target customer. These mistakes will delay your product or make it fall short of customer expectations. So often we rush to do things due to time pressure, but we always have time to do it again. Take the time to define your product, *thoroughly*.

A smartphone's definition includes its industrial design (the form factor), user interface, features, and specifications to be met. To build this smartphone, a manufacturer will need to define elements like the chips, memory, display, battery, camera, electronic components, antenna, printed circuit boards, mechanics, charger, SIM card, and accessories like headphones. In addition, the manufacturer will need to choose an operating system, wireless-protocol software, software applications, and software tools such as over-the-air updates. The manufacturer will also need to define the service and repair needs and material, tools and support for its sales and marketing teams—collateral. Finally, it is very important to have a timeline of what is needed, and when, to secure a product launch.

In late 2001, our product management department at Sony-Ericsson defined the T610 with its sixty-five thousand-color display. We were poised to cause a major disruption at a time when most phones had monochrome displays and a few had four thousand colors. But to achieve our vision, we needed a special chip to drive such a display—a chip that did not exist. We set an aggressive schedule to have this chip developed by one of our trusted suppliers. With nine months left to launch the phone, this supplier informed us that they could not meet the delivery date. Without this chip, we would not have our game-changing phone. I was CTO at the time, and my team and I scrambled to find a solution. We had three months to find a solution and another six months to incorporate it and launch our phone. Luckily, a third-party supplier had a chip and was willing to make a minor modification so we could use it. We also had to develop new software to use this chip. The engineering team worked overtime to do this, and the phone launched on time, was an immense success, and generated $3 billion in sales. Had we had a truly complete roadmap with every critical component qualified in time alignment to support our product launches, we would not have had to scramble and put our transformative product launch at risk.

A multiyear product roadmap also acts as the nucleus to provide visibility and align different functions of the company to produce a string of products. It becomes the blueprint that each department follows. Engineers innovate and build solutions to the product roadmap's specifications, purchasing buys components to these specifications, supply chain plans how to build such products for the best cost, and sales and marketing plan how to market and sell these products. Ideally, each department should create execution plans based on this nucleus and share them with other departments. Alignment is key.

To maintain the above alignment, I made sure my roadmaps were maintained in a single document, updated every month, and sent to every department every month. This allowed everyone to know what had changed each month and what needed to be done to adapt or change course. If such coordination does not happen, departments are liable to get out of sync and will likely miss targets. Changes in the roadmap are common, especially for products further out in time. New market trends and innovations from within or outside the company can be disruptive. Thus, it is essential that the company develops a process to monitor changes and adapt the roadmap to be current. A good process is one that solicits input from all departments of the company to refine the roadmap and make it as strong as possible. When it comes to seeing attacks, a three-hundred-and-sixty-degree view is better than a sectional view.

Companies that are unable to define clear multiyear roadmaps often must react to market trends and competition. These late movers are at risk of losing market share. In my experience, I have found that most companies have roadmaps, but they are not as complete as they could be to drive every part of the business for success. For example, a semiconductor manufacturer may have a great roadmap for chips, but seldom do they have a great roadmap for the software that makes their chips winners.

Alternately, consider hydrogen fuel cells that power vehicles such as the Toyota Mirai and Honda Clarity. Fuel cell electric vehicles (FCEVs) are especially efficient for long distance transportation of goods, such as cargo carrying trucks.[101] They also reduce the carbon footprint significantly. However, hydrogen is not naturally available and has to be produced using methane by a process called electrolysis. Until there are fueling stations that can produce cheap hydrogen, this amazing innovation will lag behind battery electric vehicles (BEVs).

Robust product roadmaps will increase your chances of being a first mover and help you stand apart from your competitors.

Convert Disruptive Ideas to Disruptive Products

So often, as I have seen in my career, companies identify brilliant ideas that could lead their products to large market share, but they ultimately fall short. The two main reasons for this are because their plans are not well thought through and because they get distracted, lose focus, and don't execute well. In the end, the product does not turn out to be what it was meant to be. This is fatal.

To make a disruptive product from a disruptive idea, many things need to come together. Delivery of a disruptive product requires

- defining your product's winning proposition; and
- planning and executing every step that realizes that proposition.

I will use the famous Harvard business case study on Southwest Airlines to illustrate my point. Southwest Airlines entered a crowded U.S. market in 1993 amongst a field of eleven competitors.[102] Their product was a service—airplane travel.

Their strategy was to enter as a budget airline with a twist. Their benchmark for pricing wasn't other airlines but any form of transportation, including automobiles. This was radical thinking. Could it be done?

This meant they had to streamline their costs to compete with people driving between cities instead of flying. They knew what it cost to drive between cities, and that was one important data point in their model. They must have also estimated how many passengers would fly with them at various ticket prices. To be profitable, the cost per passenger had to be lower than the ticket price.

The main costs of running an airline includes cost of airplanes (buy or lease), fuel, airplane maintenance costs, landing costs at airports, gate occupancy costs (depending on how long the plane is parked at the gate), labor costs (people who work for the airline), food and drinks for passengers, and marketing costs to get passengers to fly in your planes.

To optimize their costs, Southwest flew one type of aircraft (the Boeing 737) and used relatively newer planes to reduce maintenance. They solicited ideas from their pilots to reduce fuel costs. They flew directly between smaller airports that had lower landing fees. Several other airlines used a hub and spoke model—flying to hubs and making connections to the destination. Southwest expedited boarding and deboarding passengers, reducing gate occupancy time. They served drinks and peanuts but no food, eliminated paper tickets, and used direct internet marketing—no travel agents or intermediaries. This made them very cost competitive. I am sure they iterated their plans many times to get their costs right to secure profitability.

Cost was not the only factor. They modeled the most convenient times for their target passengers to fly, made booking tickets easy, simplified the boarding process, made passengers feel welcome on the plane, and made sure that passengers were okay trading no food for a cheap ticket.

Well, it worked. Southwest has morphed since those early days. They may not even be the cheapest airline today. However, they are the only domestic airline in the world that has been profitable for forty-seven years.[103]

Define Products Using Scientific Methods

I will assume companies define products to maintain or gain market share (revenue or number of units) and generate profits. That is, they want to maximize their return on investment or ROI.

A product with the greatest set of specifications but poor business-case assumptions will invariably fail. The product may cost too much, destroying its profitability, or be late, missing its market opportunity. Once a company has sunk a lot of money into the development of a product, I have rarely seen it be stopped on account of a bad business case. The result is lost opportunity, lost revenue, and lost profits.

I use a model called Design for Growth—this is an iterative process that creates a business case for each set of product assumptions and allows planners to evaluate outcomes and pick the right option. It is not foolproof, but it adds rigor to the product-creation process.

Recall that earlier we stated that every product has a price shelf, or a price range that the market will pay for the product. The market leader usually sets the price range, as well as the product's *benchmark score*, which establishes the expected product-value proposition at this price range.

For example, the benchmark score for a laptop can be calculated from a combination of seven attributes:

- Performance metrics, such as computational speed for various applications
- Start-up time
- Hours of continuous usage on a single charge of its battery
- The laptop's weight
- How stable is the laptop—does it rarely crash?
- Security—is it immune to viruses?
- Does it have appropriate connection ports to plug in projectors, memory devices, and other extras?

One such benchmark score could be net promoter score (NPS)—how your customers rate the laptop. Your product must compete against the market leader and, hence, can be measured relative to the leader's benchmark score by a *product score*. Alternately, in the absence of a leader, you can set your own high bar through customer surveys.

The *product score* is the rating a customer or user would give your product based on the same calculation used to set the benchmark score. The better your product's score relative to the benchmark score, the higher the probability of taking market share and securing the higher end of that shelf's price range. The worse the score, the higher the probability of being at the lower end of the shelf's price range and/or selling in lower volumes.

As an example, assume the leader sets the benchmark score of 70 points and this score has allowed them to secure 40 percent of the market at a shelf price of $800 to $1,000. If your product score is 55 points—which is 15 points below the leader—you will most likely need to price your product at the lower end of the price range ($800) to be able to sell it. On the other hand, if your product score is higher than the benchmark score, say 80 points, you are likely to take share from the leader.

This correlation (or mapping) of product score to market share (number of units sold) is the *share function*. From this share function you can create a *share gain* table, as shown below, which predicts how many units you can expect to sell for each product score value.

Product Score (100 max)	Market Share	Predicted Units Sold
80	50 percent	5,000,000
70	40 percent	4,000,000
60	20 percent	2,000,000
50	1 percent	100,000
40	0 percent	0

Observe in this example that the share function is non-linear. Uniform drops in product score causes disproportionate drops in share (units sold). That is, as you go from a product score of 80 to 70 (10 points), you lose one million units (20 percent drop), from 80 to 60 (20 points) you lose 3 million units (60 percent drop) and from 80 to 50 (30 points) you lose 4.9 million units (98 percent drop).

Your objective is to design your product to secure a product score that maximizes your market share potential.

There are two cautionary notes on calculating the share function and share gain table.

- You must correlate and back-test the share function versus market-share to make sure it is realistic and not biased. This share gain table will also change with time as the benchmarks evolve.

- It is not enough for your product to only secure its desired score. The product must be delivered on time, with the right quality, and you must invest in sales channels and market the product to ensure the product is promoted and sold to secure a corresponding share. The analogy I give is winning a car race—to win, you need to have a great car, great driver, and fuel. You cannot just have a great car and win.

Once constructed, this share gain table will allow you to make design choices and evaluate profitability via the flow chart shown in Figure 8 (see next page). Start from the bottom and work your way up.

First, you compare your product score versus the competitors' product scores. This comparison determines your share function. This share function is mapped to volume (of units) you can secure at that shelf price, using the share gain table. Next, you can calculate your revenue by multiplying the volume of units by the shelf price. From this revenue, you subtract your product cost (cost of goods sold) and operating expenses to calculate your profit.

To illustrate how this model helps with choices, I will use equipment used in movie making as my example. Imagine you run a company that builds and sells workstations for creating visual and special effects (VFX) and computer-generated imagery (CGI) for movies. These workstations use powerful computer and graphics chips that run sophisticated software. Movies like *Jurassic Park, Avatar, Lord of the Rings, Toy Story,* and *Gravity* all used VFX and CGI extensively. VFX and CGI artists use these machines to create spectacular scenes and animations.

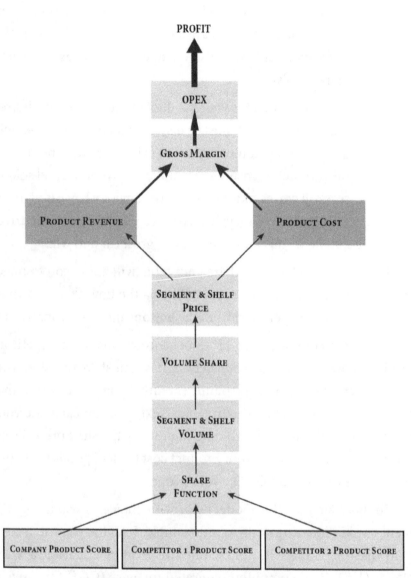

Figure 8: Design for Growth Model

Your company is trying to expand its share in this market, where there is an entrenched leader. There is a real opportunity because customers want the option of another competitive supplier. However, you are unable to meet the benchmark specifications (product score) set by the leader. The engineering team decides that it must make its workstation much more powerful by using higher performance computer and graphics chips and increasing its software development to improve its product score.

The more powerful chips add to product cost, and more software effort increases operating expenses, both of which dilute the profit in the business case. However, by making this choice, your company can create a product that exceeds the benchmark specification (product score), which in turn is likely to capture more share and increase revenue to offset the increase in cost, thereby increasing profits. You may also decide you are willing to accept lower profit, at least for a while, to gain market share.

One can use the flowchart in Figure 8 to iterate design choices and associated costs to determine the best return on investment. You may also conclude through this exercise that the opportunity is not worth pursuing because the costs are way too high, it takes too long to build the right product, and the risk (based on what else you need to do) for generating a good return on investment is too high.

When one uses this model across the product portfolio, it becomes more powerful because you can blend revenue and gross margins across multiple products to arrive at a portfolio that optimizes your business revenue and profit. You should run this model on each product by sales region and analyze the results. If I had to prioritize, I would first weed out less attractive (lower profit) products and then less attractive sales regions (lower revenue) for a given product.

A critical aspect of this model is to capture both the product's cost of goods sold and operating expenses accurately. Often, this part of the exercise is not done thoroughly, and it manifests as a bad business case. Make sure you capture all costs in as much detail as possible. These costs must be projected for the entire duration of the product lifetime and reflect anticipated cost changes. The quality of the model depends on the rigor one applies to create the model.

It is equally important to track how one performed against the model by checking what the company committed to achieving when the business case was approved, and execution began against what was realized when the product was sold. I call this analysis *Say-Do*. This Say-Do check helps refine the model and assesses where things possibly went awry.

This process must be owned and run by a department in your organization that has the technical and commercial skill to define, model, analyze, and optimize the product roadmap by collaborating with the rest of the company. In my experience, when this process is centralized in one department like product management, it results in powerful roadmaps. When the function is distributed throughout the company without clear responsibility, the result is poor. Ownership and accountability must go hand in hand.

Prioritize What Customers Need

Product managers in most companies use extensive sets of feature and performance benchmarks (metrics) to compare their products with competitors. These are all valuable, but what matters most is what customers care about and need because they are the ones who buy your products. You can only get this feedback by talking to your customers. This does not mean you take everything a customer says literally and address it. The key is to distill customer feedback into what they like or dislike about your product—and more importantly, what they like about your competitor's product.

When you listen to your customer and create a consistently positive experience with your products that customers cannot find with competing products, you build *brand equity*—value, loyalty, and trust. It is building stickiness.

Some outstanding examples of companies who have built strong brand equity are Starbucks and Tylenol.[104] Starbucks coffee is not just a beverage but is designed to make a connection with its customers. This is evidenced by its loyalty program that has 26.4 million customers as of early 2022.[105] There are even more dazzling statistics: about sixty million people visit the over thirty-one thousand global Starbucks cafes each week, which translates to more than three billion visits per year, with regulars (about 20 percent) visiting the café sixteen times per month.[106] My calculation says each one of these frequent customers spends $500 per year on coffee!

Tylenol from Johnson and Johnson is an over-the-counter pain relief drug. It is amazing that it is chosen by consumers 26 percent more than its competitors.[103] Some of this band equity is achieved by marketing, but in the end, the proof of the pudding is in the eating— the product.

The consumer industry uses a metric called Net Promoter Score (NPS).[107] It is a great metric to compare products based on customer preference.

The way this metric works is as follows. Every rater (consumer) gives the product a score between zero and ten.

- A score of zero through six means "I don't like the product" (detractors).
- A score of seven or eight means "I don't care" (passive position).
- A score of nine or ten means "I like the product" (promoters).

Promoters recommend the product and detractors don't. If one hundred people rate the product and you have forty people who are promoters, thirty people who are passives, and thirty people who are detractors, then your score is calculated as follows: 40 percent promoters minus 30 percent detractors equals an NPS score of 10 percent. You ignore the passives.

As per Customer Guru's 2020 data, the Samsung Galaxy phone has a score of 67 percent and the iPhone a score of 63 percent, which are very good scores.[108] Some other companies with impressive scores are Costco (79 percent), Starbucks (77 percent), Sony (61 percent), and John Deere (54 percent).[109] It is possible to get negative scores if there are more detractors than promoters, which is an awful position.

NPS is a telling metric because the detractors also explain what they did not like about the product. If you correlate your product's NPS against a competitor's NPS, it will tell you what you need to fix; otherwise, you are not in sync with your market and will lose share to that competitor.

In my experience, you do not have to be the best for every feature and attribute. You must be the best at what customers care about and use. For the remaining features and attributes, you need to be within the zone of competitiveness or good enough. This target should be the focus of the product-management and engineering teams' work.

NPS is useful for end products such as cellphones, TVs, cameras, laptops, wearables, and enterprise application software. However, it may not be suitable for all products—for example, it is not the best gauge for intermediate products like automotive spares, semiconductor chips, software, and other components that are used to build end products. Intermediate products are better measured by metrics such as:

- How compliant is the intermediate product to customer specifications? This can include cost, quality/reliability, performance, and other requirements that impact the end product's NPS.

- How easily is the intermediate product integrated into the next-level solution?

- How does the intermediate product perform under different use-cases that the customer specifies?

- How well is the intermediate product supported by the company selling it?

At EMP, we sold chips and software to original-equipment manufacturers (OEMs) who built mobile phones. We sold intermediate products. In this business, a key metric for our products was compliance with wireless-operator specifications. Every operator (e.g., T-Mobile, AT&T, Vodafone Japan) issued a detailed specification of features and performance, almost four to five thousand items, that our platform had to be compliant with. Without this compliance, our customers, the mobile-phone OEMs (e.g., Samsung, LGE, Sony-Ericsson, Sharp), would not buy the platform because their mobile phones also had to comply with these specifications. We invested to secure this compliance by having dedicated people work out of each major operator's facility to collect requirements and constantly feed them to our engineering teams, who ensured that our products met these requirements. The high level of compliance made our product one of the platforms of choice.

NPS and compliance to wireless-operator specifications are two specific examples. The exact metric or metrics you end up using for competitiveness must be relevant to your business and your customers. Whatever you chose, be the best at what your customer values and wants.

Build Stickiness Through Customer Investment

In chapter one, I defined stickiness as a customer's aversion or barrier to switching to a competitor's offering. Fostering and maintaining customer loyalty and giving customers reasons to stick with you are crucial to maintaining your company's success. Stickiness happens when customers begin to like and trust your products. But stickiness grows when customers invest in your products and do not want to abandon their investment until they have a bad experience.

The following are examples of businesses that have sticky products, which I have either used or worked with closely.

- **Credit Cards:** Take a service business such as a credit card that one has used for years, which has not experienced any fraud and offers great benefits like cash back, low APR (annual percentage rates), loyalty points, etc. In this case, the stickiness is trust and benefits.

- **eCommerce Platforms**: Many online stores build their business on a Software-as-a-Service (SaaS) platform such as Shopify. The online store invested money and effort to build on this platform, along with applications and processes that their customers have adopted and now use to drive the online store's business. The cost of uprooting the platform, applications, and processes and moving to a new SaaS platform is both expensive and disruptive for the online store's end customers. In this case, stickiness arises from investment in a solution that is working well for the company's customers.

- **Enterprise Applications**: Enterprise application software offered by companies like Salesforce is bought and rolled out widely across sales teams. This application is now an integral part of the company's revenue-generating process. The sales team has invested a lot of time into learning to use it, and it is now an indispensable tool for them in their daily jobs. In this case, the stickiness is the time, relearning, and disruption caused when uprooting the existing system for a new one.

- **Licensing**: Some companies have intellectual property

portfolios (e.g., patents, unique building blocks for products) that they license for a fee to other companies. When this intellectual property is essential for building your products, you have no choice but to take a license. Companies like Qualcomm and ARM are examples of licensors of important technology to consumer electronics companies.

- **Manufacturing:** Consider a manufacturing company that helps you manufacture your products at the stated cost, which helps you reduce costs with time. This manufacturing company delivers on time, will carry inventory on your behalf (supplier-owned inventory), and has invested or is willing to invest in production capacity to meet your growing demand. In this case, the stickiness is the reliability of supply and value-add to your business that you as a customer place on this manufacturer.

- **Mission Critical Software:** Consider embedded software such as an operating system that is safety certified and deployed in mission-critical applications such as automobile electronics that control driving functions, nuclear power plants, medical-surgical equipment, and high-speed trains, which have not seen a failure in years. Stickiness in these cases is quality and reliability, which are paramount in such applications.

- **Smartphones:** The iPhone and Samsung Galaxy are the two premier smartphone brands. The phones under these brands have beautiful form factors and user interfaces that their customers are familiar with. Switching from one phone to another entails the inconvenience of learning a new user interface, which is a cost that the user may not want to invest in, plus they will need to transfer content and contacts from their old phone to a new one and possibly move over to a new ecosystem (such as the application store) that their phone supports. The stickiness, in this case, is usability of the device, its utility and desirability to the user, and the inconvenience and effort to switch to another device.

- **Sports Apparel:** Nike's products are associated with quality, innovation, determination, motivation, and prestige—created through their collaboration with world famous athletes and evocative ad campaigns.[110] Its swoosh logo and "Just Do It" slogan are immediately recognized and sought after—driven by positive brand association.

Many of these examples are similar to ones I provided for product differentiation. This illustrates that differentiation and stickiness are interrelated. Product differentiation that increases your stickiness with the customer is what you really want.

In every example above, the key element to stickiness is the high switching cost for the customer. If the cost to switch is *low or worthwhile*, then customers can be convinced to give a different product a chance.

Examples with a low barrier to switch include:

- T-shirts, where many retailers differentiate only on price.
- Self-serve gas stations. Do you care which one you go to?

Worthwhile reasons for a customer to switch or provide access to a new supplier include:

- A disruption in technology. Customers may want to look at alternatives to make sure they get the best.
- A company policy to have a dual-source supply chain for supply security.

My earliest opportunity to create a sticky product was in 2003 at EMP. 3G networks were being rolled out across the globe, and mobile-phone manufacturers needed 3G chipsets to build 3G phones to meet the market demand. EMP had many entrenched cellular-modem-chip competitors, but no one had launched a 3G solution. This was the opening we needed. We proceeded to build our platform based on five compelling value propositions for the customer:

- **Global Roaming:** It would be a global platform that supported radio-frequency bands across all major regions, so people using phones with our platform could roam across the world. 2G phones did not allow this. You had to carry multiple phones.

- **Fall-Back Mode:** It would be backward compatible with existing cellular 2G and 2.5G standards, allowing usage on these legacy networks if coverage for the newer 3G standard was not yet available.

- **Reduce Customer R&D Cost:** We would integrate the chips and software as a platform that would be tested across major wireless carriers' networks and customer use-cases. Essentially, we would do a lot of the heavy lifting that our customers did and reduce their R&D costs.

- **Time to Money:** The platform would allow our customers to build a phone rapidly, thereby reducing the time-to-market and creating faster time to money, for them, from their sales.

- **Ability to Differentiate:** Our platform would support a host of new multimedia applications that the new 3G standard enabled, and customers could readily exploit these capabilities offered on our platform via application programming interfaces (APIs).

Customers were intrigued with our value proposition and gave us a shot. Those of us who interacted with customers had experience in building phones. We were phone designers and manufacturers before we went into platforms. Therefore, we were able to have credible discussions with customers about improving their development process and time to market using our platform. Our credibility came from our knowledge and experience. Customers found this very valuable, and to them, we were more than a supplier—we were consultative partners.

We executed to our plan and promise, and within two years, we won over fifteen phone manufacturers. Some customers invested heavily in our platform and built a skyscraper of optimized applications with it. This made our platform very sticky for them. Their investment in our platform would remain as long as we kept delivering stable platforms that helped them sell their phones profitably.

In summary, to create stickiness in products, focus on three things:

- Build reliance, so that the customer believes they must work with you, through high-touch engagement and knowledge.
- Deliver meaningful value propositions through your products that bring *higher commercial value* to your customers, such as:
  - Shorter time-to-market
  - Lowering the customer's cost for development
  - Access to an ecosystem that acts as a convenience to them and, hence, is a value multiplier in favor of your product
  - Quality and reliability that enhances their brands
  - Value-add services that reduce their total cost and cash outlay
- Make your product the foundation upon which your customer builds a tall building—if successful, it is unlikely they will tear down the building for a new foundation, even if a competing foundation has some interesting attributes.

Constant Self-Assessment – Quadrants of Truth

When companies are not growing in revenue and profit, they are usually not adequately addressing their market opportunities, or they do not have the right product portfolio. That is, they have gaps in their product portfolio—they are lacking sales in addressable markets (coverage), or their customers do not feel the company's products are attractive to buy and hold on to (stickiness).

You need to constantly gauge the revenue and profit growth trajectory of your company looking at the Quadrants of Truth in Figure 9. This figure plots a company's position along two axes: coverage and stickiness. Coverage is the ability to address many segments and geographies of the available market, while stickiness is the customers' reluctance to switch from the company's products and is thus a measure of the company's attractiveness or competitiveness.

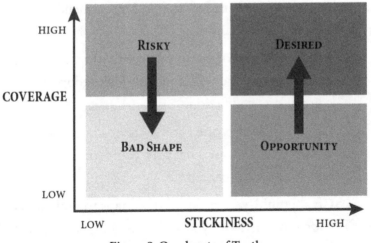

Figure 9: Quadrants of Truth

Being up and to the right in Figure 9 is the best position. The arrows indicate the potential direction a company may take. For example, if the company is in the Opportunity quadrant, it has the potential to go to the Desired quadrant by expanding its coverage. If it is in the Risky quadrant, it is likely to drop down to the Bad Shape quadrant when it loses market share. While less likely, a company may have a major quality issue and lose its stickiness, moving from the Desired to the Risky quadrant. The goal of the company is to get to the Desired quadrant through thorough planning and execution. It goes without saying that in getting to the Desired quadrant, the products must also generate a good profit.

Constantly review your position via the quadrants of truth and plot where you and your competitors are placed. Use this assessment to urgently adapt your roadmaps and operational plans to get to and remain in the Desired quadrant. In doing this assessment, be proactive and not reactive.

Summary: Products Creation
The East Tower

Products create revenue and build brand value for a company. To ensure the best possible chance of success, I recommend the following principles for product definition:

- Intersect transformational trends through systematic research using the ORCa model. Make educated bets with courage and conviction.

- Be a first mover as often and as far in advance as possible. If you are late, look for what your competitors don't, wont, or will do to leapfrog them.

- Create multi-year product roadmaps to build a deep and wide moat between you and your competitors, an endless barrage of projectiles to win new territory, but also to serve as the vehicle that aligns product creation in your company.

- To transform brilliant ideas to disruptive products, you need many things to come together. Plan well, be laser-focused, and execute.

- Define products using scientific methods. I use the Design for Growth model to iterate design choices around a product score and share function to maximize my return on investment. Conduct Say-Do analyses to refine the Design for Growth model and product-definition process.

- Use customer-centric metrics, depending on your business, to increase the competitiveness and customer appeal of your products to build your brand equity.

- Build stickiness through value propositions for your customers, making them invest in your product and making it an integral part of their value creation system.

- Use the quadrants of truth to constantly assess where you stand in your market proactively and adapt your plans with urgency.

In this chapter, I described a process for defining winning products. Just defining them won't get you far. It is useless to have the sketch and design of a grand protective tower on the perimeter wall that is far too expensive to build, takes long to build, or will crumble with time. You need to build products and deliver them at the right cost, right quality, and on time for them to be effective. In the next chapter, I will describe exactly how you can go about achieving just that.

6

The West Tower
Product Delivery Builds Your Arsenal

You have conceived the coolest product. You have devised the best strategy to launch the product to generate a lot of revenue and profit. But can you deliver? Will your product be on time to meet a market window of opportunity, be of high quality, and be produced at the right cost?

Castle towers were strategically placed to defend a castle. They came in many shapes: rectangular towers, round towers, horseshoe towers, and even hexagonal towers like the ones at the Caernarfon Castle in Northern Wales or the octagonal towers at both the Caernarfon Castle and the Castel del Monte in the Apulia region of Italy.

Rectangular towers were easier to build and provided a large amount of internal space for soldiers. However, their corners were weak and subject to mining. That is, the enemies could get close to the wall and begin to dig a tunnel (mine) to get inside the castle. Due to the tower's shape, archers could not fire upon the tunnellers, as there were blind spots. Round towers eliminated this issue and were stronger against projectiles—their semicircular shape could bear a stronger hit. However, round towers had less moving space for soldiers than the rectangular towers, unless they had a very large diameter. Horseshoe towers were D-shaped. The semicircular part of the D faced the enemy, and the flat side of the D faced the interior of the castle. This shape combined the advantages of the rectangular and round towers.

Embrasures or long vertical slits were placed along the wall of the towers at multiple firing positions. Sometimes these openings were designed to be narrow on the outside (facing the enemy) and wide on the inside to give soldiers room to maneuver their position and weapons for the best angle to shoot from.

During peacetime, towers were used for storage and as accommodations for soldiers of the garrison.

A tower's utility and its protective and defensive capability were influenced by its shape, construction materials, and location. Likewise, a product's effectiveness is defined by its quality, cost, and timing, which I collectively call product delivery.

I will use the West Tower to symbolize these three critical elements. When you get these elements right, you truly have an armory of effective weapons—your winning products. When you don't, you will be left with great-looking weapons that are not effective.

Product delivery is not as glamorous as product creation. It is about process, discipline, and doing many things right every day until the product is launched. You are making sure your product is released on time with the right specifications, including at the right cost, and with high quality. You need to be hyper-focused on the little things that must come together piece by piece like a jigsaw puzzle, being vigilant to what is off-track and correcting each departure from the plan rapidly.

Let me tell you an interesting story about product cost, the first of our three critical elements. Bluetooth was the brainchild of Dr. Nils Rydbeck, the first CTO of Ericsson Mobile Phones,[111] who I had the privilege to work for. One afternoon after lunch, he handed me a paper napkin on which he had written, "invent a 10-meter wireless link."

The need for a short wireless link grew out of solving a set of compelling-use cases. A laptop could connect wirelessly via this link to a cellphone, which could connect to the internet, thereby making the laptop always connected to the internet. What a boon for a businessperson in an era where WiFi was not available widely. It would be so much more convenient to play music from your phone to your headsets without clumsy wires. We could enable safer driving by synchronizing our cellphones to our car speakers and microphones to make hands-free calls rather than driving holding a phone to one's ear. Accidents caused by eyes off the road could be dramatically reduced.

Bluetooth, although this was not the original name, was born and realized thereafter thanks to several contributors, but none more so than my brilliant colleagues Jaap Haartsen and Sven Mattisson. When Bluetooth was defined, we thought a cost of $5 would make it very attractive to the market. The anticipated uptake happened only when the cost got below $1, and when the cost fell below 50 cents, widespread adoption and concomitant volume growth occurred—analogous to the proverbial hockey-stick graph. Today, Bluetooth has moved from a product to a function in a larger semiconductor chip and costs pennies—cost can make or break a product's widespread uptake.

Hyper-competitive markets are unforgiving, and when quality or time to market goes awry, companies lose a lot of money, and in the extreme, can collapse—regardless of their size.

In 2016, Samsung's Galaxy Note 7 had a battery issue that is reported to have cost Samsung $10 billion and market share before the company fixed the issue.[112] Samsung conceded their pole position to Apple and opened their share to Xiaomi and others. To Samsung's credit, they bounced back brilliantly, to the top, through execution and winning back customer's trust.[113] Imagine if the next phone they had launched had also had a major quality issue. I doubt they would have recovered from a double hit.

For decades, Intel led in processor chips for laptops, desktops, and servers because they had the best semiconductor technology powering their chips. They were typically two years ahead of any competitor. In 2019, cracks surfaced in their delivery, [114] and they have since fallen behind in semiconductor technology leadership versus TSMC and Samsung.[115, 116, 117] This has allowed competitors who use TSMC and Samsung to take a sizable bite out of Intel's market share and value, costing the company billions of dollars in opportunity. However, Intel is investing heavily to regain its technology leadership with several ground-breaking innovations.[118]

To secure flawless product delivery, you need to

- rigorously follow systematic processes;

- be focused and execute with discipline every day; and

- be realistic about capabilities and timelines.

Invariably, when I have seen products delivered late, with poor quality and higher-than-planned costs, it is because these three rules have been violated.

Product delivery is all about experience and details. Hence, you will find that most examples in this chapter are from my experiences. You will also find that I go into detail to explain the core issues that impact product delivery. With hope, the principles and lessons I explain should translate to several industries.

Product delivery requires every member of the project team to know what to do every single day and to do it right. This takes process, focus, and discipline. Furthermore, products that have unrealistic timelines force teams to take shortcuts and miss targets. Putting undue pressure on the engineering team is silly. As a leader, you can always browbeat the team into giving you the answer you want to hear but not the product you want at a desired time.

In the autumn of 2004, six months after EMP had turned profitable, we defined an all-new and even more advanced 3G platform for mobile phones. This new platform would support higher-data-rate applications such as faster downloading of emails with attachments, web-browsing, and streaming video and music. More importantly, it would reduce the cost of our prior 3G platform by half. It was a transformational platform and would take over two years to launch, occupying three-quarters of the company's engineers.

Two of our competitors had promised our largest customer a similar platform a whole year earlier. I was incredulous about their claims because they had not launched a single 3G product successfully.

Yet, there were many tough meetings with the customer and cellular operators on why we were late. I was pressured to compromise on my specifications to get the platform out sooner. The consequences of being late were dire. Being late meant that competitors would get an opening to displace us. However, upon consultation with my team, I decided to stand steadfast in my plans because none of us had conviction that we could build a good product any earlier.

The CEO of one of the world's largest cellular operators was upgrading his network to support high data rates based on the availability of platforms such as ours. He was investing billions of dollars, and if customers did not have phones to use on this upgraded network, it would be a premature investment with no return.

I was summoned by this CEO to explain my schedule in detail. I explained that for widespread uptake of 3G phones with high data rates, cellular operators had to meet certain cost points. To build such a platform at the target cost points, it would take a certain amount of time and there were no shortcuts. The CEO agreed with me, as he knew the business well. At that time, operators subsidized phones and recovered their costs from monthly service fees. A lower-cost phone would mean smaller subsidies. "If you truly believe you can drop the cost by 50 percent and meet our specifications, do not change your plans, because we need your cost structure and feature set to make 3G phones affordable," he told me.

EMP delivered on time with the features, cost, and quality we had promised. Interestingly, two of our competitors who had promised my largest customer a platform a year earlier failed, as expected.

In the following sections, I will outline my approach to securing product cost, quality, and time-to-market. I refer to time-to-market as new-product introduction, or NPI.

Product Cost Management – Constraint on Choices

In every business I have run, I have followed the same core tenet: the market sets product price, and the company controls product cost. It has always been a priority for me to control product cost to secure the right gross margins.

Building products at target cost requires that you make it a key parameter in product definition. It is not an outcome of all the other choices you make but a constraint on the choices you make.

Focusing on cost is a discipline, just like every other discipline in building and delivering a product. It begins by setting product cost as a key parameter in the definition of the product and making every department involved in product delivery aware of its importance. The departments that influence product cost are:

- Product management (product definition)
- Research and development or Engineering (product design)
- Purchasing (product parts purchasing)
- Manufacturing (production)
- Quality (specifications, warranty, and returns)
- Services (repair of returns)

The product management department defines the product to be built and must be judicious by using cost as a constraint on the definition and specifications. They cannot specify a high-cost product and expect engineering, purchasing, and manufacturing to miraculously reduce cost. The engineering department designs and builds the product and, hence, has the most influence on cost. Manufacturing and quality departments have requirements that can decrease or increase the product cost. If these requirements are ignored, you could end up with a product that does not meet cost targets. Services and repair departments will have requirements on product design to facilitate lower-cost repairs. For example, if a product is hard to open up, the repair center may have to break the casing and replace it. This adds to repair costs. Similarly, the purchasing department may have negotiated lower-cost parts, while the engineers may have defined the product with similar but more expensive parts. To avoid such disconnects and missteps, I involve all relevant departments early in the definition phase of a product.

Every one of these departments must know what the cost targets are for a product over its lifetime, and they must create plans and proposals to secure these costs. They must also build a cost reduction roadmap for each product, with milestones for delivering improvements. When there is such collective focus, you realize the maximum cost reduction.

The following series of examples helped me formulate a process for product cost improvements.

In their book *The Discipline of Market Leaders*, Michael Treacy and Fred Wiersema discuss three value disciplines that companies have adopted to gain market leadership.[119] These are customer intimacy, product leadership, and operational excellence. The authors use Walmart to highlight operational excellence. Walmart was laser-focused on managing the cost of their products through a highly optimized supply chain and tough-as-nails approach to cost-cutting. Their low-cost-of-goods focus has made them so dominant that they put many competitors under severe financial pressure by selling products at large discounts in the U.S. and abroad. One foreign casualty was Comet, a discount retailer in the UK.[120] In the U.S., Walmart superstores effectively retired many small businesses.[121] Ever since I read this book, I have been paranoid about competitors adopting Walmart's mindset before I did.

A second example is the affordable fashion company Zara, owned by Inditex, that disrupted fashion retail.[122] Zara sells clothing, accessories, swimwear, beauty products, and perfumes. I believe Zara's success stemmed from having a very tightly managed and fast supply chain. Fashion is trendy. Zara was able to react quickly to trends by locally sourcing products that were sold in local retail outlets, thereby reducing lead times. They used just-in-time inventory (building products only when they are needed) so they did not have to carry a lot of stock. They replenished their stock only based on true demand. They could do this because they could deliver rapidly, typically less than three weeks, which is amazing in the fashion retail world. Many fashion companies outsourced work to Asia to lower cost, but Zara chose to source it close to where they sell because they secured so many other cost efficiencies that offset the cost of sourcing from Asia. Zara's model demonstrated to me that controlling cost is strategic and multifaceted.

The best personal example I have is from my time as a general manager at Ericsson during the late 1990s. The cost of a 2G mobile phone (conforming to a North American standard) in those days was $240. We created a systematic roadmap for how to reduce the cost by making plans with each of our different cost-control centers: engineering, purchasing, manufacturing, quality, service and repair all had synchronized targets. Our plan included reducing discrete electronic-parts count through integration into a smaller number of semiconductor chips, using cheaper molded plastic instead of metal for the frame of the phone, dual sourcing of parts (creating price competition among suppliers), optimized manufacturing (higher production-line utilization), higher quality (lower returns, repairs, and warranty costs), and eliminating operational inefficiencies. The net effect was that we reduced the cost of phones from $240 to $65 in three years while improving functionality and quality.

With these experiences in mind, I recommend the following process to address cost reduction. These principles are equally applicable to companies that manufacture and sell goods and those that sell services.

- **Step One:** Establish a strategy for cost reduction by looking at all the aspects of your cost to produce your product or service. Try and break down your product or service cost into its elements, analyze what contributes to the cost of each element, and assess if cost can be reduced by investing effort (a value-based engineering approach). Prioritize the effort on those items that get quick wins, as success is a motivator and reinforces validation.

- **Step Two:** Depending on your product or service type, establish relevant cost-control centers (departments) where each center has a role to play in the reduction of costs. Involve all teams early in the product design cycle, making cost a forethought rather than an afterthought.

- **Step Three:** Assign practical targets and appropriate time frames for achievement for each cost-control center corresponding to each product. Encourage each group to be creative and innovate to reduce costs. Appoint a champion for each relevant cost-control center listed above. The champions must know the business and be empowered to enlist support across the organization to secure targets, or they will fail. Cost reduction is a collective, not an individual, responsibility.

- **Step Four:** Review the targets and progress with a regular cadence to understand the status. At each review, the gaps to targets must show a trend toward closure or be refined, as keeping actions open for a long time just creates huge unread lists. In my businesses, I held bi-weekly meetings with each of the champions to assess progress. These periodic reviews need to be constructive. The business leader must listen, suggest, and coach so meaningful progress can be made. When people participate and are recognized for progress, it fosters ownership and increases the drive to accomplish the task.

- **Step Five:** Finally, if any change to cost targets in the approved business case is uncovered during design or any phase in producing the product or service, ensure that it is escalated to product managers (who own the product or service business case), so they can take appropriate actions. This means creating a list of actions to get back on track to the target cost. Any final variance from the target that is not budgeted needs to be escalated to the general manager, as the business case is at risk, and this could impact the company for years.

Even when you have a well-oiled machine to drive cost down, you can get surprised due to trade regulations and tariffs, which require vigilance and creativity. In the late 1990s, we were selling phones in Latin America. A regulation under the auspices of MERCOSUR (the Southern Common Market) added a large tariff on our products based on the country of manufacturing origin. If memory serves me right, this tariff was around 26 percent. It essentially wiped out any profit margin we could make on our phones. However, if phones were assembled in member countries, they were exempt from this tariff. We created a plan to ship kits of phone parts (called complete knock-down kits, or

CKDs) to Brazil and assemble phones in that country. With time, we began manufacturing and assembling phones in Brazil, which eliminated the tariff that was wiping out our profit margin.

Watch Out for Variants

Product variants or stock-keeping units (SKUs) are necessary, as one product cannot satisfy different requirements for every segment or geography of the market.

In more than one company I worked with I observed that a product or business manager decided that we needed a variant to fill an immediate revenue opportunity. The cost of creating a variant was low, so it was often created.

However, all the downstream impacts of creating a variant are often ignored, like maintenance and administration costs that dilute company profits. It could also be the variant has lower gross margin because it was made to fit "an opportunity" and its cost did not match the lower price it was sold for. If this variant is sold in high volume, it will dilute the gross margin of your portfolio.

Consider the many electronic products we use every day—laptops, smartphones, tablets, smartwatches, smart speakers, and TVs. Every one of these products has a physical electronics device (hardware) and software that makes it run.

As an example, let us say our business makes and sells one of these products with three product variants in the U.S. to address a high-, mid-, and low-market tier.

So, we have three sets of hardware (devices) and three sets of software. We now decide to add three more regions—Brazil, Mexico, and India—and sell products into these areas. However, each region requires some change in the devices and a new version of software. So now, we need three products per four regions, which equals twelve hardware variants and an equivalent twelve software variants. What if one had fifty products and twenty regions? This explosion of variants comes with two associated issues: potential gross-margin dilution and added cost.

First, check whether the product variant for a segment or geography has a good business case. If it is dilutive to the portfolio gross margins, be careful in creating the variant.

Second, the explosion of variants comes with added costs such as:

- The additional development and production cost for each variant.

- The maintenance costs for all variants. Your laptops, smartphones, tablets, smartwatches, smart speakers, and TVs are all updated with software regularly. Every time there is a bug that is corrected in the software, all the variants using this software must be updated. Before updating each device with the new software, it must be tested on every variant to make sure it works on each of them. This is time consuming and expensive work.

- The complexity of ordering parts, manufacturing, and inventory management, which goes up exponentially as variants grow. This gets a lot harder to manage if demand forecasts from each segment, sub-segment, and geography for the variants are not predictable, creating extra inventory.

- The effort expended to continuously reduce the cost of each variant with time to stay profitable.

- The growing administration costs to keep track of all variants/SKUs and their configurations in the system.

As these costs add up, it dilutes profits. As such, one needs to constantly prune and manage these variants to keep costs in check.

One may ask what happens with variants for software? This is not as complex as variants that have both hardware and software. However, even with software, variants could create a lot of work and added cost.

My favorite example on managing variants is McDonald's, the highly efficient, multi-national fast-food restaurant. As of March 2020, they had thirty-eight thousand restaurants in one hundred and twenty countries.[123] The secret to their success over eighty-two years is that they constantly innovate and update their menus based on customer research while also maintaining fixed menus that don't vary. This allows them to streamline their supply chain, operations, and administration to manage their costs and remain profitable.

Regarding variants, the bottom line is that you should only create them if the business case justifies the variant. And you should prune variants constantly by determining if they are necessary.

In a semiconductor company where I ran a multi-billion-dollar product line, we had more than ten thousand variants. I decided to do a Pareto analysis of these products. Essentially, we created a histogram of sales demand over the past two years for each variant. This analysis showed that three hundred parts generated 92 percent of our revenue and almost all revenue came from only three thousand of the parts. In essence, we could eliminate more than seven thousand variants and reduce the associated maintenance costs with almost no impact. After we had decided which variants to prune, we issued an end-of-life notice to customers. Customers that really needed the product variants placed last-time orders.

Product Quality Management – Forethought Versus Afterthought

Product quality refers to a product functioning to its manufacturer's specifications over its lifetime.

In 1998, I was a newly appointed general manager of Ericsson Mobile Phones. We sold products in North America, Latin America, Australia, and New Zealand. In my very first year, our phones encountered a return rate of 20 percent. These returned phones had to be repaired and re-shipped to the customer. The cost of this quality issue was astronomically high. To illustrate the magnitude of the problem, assume we sold five million units per year. This meant a million of these units might be returned for repair, and each repair and ship back to the customer cost us $50. Thus, our potential recall and repair cost would have been $50 million.

This had a serious impact on our cash flow, but a far worse impact on our brand reputation. Customers who sold our phones were livid, as we were hurting their business, and trust was eroding. Turning up to every angry-customer meeting made me feel like a cat on a hot tin roof. Excuses ignited more passions.

Customers were frustrated because we really did not have a plan. Instead, we spent the time explaining everything that went wrong. Customers wanted to know the time of day, and we were explaining how the clock was built—they simply wanted to hear what we would do to keep this from happening again. They also wanted to know if I was up to my job as general manager to solve the issue. Why did they need to buy products from someone who did not know how to build a high-quality phone? This was a defining moment for me.

It took me six months to think through a plan. Fortunately for me, I got to listen to a great talk on product quality from a Japanese supplier. The speaker's message was clear—quality requires a mindset shift. He used an example that left a lasting impression. He said there is a difference between building a high-tech product and growing vegetables. The output of the vegetable crop is less controlled in quality. The farmer can harvest the vegetables and send the best to the market and consume the rest. He said this was not the right approach to use for high-tech products.

I realized that quality, along with cost, had to be a forethought and not an afterthought. Quality had to be built into our products, integrated into their development, and not monitored by a department of statisticians.

Part of our problem was that we had grown too fast as a company and had not focused on quality, as we should have. We did not control what components we used, we did not monitor our suppliers and factories tightly, we did not test our products adequately, and quality was not designed into our products.

To address these shortcomings, my team and I came up with a set of seven must-follow rules:

- Change the design philosophy (quality first).
- Mandate the use of a qualified component list.
- Expand product testing.
- Enforce supplier quality management.
- Tighten manufacturing and repair quality management.
- Add a failure analysis lab.
- Make quality a key business metric.

While I will focus on my description of these rules for a mobile phone, the principles in these seven rules apply to devices, software-only businesses, and service businesses. However, you must adapt these rules in the right context, and some rules may not apply.

Change in Design Philosophy – Quality First

We analyzed the mistakes that we had made in our phone design. Most of our issues arose from battery connectors and display connectors. These connectors attached the battery and display to the printed circuit board, which carries all the electronic circuits that make the phone work. We had used connectors that were easier to assemble in

173

our factory but became less reliable over time. As the phone was used, the connections wore out and created failures. This taught us to never compromise in areas where the cost of failure is orders-of-magnitude higher than the component or assembly cost. We called this approach "quality first."

Qualified Components

Our engineers were only allowed to use components from our qualified-parts list. The qualified parts were rigorously reviewed for cost, performance, reliability, and manufacturability. This list was maintained by our purchasing department. A secondary benefit of using qualified parts was that it reduced design time. This was because we had tested and characterized each part and knew how it worked versus using an untested part. Characterization is done to assess how the part will perform over a variety of conditions such as temperature, for example. With an untested part, engineers had to spend additional time characterizing it and understanding its behavior under various stress conditions. This added risk to our delivery schedule.

Detailed Product Testing

We had good hardware and software component testing in place. However, we needed more system-testing, use-case-testing, and stress-testing. System-testing is where you test the entire phone, exercising all its functions in the real world on live cellular networks. Use-case-testing is where you subject the product to standard ways a user may use it over its life. Stress-testing is where you accelerate failure of the product through harsher conditions than the product would normally experience.

One example of a combined use-case-test and stress-test of a phone is to simulate accelerated wear and tear and make phone calls. An ingenious engineer came up with a test where we placed phones in a tumbler along with rocks and tumbled the phones for twenty-four hours, then used them to make phone calls. The tumbling with rocks shredded the phones' outer casings, but the electronics, displays, batteries, and frames had to hold together and still allow the phones to work. If the phones could make reliable calls and still display data on their screens over the duration of tumbling (24-hours), then the phones passed the test.

We chose this measure to simulate the harshest conditions that could vibrate and shake the phone. Under this test, the connectors experienced accelerated stress and could fail. If the battery or the display connector broke or wore down, the phone could not make a call or display data on the screen.

To improve system-testing, we added personnel to test phones in the field in more countries and in diverse cellular networks provided by different equipment suppliers to get the best possible coverage of test cases. We also created use-cases that would stress the phone's software and hardware to its limits. These tests resulted in finding many more bugs that we were able to fix before launching the phones.

We also added several additional highly accelerated stresses—and life-tests called HASS (Highly Accelerated Stress Screening) and HALT (Highly Accelerated Life Testing), respectively. With time, we automated all tests, and our test lab looked like Q's lab in a James Bond movie. It got a lot of visitors and admiration. I personally gave tours.

We had a major customer in Colombia, where our phones had more than 50 percent market share. After visiting the lab, they were so impressed that the regional sales manager called to say our sales jumped to a higher share. In my study at home, I still proudly display a commemorative stamp issued by that country in honor of our phones.

Failure Analysis Lab

To accelerate analysis of failures, we added several state-of-the-art diagnostic and test tools like scanning electron microscopes and focused ion beam (FIB) machines. This was in the late 1990s, and it cost us a lot of money. With our tools, we had the ability to delaminate electronic components and semiconductor chips and inspect them for issues.

This Failure Analysis Lab gave us an independent pair of eyes on supplier issues that they, the suppliers, might not have reported or had not found. It also helped us diagnose problems faster than sending failed parts to third parties and working on their schedule to find a solution. Since this lab was located next to our engineering teams, they had access to the equipment to diagnose issues quickly and find solutions to problems in their designs.

Supplier Management

One of our suppliers provided a 10-cent electronic component that was placed in our phone's receiver circuitry. The supplier decided they were going to change the manufacturing recipe to increase their output to help meet our growing demand for these components. However, this new recipe caused these components to crack and fail in the field. When these components cracked, they essentially blocked the radio signals from traveling through the receiver path. If this happened, people with these phones could not receive calls. This 10-cent component resulted in $50 in repairs per phone.

As a result, we created a strict supplier-management program. We outlined mandatory quality tests that suppliers had to perform periodically and report back on. Suppliers had to inform us of *any planned change* they wanted to make to their manufacturing process, equipment, or material used. All changes had to be approved by us, or they could not make the change. We also initiated regular audits of their factory and processes by qualified auditors. We made all these changes mandatory and contractual.

There will be surprises in your product delivery—but nothing your supplier does, none of their processes or materials or systems, should catch you by surprise. Because surprise means increased risks and a higher likelihood that something will go wrong.

Manufacturing and Repair Quality Management

We treated our internal manufacturing sites just like we treated our suppliers. They had similar processes, protocols, and audits to follow. Every manufacturing site had to periodically measure units they produced and report the results to our engineering teams. All equipment had to be precisely calibrated. A dedicated internal team carefully monitored all excursions and deviation from our acceptance criteria and promptly handled the issues. Essentially, we stopped production until a fix was found.

Our manufacturing sites also served as our repair sites. So, we instituted strict repair processes with version control. This ensured that we could specify repairs for each version and ensure that unique problems specific to that version were fixed. This eliminated wrong or unnecessary fixes for each phone repaired.

Quality as a Business Metric

Lastly, we made quality a business metric to gauge our annual performance. This raised awareness across the company of anyone contributing to the building of the product. We also set aside time to periodically review how to improve our product quality, which we tracked via our metrics.

I have been very brief in explaining a topic that deserves its own book. Today, quality management is very advanced compared to the way it was in 1998. When we implemented the above rules along with a rigorous but practical quality-management process, our return rates dropped from 20 percent to 1.5 percent. The industry benchmark at that time was closer to 3 percent.

A year or so later, I was addressing a dealer conference. These dealers always told me how lousy my phones were compared to competitor phones, and this typically drowned out the meeting. At this meeting, I took my phone out and slammed it on a tabletop and then threw it across the room. I then walked over, picked it up, and asked the dealers to do the same with their phones. I do not believe I got a question on quality after that.

New Product Introduction – A Matter of Time

New-product introduction (NPI) is the process of building a product to defined specifications and ensuring that it can be produced to a high quality. When products do not meet these specifications (e.g., features, performance, cost, quality) and are late, the associated business case is unlikely to be achieved.

However, everything does not always go as planned. When it does not, I always protect time-to-market by compromising on features or adding resources as an added cost to the project. This is because markets do not wait for your company's products, and competitors will get ahead if you are late. Without products to sell, there is no revenue, and without revenue, you do not have a business for long.

I have used the following four principles to secure new-product introduction:

- Planned cadence
- Phase-gate process
- Delivery-accuracy metric
- Program management

Planned Cadence – Heartbeat Model

A planned cadence is a repeatable timetable used to launch products. This sets a timetable that the whole organization must understand and commit to keeping. All product-related activities are planned around this timetable or cadence. Take Apple and Samsung for example. They launch a new phone model—iPhone, or Galaxy respectively—every year like a heartbeat.

The above cadence also gives a company a timetable to ramp down an old platform and replace it with a new platform. After they launch a new platform, they should still support their old platforms with software updates based on customer demand and reported field issues. These updates are commonplace—you are probably familiar with notifications you receive on your smartphones and computers to update your software and reboot (power cycle) your device.

The biggest advantage to having such a product-launch cadence is that it allows the entire business to plan resources, make commitments to customers, and manage production on a predictable schedule.

Process – Checkpoints and Checklists

Next, you need a structured process for defining, building, launching, and managing the life cycle of a product. Most companies follow some form of a phase-gate process. We followed one with eight phase gates, or milestones or checkpoints. A gate is a decision point with entry and exit criteria. One can enter or exit a phase gate only if all requirements have been met and stakeholders have signed off.

We kept strict control of these phase gates because we knew that if we hit each of these checkpoints on time and passed the checklists, there was a very low chance that things would go wrong. Every product launch is hard—it does not matter how seasoned you are. Each launch needs the same discipline and rigor. Because things do break, and then there are many, many issues that will pop up along the way.

The eight gates we used were:

- Phase Gate 1 (Concept): The product is defined.

- Phase Gate 2 (Feasibility): All assumptions, technical and commercial, are validated and a business case built.

- Phase Gate 3 (Program Start): Resources (people and money) are committed, all specifications are ready, tools and equipment are allocated, a detailed schedule is prepared, a program manager is appointed to execute the program, and the business case is approved. This is the gate at which the decision to begin product execution—or not—is made.

- Phase Gate 4 (Feature Compliant): All features must be implemented, but the product is still not compliant with specifications, nor is it optimized for performance.

- Phase Gate 5 (Spec Compliant): The product is compliant with agreed specifications and performance requirements.

- Phase Gate 6 (Production-Ready): The product has been built in the factory, tested, and is ready for mass production at the desired manufacturing yields, cost, and quality criteria.

- Phase Gate 7 (Maintenance): The product goes into maintenance mode, where it may receive changes in components (typically to reduce cost or improve performance) and software upgrades.

- Phase Gate 8 (End-of-Life): The company decides to end-of-life the product and gives customers notice for the last-time buy.

This is a rather standard process and is followed by many hardware and software companies. There may be variations to the process, but the general principles remain.

There are two key elements to making this process successful:

- Entry and exit criteria (checklists) at each gate

- Business accountability and approvals

Entry criteria at each gate must clearly define what must be achieved in the phase. Exit criteria must validate that entry criteria are met and determine if there are any changes to the technical or commercial specifications. Changes that affect the product specification and business case must be reviewed carefully, as they have major impacts on the company's financials. The status of the criteria should be maintained via easy-to-read checklists. With complex checklists, issues get lost or overlooked among the heap of things to look at.

The criteria and checklists must be reviewed by business owners, who must then approve or disapprove going on to the next phase. When this is treated as a ceremonial review, costly mistakes are made. The success of the program relies on the approvers making the right decisions based on true status. The business owners must at a minimum include the following people: the decision-maker for the business, product manager responsible for the product, the head of manufacturing/supply chain or product delivery, the head of quality, the head of R&D, the head of sales, and the program manager. This team of stakeholders needs to be able to make tough decisions that may result in delays or even cancel the program. When the entire team knows this is a serious review, the planning is more rigorous and the content is more complete.

Two common reasons why programs go awry in execution are:

- The criteria and checklists are not prepared with rigor, resulting in poor checklists for entry and exit criteria.

- Approvers make bad decisions to pass gates with incomplete checklists or do not take these reviews seriously.

The two most critical phase gates for GO or NO-GO decisions are the Feasibility and Program Start phase gates. These are where the program is validated and large sums of money and resources are committed. When these two phases are not well-planned, there are invariably delays and business cases are not met.

For example, imagine approving Phase Gate 3 (Program Start) with incomplete or unacceptable cost data and an optimistic assumption that deficiencies and variances from targets will get resolved by the time production starts. In this case, after spending, say, $50 million on the program, if the cost variances never get fixed, you may be stuck with a product that loses money. Another example is when the team has not done sufficient due diligence to meet a critical performance target that determines the product price. Let us say the team banks their hope on recovering this shortfall in performance with a special component from a third party that never materializes. Such mistakes are expensive. As you may recall from our Design for Growth process, this product is unlikely to meet its product score and consequent business return on investment.

I have had a few projects in which we spent millions of dollars before realizing that we were not going to be successful—the product was off-track, and we had to stop the project. Those are tough decisions, but pulling the plug on a product before it is released beats throwing money and resources down a hole with no feasible return. Even if it is late in the product-development cycle, you must be ready to make the call to walk away if you see red flags and realize the product is not going to generate a good return.

In 1998, two teams in our mobile-phone division at Ericsson were competing to implement a standard called enhanced data rate for GSM evolution (EDGE). I led one. We tried for eighteen months and spent close to $40 million. My team worked hard, every project review seemed upbeat, but there was nothing concrete to show that our solution would work. We also relied on a supplier who overpromised and underdelivered. This supplier was unreliable. Assessing the situation and future spend, I decided to kill the project. Our European team delivered the technology a year later, and we adopted it. They had the capability that we did not possess. It hurt to lose the race, but it was the right decision to pull the plug. It was not the best situation for my team, but it was the best decision for the company.

It takes time and experience to recognize the right time to pull the plug on a project. This sense is honed by being dispassionate about the product and technology and rational about returns on money spent.

Ultimately, you must maintain a high hit ratio, which is the number of successful projects divided by total projects done, because competitive markets are unforgiving.

Delivery-Accuracy Metric – Aligning Everyone

Project delays result in budget overruns, lost market share, and even catastrophic consequences.

An extreme example of a project delay and cost gone awry is the Taj Mahal, a magnificent mausoleum built as a tribute by the Mughal Emperor Shah Jahan to his beloved wife, Mumtaz Mahal. This UNESCO heritage site draws more than five million visitors every year, as it is spectacular. It was an ambitious project, artfully designed in intricate detail but probably poorly planned and managed. It took twenty-two years and twenty thousand workers, overran its budget, bankrupted the Mughal treasury, and defocused governance of provinces, leading to rebellions and, some believe, even led to the colonization of India.[124]

In my relatively more mundane capacity, I have always maintained that delivery accuracy is the single most important aspect of each program. Timing is everything in fast-paced technical businesses. When you miss product-launch dates, it affects financial forecasts, disappoints customers, allows competitors to catch up, and occupies resources longer on the existing program, impacting future programs. In a hypercompetitive environment, delays can also kill your business.

That lesson was reinforced in 2006 when I was the general manager of the wireless division of Freescale. We delivered chipsets and software for cellphones and media players, and we also sold special chips to medical companies.

To be innovative, we typically chose the latest semiconductor technology for our chips. This technology gave us better performance and lower cost but was less mature, causing us to go through several iterations of making the chips, resulting in delays. We also lacked software expertise, and as a result, new features took extra time to be developed.

As I mentioned earlier, smartphone industry leaders like Samsung and Apple deliver a new generation of phones each year. The time needed to develop our solutions took us out of the running to be chosen by most manufacturers who followed such a heartbeat model.

So, we decided to only use mature semiconductor technology in future designs to reduce the number of chip iterations. By adopting the methods and processes outlined in this chapter, we were able to launch our complex chips to within one week of the committed date, which was an amazing transformation and a reflection of my excellent engineers.

However, we had a bigger problem when it came to software. Building the desired team would have taken us years. Instead, we looked to buy software and found a partner. They licensed their software to us. Based on our improved chipset roadmap and the new software license, we secured a major design win from a top-tier phone manufacturer.

Things were looking up for us. But our partner had internal problems and was unable to make their committed software deliveries—so we lost the design win and with it lots of global credibility for our delivery capability. After this, we could only sell chips to those companies who had their own software that they could run on our chips. Our growth potential was severely limited.

The lesson: Every element of the solution must be tracked with the same accuracy to meet customer deadlines. One tiny missing or delayed part could prove the difference between succeeding and failing, between landing or losing a client.

Delaying the customer can cost them heavily. A three-month delay for a phone customer means lost sales for an entire season, which can result in billions of dollars of lost revenue, diminished market share, and a weakened brand. Nothing is more important than delivery accuracy—on time at the right quality. This lesson led me to implement a metric that has never failed me.

Each program is broken down into several tasks. Each task is assigned to one or more people. Every task carries one delivery point that is the basic unit of the score. If the unit is delivered on time and with the right quality, that task gets the full point. If, for example, a task is three days late, the score for that delivery is halved, and if the task is delivered five days or more late, that task loses the whole point. If the task is delivered on time but the quality is unacceptable, the task loses its entire point.

Quality is gauged by the person who receives the output of the task (as this person must integrate the task into the next stage of product development). We would calculate the total score for the program, over the tasks that had to all come together to create the product. All the functions that had deliveries to the program, including third parties, were measured in the same way.

The delivery-accuracy metric on each program was calculated by adding up the total score achieved on the program and dividing this by the number of delivery tasks. Our rule was that all our programs executed during a year had to have an average score above 90 percent. We arrived at our metric through trial and error, trying to contain the maximum delay on a program to no more than five working days. I found that when more than 10 percent of tasks on any program were late, we invariably missed our committed delivery dates.

Furthermore, for this metric to work you must track your program status daily and address deviations to the plan immediately to avoid having a few late tasks create unrecoverable program delays. If you do not do this, you can get a great score but a very delayed program. For instance, if you have only two delayed tasks out of 100 tasks your score is 98 percent, but the delays in those two tasks may slip the program by months.

We used this metric in two ways: first, it was built into our compensation structure (bonus/incentive plan), and second, the whole company had visibility of this metric. If we did not get a certain score across all programs each year, we did not get this portion of our bonus—a meaningful amount. This applied to everyone in the business and in rating our suppliers. Then we made the score for each team visible. These metrics motivated teams to make sure they were not the laggards. It drove rigor and accountability via pride of not being the last one in the pack.

When we implemented this process in three different companies, it worked wonders. First at a semiconductor company, the average delivery-accuracy delay went down from months to a week. At a second platform company, we used this metric to deliver more than two hundred software releases every year to various customers without a day of delay. At a third company, we never missed delivering our solutions to the exacting production schedules of automobiles.

The most interesting aspect is that this metric was implemented as an honor system and people took pride in delivering accurately.

Program Management – What and When Versus Who and How

The role and responsibilities of a program manager can range greatly in a company. At one end of the spectrum, the most powerful person in terms of decision-making authority on a program is the program manager—this was the model I learned at Ericsson. At the other end, the program manager is relegated to being a schedule tracker—this was the case in several other companies I worked at. It is no surprise that at Ericsson we could deliver very complex programs on time at high quality and that these other companies were habitually late.

To be successful, the role and responsibilities of this position must be very clear, as explained in some detail in the chapter on culture.

Consider building a set of small, lightweight satellites that orbit our planet and collect data for Earth and climate observation. These satellites scan the earth and collect useful information to gain insight into natural disasters, ocean and river pollution, and weather patterns.

Building each satellite is complex because they comprise many diverse subsystems. Each satellite must have a source of power (solar cells and a battery), sensors to make measurements and control its flight path, communications to relay their data back to an Earth station and receive commands, an enclosure that can withstand the radiation in space, and so forth. These various subsystems are provided by different suppliers (companies) around the world. The satellite must be launched on a rocket such as those built by SpaceX. So, a berth must be booked on a rocket that will be launched. Once this is done, the countdown on time begins. You pay for booking your slot on the rocket and do not want to lose money by missing the launch. The rocket won't wait for you to be ready. Its launch date is fixed.

This means each of the above independent deliverables must be planned, tracked, and brought together in the satellite program to make the launch date.

So, how does this happen? To make this happen, I use the following critical definition:

- Program managers determine *what* and *when.*

- Line managers determine *who* and *how.*

A line manager is one who manages people in a department or company to deliver the product. These line managers are the technical experts, and the company relies on them to build the best product. In our example, these line managers are those responsible for delivering each subsystem from each of the different companies.

The program manager works with line managers to create an agreed-upon schedule and a budget for every subsystem that needs to come together in the program. The program manager then manages the deliveries from every team involved in each track to the agreed-upon schedule. The program manager determines *what* needs to be done and *when* each task is to be delivered to ensure the overall timeline is met. A competent program manager will hold some buffers to manage delays. It is important that only the program manager holds the buffers; otherwise, if every group sandbags their respective schedules, the product will invariably be late.

It is the program manager's job to hold teams accountable to their timelines. All programs have a critical path that interlinks deliverables. Delays along the critical path impact multiple other deliveries, causing disruptions to the timeline. When this happens, the program manager must fix each blocking issue expediently. Think of a car's transmission system—if the transmission is broken, the car will not speed up, regardless of how hard you press the accelerator. Let us say in our satellite program that the delivery of the communication unit is delayed. If the launch date is fixed, this delay reduces the time for integrating all subsystems and testing the satellite thoroughly. This may compromise quality, shorten the manufacturing readiness, and in the worst case, delay the program to lose its launch timing. As such, it is the program manager's task, in conjunction with cooperation from the line managers, to ensure that the critical path of the program stays intact.

Keeping all tracks synchronized with the critical path invariably leads to tension between program and line managers, as they are challenged to secure specification compliance, timeliness, and quality. Healthy tension is expected, but this should never get adversarial, as it is counterproductive. Therefore, roles and responsibilities must be clear.

Given the complexity of such programs and the multiple tracks, I have never found a way to have line managers manage their own tracks while also finding a way to coordinate other tracks to secure a program to be on time and meet the requirements. Therefore, in every business I ran, I elevated the role and responsibility of the program manager to complement the role of the line managers.

Program managers must be focused on three things—program cost, schedule, and compliance with specifications (including quality and product cost)—to secure their programs. For example, if they are coming up short on compliance with specifications and need more people to write software and test a feature, they should secure approvals to spend more and fix the issue. Appropriate escalation and fast decision-making must be part of this structure. The best program managers I have worked with were excellent detectives, could probe and sniff out issues, and found solutions before they needed to move mountains to have these issues fixed. These program managers had a process and method to drive closure without fuss. They were commercially minded, fact-based, and solution-oriented.

I cannot stress enough the importance of having good program managers on complex programs. They are responsible for delivering the program and must be empowered.

Timely new-product introduction can be achieved using the following recipe, namely:

- Ensure there is a planned cadence (heartbeat) that sets the overall timetable within which all programs and product-launch-related activities fit in each year.

- Create an NPI process for each program with phase gates and entry/exit criteria via checklists and approvals from engaged business leaders/owners.

- Implement a delivery-accuracy metric to drive rigor and behavior in execution.

- Ensure there is strong, empowered program management to complement line management.

Seven Sins of New Product Introduction Delays

No matter how seasoned you are, every project is hard in its own unique way. You will need to rely on process, discipline, and rigor. Expect things to break and new issues to pop up. Be prepared to stay unflustered and find expedient solutions.

In my experience, new product introduction delays for products are caused by at least one of the following seven factors. This applies to devices, software, and services.

- **Lack of Architecture Integrity:** The product architecture is a collection of building blocks organized in a framework to work synergistically. If this architecture is weak, the product malfunctions and can break when modified or stressed. Imagine building a toy house with wooden blocks. If you want to modify an intermediate layer of this toy house or build a taller house, you likely need to rebuild it from scratch, which takes additional time and effort. Also, if you stress the house by hitting it, it will fall to pieces. Products are not so different. When the product architecture is poor, it is unable to hold up when stressed by loads or when changes need to be made. Delays are caused by constantly trying to diagnose and rebuild the product to function as desired.

- **Immature Building Blocks:** Products are built with many components pieced together in an architecture. In such a structure, it is not enough that the architecture is sound. Every building block must be sound. Imagine a house that is built with a load-bearing wall that has half-baked bricks. The wall cracks frequently. The house owner will have to constantly monitor and shore up that wall so a larger part of the house does not collapse. When you build products with weak components, you experience delays caused by diagnosing and patching or replacing weaknesses. The quality of every building block you use in the product must be excellent.

- **Poor Requirements Management:** If product requirements constantly flow in as the product is being built, there is constant replanning and additional work created that delays product launches. Requirements must be managed. When you are working on a project that is two years long, customers will give you a lot of new requirements. I made sure that those requirements were vetted before they were introduced. If the requirement was going to be disruptive to the launch date or hurt quality, I would not accept it. I would tell the customer, "We cannot include the feature in the launch, but I can give it to you in a future iteration of the product (with a specific date). Of course, I am going to do it for you, but I do not have the capability to address your requirement in this release without delaying or breaking the project." Customers who need your product on time with quality will understand and engage in a rational dialogue on such compromise.

  You cannot promise 20 percent more to the customer and then turn around and tell your employees to work 20 percent harder. But many managers end up doing just that.

- **Immature Manufacturing Readiness:** If the product is hard to manufacture or produce and has poor yield, it is likely that the product will be delayed until the yield is good. This is because selling products with poor yield is a loss for the company. For example, if the company plans for one hundred units to be produced each day and they produce only twenty-five units and must scrap seventy-five units due to manufacturability issues, it makes the product launch unsustainable because the cost goes up by a factor of four.

- **Overly Aggressive Schedules and Priorities:** Poor planning and unrealistic optimism result in overly aggressive schedules that cannot be met. Being pollyannish on product schedules must be avoided, irrespective of the fleeting kudos you may get for presenting an aggressive but unrealistic schedule.

  It is equally important to prioritize projects based on your resources. Trying to do more with less is good, but not when it is unrealistic. Multiplexing your expert engineers across many projects, hoping all get done, reduces the efficiency of the engineers and makes it very likely that every project will be delayed. It is better to do a few projects on time with high quality than it is to take on many projects that are all delayed and have quality issues.

- **Inadequate or Inexperienced Staffing:** From the beginning, projects should always be staffed fully and with experienced personnel to meet NPI schedules. This applies to internal resources and your contractors. This gives the team the best chance of hitting timelines. Hoping to start lean and add resources that are back-end loaded rarely works. You reap what you sow.

- **Poor Process and Management:** Programs that have loose development processes and weak program management often run into problems and have delays. Structured development that follows a proven process and rigorous program management that manages the critical path of every program are essential for on-time launches. Program managers must manage third parties contributing to the product as well as their internal teams.

Summary: Product Delivery
The West Tower

Just as the West Tower's protective capability is influenced by its shape, construction material, and location, a product's effectiveness is defined by its quality, cost, and timing. That is, after a product is defined, it needs to be delivered on *time*, with the right *features*, high *quality*, and at the right *cost*. Useful tips include:

- Cost and quality must be forethoughts, not afterthoughts. They are essential constraints on product design choices.

- Managing cost and quality requires structured processes. The processes suggested in this chapter are frameworks and recipes that worked well for all my businesses.

- Be prudent when introducing variants or stock keeping units (SKUs). Think of all the costs when introducing them. Each variant must be justified by a business case. Variants must be pruned when they dilute profits.

- New product introduction accuracy can be improved significantly by having a planned cadence for product launches; a good development process with checkpoints and checklists that appropriate management levels review and approve; a team-aligning, delivery-accuracy metric; and strong program management.

- Pay careful attention to avoid the seven sins of new product introduction delays.

Once you define and create your products, the products must be sold. I once had a CEO tell me that if you have great products, they will sell themselves. I cannot disagree more. You need great salespeople and channels to sell your products. This is the topic of our next chapter.

7

The South Tower

Sales Channels Are
Your Pipes of Sustenance

As mentioned in the last chapter, the claim that great products sell themselves is a fallacy.

A company won't exist for long without productive sales channels. Products need to be distributed through channels and sold by salespeople. These pathways for product sales and revenue are what I call *pipes of sustenance*. These pipes or channels are critical for obtaining market coverage and converting the product into revenue in a company's addressable market. I compare sales in a company to water in a castle that is life preserving.

Fresh water supply was essential to castles. Without water, the defenders of the castle could not survive, especially in a siege. Take away the water supply, and the castle fell. Water sources outside the castle could be poisoned as well. Therefore, it was essential to have a source of water within the castle walls. Castles used wells, cisterns, and even natural lakes inside their perimeter walls as their water supply.

Castles were typically located at high vantage spots on rocky terrain, making digging wells hard. Yet, these wells were painstakingly dug. At the heart of Dover Castle in England, a well sunk four hundred feet deep feet was protected by a tower.[125] There are castles with even deeper wells, such as the Zbiroh Castle (five hundred and thirty-eight feet) in the Czech Republic and the Kyffhausen Castle (five hundred and seventy-seven feet) in Germany.[126] Furthermore, hand-digging such wells was dangerous, and raising water from such depths was laborious. The castle well could be situated in the inner courtyard and protected by flanking towers. Some wells were situated within the towers.

In other castles, such as the Warkworth Castle in Northumbria, England (circa 1370 A.D.) there was a large tower where rainwater from the roof was channeled down a shaft to a cistern (reservoir) below.[125, 127] Water from cisterns could be piped to the keep via gravitation flow or rotating wooden water wheels that scooped up water and poured it into channels.

Sales channels represent the South Tower of our castle, our "water tower"— an essential structure for the castle's survival. Just as without water, the inhabitants of a castle could not survive long, without the flow of sales, a company cannot survive very long. And like medieval architects and builders who used their ingenuity to provide protected sources of fresh water inside the castle, you need to get creative in how you structure your sales channels to realize the most revenue.

The importance of channels and salespeople should not be underestimated. Many organizations, including start-ups, focus heavily on engineering and soon realize that they are not meeting their sales projections. I suggest they reexamine their investment in sales channel coverage, their sales team, and its capability.

The growth of the venture-backed start-up Samsara sheds light on the value of a robust sales structure. The company, launched in 2015, uses IoT (Internet of Things) data and analytics to help businesses in North America and Europe streamline their fleet management, cargo tracking, and physical operations.[128] This market segment has entrenched players and geographically dispersed customers. With such competition, product differentiation alone is not enough. Samsara recognized that growth required many competent salespeople to cover the geographically dispersed market. Latka, a Software-as-a-Service (SaaS) magazine, cites that in 2019, Samsara had secured fifteen thousand customers with a staff of four hundred and ninety-five salespeople and two hundred and fifty-nine engineers.[129] That is, they invested twice as much in sales versus engineering, a statistic that stands out. Per my independent research, they have a larger direct-sales team than any of their competitors. While their products might be compelling, their approach to market coverage and winning customers has been more impressive. Just before the COVID-19 pandemic, their valuation hit a giddy $6 billion,[130] and in early 2021, it was reported that the company was considering filing for an initial public offering.[131]

Samsara is one example of a company that seems to have prioritized and optimized its sales channels, and there are many more. Having good products and great channel coverage is a better option than having great products and poor channel coverage. Having great products and great channels is the winning combination.

Having risen through the ranks of engineering and operations, I did not have an appreciation for sales or channels until I became an accidental salesperson. I was fortunate to work beside a few gifted salespeople, but as in many walks of life, you need to live through something to truly appreciate it. In most companies I ran, we did not have enough salespeople, and I got involved trying to help. I was never good at sales but being involved allowed me to realize that selling is complex.

Selling involves gaining customer confidence and credibility, closing contracts, making revenue and gross-margin numbers quarter after quarter, forecasting the next quarter's revenue accurately, not building high inventory, managing channel incentive spending, tracking competitors, negotiating new requirements with engineering and customers, working with marketing to promote products, hunting for new accounts, and pricing products to win. Yes, it is just as complex and detailed as engineering or supply chain operations.

Being a great salesperson means being a problem-solver—you are finding a solution for your client and setting them up with opportunities to enhance their success.

Building a productive sales channel requires a holistic view. To build your pipes of sustenance, you must *reach* as many customers in as many geographies as possible to *cover* your addressable market and *convert* that reach to sales or revenue. This approach will vary with the type of product being sold. However, there are some common elements that helped me create a framework for building productive sales channels in the vastly different businesses I led:

- Go-to-market strategy
- High-touch sales
- Pay for performance
- Contracts and closure
- The *push-pull* model
- Productive sales funnels
- Forecasting and fulfillment
- Managing channel incentives

Go-To-Market Strategy – Coverage, Conversion, Margin, Results

A company needs to reach and cover as much of its addressable market as possible to maximize sales. That is, your company needs to address as many geographies, segments, sub-segments, and product shelves as practical. This requires the planning, positioning, and pricing of your products to address these opportunities, as described under the chapter on product creation. However, you also need to deploy competent salespeople armed with appropriate tools to convert these opportunities into revenue.

Many companies face budget constraints that impact the size of their sales team. But money alone cannot help a company optimize its channel coverage—smart budget deployment is also needed. Which channels will maximize the chance of success in the face of competition? The answer constitutes the *go-to-market* strategy. A company may go to market in each region via:

- Direct channels: Dedicated salespeople to address major customer accounts.

- Indirect channels: Distributors and agents for smaller or intermediate customers.

- Online channels: Digital channels (websites/portals) for online sales.

- Ecosystem channels: Opportunities through suppliers and partners who can help expand the reach and coverage for the company's products.

By leveraging distributors, agents, digital channels, suppliers, and partners, one effectively creates a *sales-force multiplier*.

However, every channel has a cost associated with it because people who work in these channels charge a fee for their services, and there are associated product marketing costs. The magnitude of these fees and costs determines the achievable gross margin from that channel. The higher the cost, the lower the gross margin.

Typically, the more touchpoints there are in the chain of sales to the end customer, the lower the gross margin. This is because every touchpoint imposes a fee. For example, assume that a product goes from a global distributor to a regional distributor to a local distributor to a retail store before it is sold to a customer. There are four touchpoints in this chain and the fees collected at each point further dilute your gross margin. This chain of fees is called *margin stacking*.

In addition, all these channel touchpoints must be managed. This includes supplying product-related material (referred to as product collateral) to support product sales, engineering support (called field or application engineering), and marketing investments. Thus, both margin stacking and channel support costs need to be factored into a company's go-to-market plans.

In making go-to-market plans and picking my channels, I have relied on three criteria.

- First, identify channels with *fast conversion rates*. Conversion rate is the rate at which the channel can sell its product inventory. If inventory is irrelevant, as in software products, then ask: Is the channel meeting or exceeding its sales forecast in each sales period?

- Second, assess the *net return on investment* in each channel, considering all costs, including incentive and marketing costs.

These two criteria can be used to prioritize those channels that have fast conversion of products to revenue, and a good return on investment.

- Third, you should validate the continued value of each channel with additional metrics such as revenue growth, winning new customers, and the ability to sell a broader array of products. Are your channels productive? When there are gaps or non-performance in these channels, as indicated by your desired metrics, you should immediately address the deficiencies with targeted plans for improvement or prune these channels accordingly.

High-Touch Sales – Competence and Engagement

Product sales can be classified broadly as *high-touch* and *low-touch*.

A high-touch sales model requires close interaction with the customer through the entire sales cycle, from the introduction of a product to signing a contract, purchasing of the product, and after-sales support. This sales model is typical for complex and technical products such as computer chips, medical equipment, avionics, robotics, and software for automotive and industrial applications. These sales teams are very knowledgeable about the product and the customers' businesses, so they can advocate for how their product meets customer needs and adds value. High-touch sales require salespeople to be consultative sellers who have a deep understanding of their customers' needs and can formulate solutions to solve those needs.

A low-touch sales model, on the other hand, involves far less customer contact. Many of the product attributes can be read on a web portal or specification sheets, and the customer may request a trial to evaluate the product before buying. The best example of low-touch sales is Amazon Prime an online portal where you can browse through products and complete your purchase. If you don't like the product, most of the time you can ship it back.

All businesses I led had a high-touch sales model, and the sales personnel typically came from product and business-development backgrounds. Further, many of these salespeople had worked in the customers' businesses. Therefore, they knew the customers' businesses and understood what *unique selling points* (USPs) should be used. They knew who in each customer's business made decisions and what the path was to get a decision. This knowledge gave these salespeople credibility and helped them sell on product value and not price alone, thereby preserving gross margin. Further, the successful high-touch sales leaders I knew were driven to close deals within defined time frames and knew how to prioritize.

High-touch sales are engagement-driven, where the sales lead has the customer's attention and keeps the sales process moving from one step to the next. This involves the ability to solve technical, commercial, and contract issues quickly. To do so, it is useful to appoint a product technical expert and a legal authority to support the sales lead, forming a triumvirate on an account. This triumvirate will be more adept at solving issues faster than if a sales leader must relay concerns to individual departments and wait to get help.

I observed that, most often, when a regional or account sales team lacked such competent sales leaders, as described above, it invariably led to poor sales in that account or region. This then is the first step to fix the problem: Hire the right sales leader. The right sales leader will also build you the right sales team.

The best salespeople are curious about the product they are selling. They study the product and are great at talking to the customer, listening to the customer's challenges, identifying opportunities, and suggesting solutions. Top salespeople love to close deals and regularly beat their sales quotas. They are driven to earn healthy bonuses.

An average salesperson, meanwhile, is satisfied with a paycheck. They are order-takers. And when the customer asks for more information about a product, they bring in an engineer or product manager to answer the customer's questions. When salespeople do not have product training and do not study the product, they are less likely to appreciate the customer's challenges and uncover opportunities and solutions. As a result, many find it hard to sell on value and instead sell by discounting price.

Informed Customers

Believe that your customers are knowledgeable. Customers are more informed than ever about products—in today's digital world, they can research products, read reviews, and check ratings or feedback on your product from different sources.

You may recognize the following behavior when you go to consumer-electronics stores, as I have experienced. Most often the salesperson will begin to pitch me features of the product I should be interested in. Rarely do they ask me, "What are you looking for in the product?" If you are like me and are one of those people who does not buy just based on trusting a brand, I am sure you have many questions based on your research about the product you are looking for. This simple observation has taught me that it is better to ask about your customers' requirements and then pitch why your product's features address those requirements.

I encountered an amazing salesperson for American Girl dolls. These popular dolls have names, faiths, social classes, and stories that children identify with. Years ago, I had come back home to Cary, North Carolina, late on the 22nd of December from a trip abroad, completely forgetting to get my young daughter a gift for Christmas. I knew what she wanted. The next day, I anxiously called the American Girl manufacturer, and their online sales representative asked me what I was looking to buy. I asked him if I could get a doll named Samantha that could be shipped to my home by the 25th. He said he would find a way to make that happen. He then engaged in a conversation with me, asking questions about my daughter. As a proud father, I began to expatiate, and soon enough, he was pitching me all the accessories this bright and creative child might want with her gift. I bought most of the things he pitched. He had tapped into a powerful sentiment—a father wanting to make his daughter very happy.

Unless they tell you otherwise, assume that your customers are well-versed in what your company offers and what they want. They may have narrowed down their choice between two companies, and it is your salesperson's job to steer the sale in your company's direction.

This also gives you an opportunity to show why your product brings a higher value to the customer than your competitor's product can. An informed customer is likely to appreciate those finer points.

Consultative Selling

Consultative selling is the best form of high-touch sales where it involves being your customer's advocate and consultant—not a vendor looking to fill an order. Helping your customer achieve hard and strategic objectives creates a deeper relationship. Let me share a personal story to illustrate this point.

At Ericsson, we sold wireless infrastructure equipment and phones. We were a leading global player and were often consulted on technology decisions by major network operators. One such operator was planning on replacing their nationwide network with a new network that offered a better path to future evolution. This was a major decision. The operator was faced with choosing between two technologies from two different camps, both with pros and cons. It seemed as if there was no clear winner. Everyone seemed convinced that the choice would be made based on the spend for the network equipment.

I was not convinced. In those days, network operators subsidized phones. That is, if a phone cost $300, they might price it at $150 to make it affordable for customers and then recover this subsidy via the monthly service fee. This operator purchased around 30 million phones per year, and hence, the subsidies took a big chunk of expense out of their annual income statement.

During my time as general manager of Ericsson's American phone division, my colleagues in the infrastructure division and I were invited to present our proposal. I went into the meeting with two slides. The first one showed a comparison of the two technologies as it related to the cost of a phone. The second slide showed a relative cost curve over time that I had estimated, anticipating how the technologies would evolve. This relative cost curve showed that our proposed technology would be cheaper by at least 15 percent, for many years to come. This was because there were more suppliers building our proposed technology, the technology was produced in higher volume to provide economy-of-scale benefits, and the technology was more mature and, hence, more optimized for cost.

If my estimate held true, this operator would save over $2 billion in subsidies each year.

After evaluation, the network operator chose the technology we had backed. Six or seven years later, I met one of the decision-makers from this network operator in Stockholm. He told me that my slides on the cost evolution of the phones and consequent subsidy savings was a critical factor in their decision.

Understanding your customer's decision criteria is essential to winning any deal. After this experience, I always tried to find out what my customers cared most about in a deal so I could formulate a winning solution. This is particularly important when you want to break into something new and big, as we did on the network switch-out.

Pay for Performance – Reward Excellence

While it is critical to hire the right salespeople, it is equally important to *pay for performance*. The design of sales compensation and incentive plans must motivate the sales team to hit or exceed targets. When targets are irrationally difficult to achieve and compensation is not commensurate with contribution brought to the company, it is hard to retain talent. Good salespeople are hard to replace—not to mention the lost time and effort invested in training them.

It is important that sales compensation plans are easy to understand and calculate. This provides visibility to the salesperson, enabling them to track their earnings. Every business I ran adopted a slightly different model, but the core idea for compensation was made up of three elements:

- A set of targets (not more than five)
- Achievement versus each target set
- A payout formula

Examples of targets could be in-year revenue, design wins that translate to future revenue, winning a new customer (new logo), and share of a customer's total spend (also known as *share of wallet*).

The payout is a weighted sum of the achievement to each target, where the value of each weight depends on what the company needs to achieve in its annual operating and long-term plans.

A simple payout scheme for each target works as follows: Set a minimum threshold for achievement to begin payout, and thereafter, increase the payout linearly up to a maximum payout level. Once a salesperson hits the maximum, there is no further payout.

Assume that the payout threshold is 80 percent achievement to the target and the maximum payout level is 400 percent (cap). For very percentage of achievement above 80 percent, the salesperson earns 5 percent of their payout until he/she hits the cap.

For example, let us say a salesperson hit 110 percent of their target or quota. This is 30 points more than the threshold. So, this person would earn 150 percent (30 times 5 percent). If the target payout was $100,000 this person would earn $150,000. A second salesperson is very successful and sells 180 percent of their target. This is 100 points more than the threshold. So, this person should earn 500 percent (100 times 5 percent) but this hits the cap or maximum which is 400 percent. If the target payout is $100,000 this person would earn $400,000. Then there is the unfortunate salesperson who hit only 70 percent of their target. Since this is below 80 percent this person does not get a performance payout.

If your salespeople are making a lot of money and you are setting good targets, it is safe to assume your company is doing well.

Contract Closure – Don't Get Stuck

One of the hardest parts of sales is getting closure on contracts. Until you have signed contracts, you do not get purchase orders and revenue. Negotiating contracts can also be stressful.

In the 1990s, I read a terrific book on negotiation by Roger Fisher, William Ury, and Bruce Patton, *Getting to Yes: Negotiating Agreement Without Giving In*. They outline four principles that helped me develop my model for negotiation:

- Separate the personality of the negotiator from the problem.
- Focus on outcomes, not positions.
- Compromise.
- Use objective criteria when dealing with difficult situations.[132]

Let me share a few takeaways from the numerous contracts I negotiated successfully, the largest one being around $2 billion in value. What is interesting is that none of these deals took more than ninety days to close, despite my being told that closing typically takes the better part of a year.

There are three useful rules that have helped me close deals:

- Create balanced contracts.
- Deal with a decision-maker.
- Break standoffs or stalemates by proposing solutions.

When contracts are one-sided and favor the buyer or seller, it typically takes longer to close, as the disadvantaged party works to balance the agreement. The exception is when the buyer or seller has no choice but to sign.

A balanced contract is one that appears fair to both parties. I do not know if any contract is perfectly fair, but one can get close. To create such a contract, one needs a deep understanding of one's own business and that of the customer's to assess each party's risk objectively and propose contract language that mitigates such risk. Typical areas of contention are pricing, payment terms, confidentiality periods, warranty, indemnity, liability clauses, and termination for breaches, the hardest being those that have punitive payments and consequences. Each potentially contentious term needs cogent arguments backed by precedence or proof of why the terms are what they are. Logic and proof usually work with a motivated buyer.

For example, it is not uncommon that a buyer asks for high liability for product failure. In this case, it is important to assess where your product plays into the customer's product solution. How does it impact the product solution, and what influence do you as a seller have on controlling the final product quality? As a seller, it is fair that your risk is proportional to factors you control, and the percentage value of your product relative to the total solution value. Most reasonable buyers will be willing to entertain such a discussion and appropriately adjust liability.

As an example, let us say you are supplying a component for $1 that will be installed into a $500 mission-critical computer for a high-speed train. The buyer wants you to indemnify them for unlimited damages in case of a failure associated with your component. This is an ask that you cannot afford. Further, you have no way of influencing their design or the product readiness for launch. So, your risk is high. One way to resolve this ask is to offer to test your component to the buyer's specification and use-cases, and if it passes their criteria, the liability will be limited to something reasonable. If the buyer's real concern is for the supplier to be truly diligent in designing and testing its product and not be negligent, then they may accept your offer. If, on the other hand, their goal is to spread their risk and liability across the supply chain, they may not accept your offer. The bottom line is to try to understand what your customer truly cares about to find a solution. In this regard, there is no harm in asking.

When negotiating a contract, it is essential to deal with a decision-maker or at least have access to one. When you negotiate with those who do not have the authority to agree, they have a propensity to take but not give anything in return. This is an unproductive discussion, and you are literally negotiating with yourself. Avoid this as much as possible. Decision-makers have authority and are usually motivated by business arguments to close deals. Therefore, they are a more balanced partner in the discussion. They are also likely to have "asks" and, when these are met, to be more inclined to reciprocate and reach an agreement.

Finally, when stuck on a difficult topic, it is unwise to get into a stand-off or stalemate. As people dig-in on positions, discussions become contentious and unproductive. Whenever I was stuck in such a situation, I asked questions to understand what was behind the buyer's position. I then asked for time to come back with solutions to their concerns. Typically, when you take a proactive position to find solutions and offer rational alternatives, the other party is more inclined to reciprocate. It is hard not to thaw with warmth—in this case, warmth being solutions. The negotiations are moot if the other party has limited interest in closing the deal.

Whenever I try to find a solution to a difficult term in a contract, I assess the risk in agreeing to the client's position. What would my worst-case loss be, and is that even likely? My advice is to avoid being overprotective by modeling the absolute worst case; be practical and prudent.

There are cases where the buyer is intransigent, and then, you must make a business decision to proceed or walk away. Companies that take such hard positions rarely succeed in the long run, as the counterparties hate working with them and will move away or be less accommodating when there is an alternative.

In summary, to expedite closing contracts:

- Have balanced contracts.

- Understand your business and that of your customer, including their pain points and what they value.

- Have facts to back up your arguments on each contentious term in the contract.

- Negotiate with or have access to a decision-maker.

- Avoid getting stuck in a stalemate by asking questions and proposing solutions.

Push-Pull Model – Lowering Channel Resistance

The power of the *push-pull* model dawned on me when I was running EMP.[133, 134] This model occurs when your customer *pushes* your product and the customer's customer *pulls* your product. When this effect is created, your sales improve dramatically because both ends of the sales pipe are open to sales flow and there is low resistance. This model is shown in Figure 10 (see next page).

I liken sales to water flowing through a series of dams. Unless the sluice gates of all dams downstream are open, the water gets blocked. In this case, water is your product, and the downstream dams are your customers, your customers' customers, and their customers. Every one of these parties must open their sluice gates for your product to flow through. It is even better if your customer pushes your product, and their customer creates a pull for your product. This removes all resistance, and your product will flow rapidly through the channel.

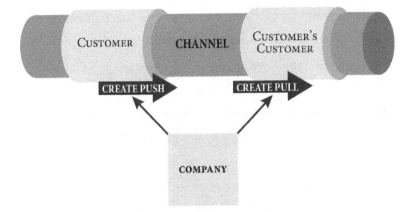

Figure 10: Push-Pull Model

When you are a cellphone platform supplier, as we were, you must pass through two sluice gates: your customer and the customer's customer. Our customer was a phone OEM, or original equipment manufacturer (e.g., Sony-Ericsson, LGE, Sharp), and the customer's customer was a cellular carrier or network operator (e.g., AT&T, Vodafone, Hutchison). Our high-touch sales team engaged with the OEM. But we had to also focus on the customer's customer. So, we assigned a dedicated expert from our team to work with each of the top cellular carriers. We requested that our dedicated experts be paired with a champion for our solution, appointed from the wireless cellular carrier's team. Our experts were co-located with the champion, at their workplace.

The wireless carrier saw benefit in this arrangement because our expert and the champion worked together to align our solution to the wireless carrier's specifications. This expert-champion pair would feed gaps in compliance back to us, and we would modify our solution to be compliant. As a result, when our solution was ready, it was highly compliant with the cellular carrier's specifications. This allowed the cellular carrier to list our platform as a compliant product, which in turn increased our customer's confidence in adopting our products. The compliance created the pull, and so when our customers pushed their products with our platform, the resistance to technical acceptance at the cellular carrier was reduced, if not eliminated.

Our experts were part of our product management team, and this allowed them to influence features on our product roadmap to be compliant to the cellular carrier's specifications. This arrangement ensured that we were positioned to design for both our customer and our customer's customer.

As a cautionary note, if the company is not willing to invest in the push-pull model, it will not work. The worst thing to do is attempt to implement it half-heartedly, because when it does not fulfill a promise to your customer or customer's customer, it leads to distrust.

By investment, I mean:

- Allocate the right resources to engage with the customer and customer's customer and collect both parties' requirements.
- Pay detailed attention to what opens the sluice gates for your customer and customer's customer. In the example above, it was compliance with the cellular carrier's specifications.
- Ensure that your product management and engineering teams can comply with the required specifications in a timely manner.

If this investment is an issue, I suggest trying it in phases, one customer at a time, starting with the one you will have the most success with.

Productive Sales Funnels – Time to Money

Sales funnels are used to categorize a sales team's opportunities in phases or stages. The first phase is the identification of an opportunity, and each successive phase represents an advancement through the funnel until the last phase, which is an actual sales order.

The question is, how do you make this funnel productive, converting opportunities to revenue, especially if you are short staffed? A model can help you pick the most probable opportunities. The model I used was based on two criteria:

- What opportunities are worth pursuing?

- How fast can you convert real opportunities into revenue (velocity)?

There are numerous models to qualify opportunities, starting with the IBM B.A.N.T. model introduced in the 1960s and the N.E.A.T Selling™ model proposed by the Harris Consulting Group, alongside many more.[135, 136] B.A.N.T. and N.E.A.T. are acronyms for four essential steps in assessing if a sales opportunity is worth pursuing.

I personally like the N.E.A.T model, which identifies an opportunity as being worthy of pursuing when:

- The customer has a real need (N) that you must validate.

- Your solution has an economic (E) impact or brings a commercial benefit to the customer.

- You have access (A) to a decision-maker.

- The customer will buy within the time frame (T) of your sales cycle.

Once you have recognized opportunities that meet these criteria, the next step is to rank them based on a score. For the score, I used a combination of the probability of success and the potential revenue. This score ranked each opportunity. I pursued opportunities in rank order from most likely to least likely.

The next step is to determine how fast this opportunity is flowing through your sales funnel, which is a measure of the velocity of progress. If the flow is slow, it can mean there is a technical issue, a commercial issue, a legal (contract) issue, or a combination of these issues.

Assess if these issues can be overcome in this sales cycle, and if not, move this opportunity for closure to a new period or discard it as lost. It is crucial to decide so your sales team is not stuck wasting time on less likely opportunities.

If one does not assess this funnel regularly, prioritize, and prune opportunities, one is bound to have efficiency issues and longer-term sales shortfalls.

Forecasting and Fulfillment – Pulse of Revenue

This is where the rubber meets the road for sales. Every company must make educated predictions (demand forecasts) of what they can sell in each period and have the products to sell to *make their numbers*. When the company gets this consistently wrong, they will fail. In my view, this is the most critical function of sales operations.

I have worked at companies that had a rigorous process for forecasting and fulfillment and others that depended on the in-house oracle to opine on a forecast. In one business, the oracle was very knowledgeable and predicted revenue to an accuracy of 85 percent. This is just not good enough though, because you cannot miss your numbers by 15 percent every quarter. When we switched from educated guesses to a forecasting process, we hit our numbers like clockwork.

To create reliable demand forecasts, you must first understand the linkages and dynamics of your sales channels.

Understanding Your Channels

Figure 11, shown on the next page, is an illustrative sales channel that I will use to explain linkages and channel dynamics.

Figure 11 illustrates a sales channel in the auto industry where a Tier 2 supplier sells to a Tier 1 supplier, and a Tier 1 supplier sells to an OEM, who in turn sells to their customers. The product in our

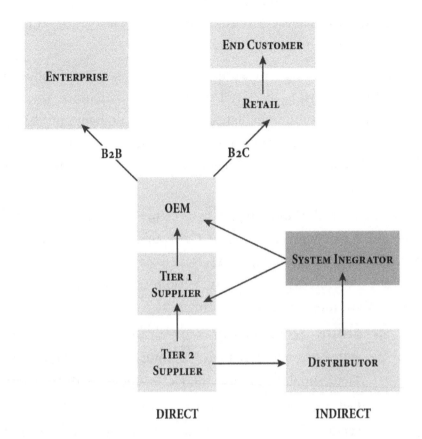

Figure 11: Sales Channel Illustrative Example

example is an infotainment unit that occupies a central spot on your car dashboard. These infotainment units are built by Tier 1 suppliers (e.g., Bosch, Visteon, Harman, Panasonic, DENSO). These Tier 1 suppliers buy software and semiconductor components from Tier 2 suppliers (e.g., BlackBerry QNX, Greenhills, Google, Qualcomm, NXP, Renesas) and use these components to build the infotainment unit. Next, the Tier 1 supplier sells the infotainment unit to an OEM (e.g., Ford, GM, Toyota, Jaguar Land Rover, Mercedes). The OEM installs these units in cars and sells cars to enterprises such as Hertz and Avis and to dealerships (retail), who in turn sell to end customers. Sales between two enterprises like Ford and Hertz is called business-to-business or B2B. Sales between a business to a customer (even via a retail dealership) is termed B2C in Figure 11.

Assume your company is a Tier 2 supplier that sells semiconductor components (chips) to the Tier 1 supplier and distributors. The Tier 1 supplier builds an intermediate product (infotainment unit) based on your chips and sells this product to the OEM. The OEM installs this intermediate product into their cars, which are sold to enterprises and retail customers.

To create its demand forecast, your company will need to understand the demand forecast from the Tier 1 supplier, the OEM, and the distributors, as shown in Figure 11. Next, your company will need to correlate these forecasts with sell-in, sell-through, and sell-out data to validate these forecasts. For those unfamiliar:

- **Sell-In** occurs when you sell your semiconductor chip to your customer (Tier 1 or distributor). In Figure 11, it is the Tier 2 supplier selling to the Tier 1 supplier or distributor.

- **Sell-Through** occurs when your customer (Tier 1) uses your semiconductor chip to produce the infotainment unit and sell this product to their customer (OEM). In Figure 11, this is the Tier 1 supplier selling to the OEM.

- **Sell-Out** is the ultimate sale of the end-product (car containing the infotainment unit which contains your chip) to the enterprise or end consumer. In Figure 11, this is the OEM selling cars to enterprises or the end consumer via the retail channel.

These three numbers determine the status of inventory in the channel. Let your product sell-in be 1 million chips. Next, seven hundred thousand of your chips are used by the Tier 1 supplier to build their infotainment units, subsequently sold to the OEM. These sales from the Tier 1 supplier to the OEM constitute sell-through.

Next, the OEM installs these infotainment units in cars and sells 600,000 cars to its enterprise and retail customers (sell-out). Let us assume that you also sold 100,000 units to distributors, but these have not moved beyond this stage.

The above data says 300,000 units (1 million sell-in minus 700,000 sell-through) are sitting in inventory at the Tier 1 supplier, and 100,000 units (700,000 sell-in minus 600,000 sell-out) are sitting in inventory at the OEM. Another 100,000 units (100,000 sell-in minus 0 sell-through) are parked with distributors. The total inventory in the channel is 500,000 units of your chips (300,000 at the Tier 1 plus 100,000 at the OEM plus 100,000 at the distributor) in one form or another.

This inventory in the channel will influence your next demand forecast based on how fast the channel will consume this inventory. Your company must estimate and track this inventory and the associated consumption rates, adjusted for seasonal trends, every three months (a financial quarter), at each of these downstream dam's sluice gates in the sales channel. These dam sluice gates are the Tier 1s, OEMs, and distributors, because they control the flow of products in the above channel.

Based on the inventory and consumption rates in the channel, you can plan how much new product to produce. You must take additional considerations into account.

If you produce too much, you will carry more inventory, locking up cash. If you produce too little, you may short the customer, and they may be upset because they have lost revenue—or worse, replace your solution with another if they have a second supplier for the same product (*dual-sourced*).

This problem gets more complicated as new products are launched to replace old products. If old products are stuck in the channel when your new products arrive, they can hamper the sale of new products. For example, assume the company did not properly plan a launch and sold-in a lot of its older products into the channel just before new bet-ter-performing versions came out. The channel will want to deplete the old inventory before launching the new version. This would cause a tepid launch of the new products.

Alternately, imagine the company produced a lot of the old prod-ucts and these sit in inventory while the new products are launched. The old products may have to be scrapped or sold for very low prices, which in turn may cannibalize sales of the new products.

A Model for Forecasting

Ideally, you want to forecast and build products to meet your sales revenue and minimize inventory. Is this possible and can this be done consistently? The answer is yes—if you are disciplined and scientific about it.

When demand forecasts are optimistic (forecasted demand is far greater than true demand), the company builds too much product, and its inventory grows. This locks up cash, increasing your working capital. Inventory for newer products typically gets consumed in the following selling periods, but inventory for older products, with dying demand, will at some point have to be written off.

Further, when demand drops, the company is stuck not only with finished-goods inventory but Work-in-Progress (WIP) and material that has been ordered (typically items that have long lead times to man-ufacture). Inventory is not the only problem. Manufacturing capacity must be planned and reserved ahead of time. Well-run factories do not have a lot of excess capacity and have high utilization of their installed resources. As such, when demand forecasts are optimistic and manu-facturing capacity has been paid for but not used, it raises the cost of the product, which lowers gross margin and dilutes profit. The reason is that the manufacturing cost is amortized over the total number of products produced. If the number of products produced is lower than the available capacity, then the cost per product goes up.

As a simple example, let us assume your installed capacity costs you $10 million per year to produce one million products. Therefore, the cost of your installed capacity per product is $10. If you produce only 800,000 products, the cost for each product is $10,000,000 divided by 800,000, going up by 25 percent to $12.50. Now, if you outsource manufacturing to a third party, it may not be any better. In this case, when the volume of your product drops, you are likely to be charged a higher price by the manufacturer.

On the other hand, when forecasts are pessimistic (forecasted demand is lower than true demand) the company does not build enough products and there is a shortage of products to sell. This reduces sales and the shortfalls open opportunities for competitors to take share from the company.

To facilitate accurate demand forecasts and match supply, I employed a three-step model led by a dedicated business operations manager. The business operations manager would collect a reliable demand forecast from the sales operations team (step one). Next, the supply chain operations team would determine what material they needed to order and build to meet the forecast (step two). The business operations manager would then reconcile these inputs along with business rules to create a report for senior management to review, make final adjustments, and approve the plan (step three).

Step One: Reliable Demand Forecast

I asked my teams to create two forecasts, a long-term and a tactical forecast, every month. The tactical forecast was what we had to build for the quarter to make our revenue numbers. The long-term forecast was a rolling month-by-month prediction of demand for the next twelve months. This forecast needs to be directional rather than exact. We used this forecast to place orders for long-lead time items, especially important during times of shortages. Take the recent shortages of semiconductor chips due to the COVID-19 pandemic. Some critical chips have a fifty-two-week lead time (i.e., the time between placing an order and receiving the chips). If I only had the tactical forecast, I would not have been able to place timely orders for these critical chips.

For the tactical forecast the sales team creates a demand profile *by each part number,* for each individual channel and region that the company plans to sell into during the given period, based on:

- Solid forecasting models
- Knowledge of the inventory at various stages in the channel
- Good sell-in, sell-through, and sell-out data (consumption rates)

The quality of the demand forecast depends on the three bullets above and a very thorough understanding of one's channels and sales dynamics.

In my businesses, every sales team created a sales forecast for the channel they were responsible for. We aggregated all these forecasts into a total forecast—therefore it is called a bottom-up forecast.

Next, we used two well-known demand forecasting models to validate these sales forecasts. These are the Bass diffusion model [137, 138] and the Holt-Winters or triple-exponential-smoothing model.[139] Both these models are available as software packages but can also be built rather easily.

The Bass Diffusion model is used to model sales forecasts for new-product launches. Using historical data of prior launches of our products in similar markets, we could forecast the sales of the new product. The model also allowed us to include the influence of price and marketing efforts on new sales.

The Holt-Winters model is very useful to forecast sales for products that have been launched and are being sold in channels. This model allowed us to include trends and seasonal variations. My sales operations team would use this model to validate sales forecasts in each channel.

Once the total sales forecast was validated, it was reviewed and adjusted by appropriate levels of management in the company to create a final sales demand forecast for the period.

Step Two: Supply Forecast

In this step, the supply chain team needs to assess what they can produce in the period compared to the demand forecast. They need to determine how much inventory they have on hand and how much material they have ordered to produce new products. I call this an assessment of the true inventory. The company's true inventory by part number includes what is in finished goods stock, WIP, and material on order that will enter production to produce products for that selling period. That is, carefully account for all material available for manufacturing and on hand to satisfy sales demand for the forecast period in question. This allows the supply chain team to determine what additional material they need to order and possible expedite.

Next, the manufacturing team needs to determine the manufacturing yield of every part number to calculate the true output for the forecast period. If your yield is 90 percent this means for every one hundred units you produce, only ninety are available to be sold. You must factor in this loss when you determine how much to produce.

Bad inventory data and poor manufacturing-yield data will result in too much or too little supply forecasted. So, it is critical to get this right.

The supply chain operations manager would respond to both the long term and tactical demand forecast—create an order plan to purchase long lead-time items corresponding to the long-term forecast and create a build plan for the tactical forecast.

Step Three: Reconciliation of Steps One and Two and Ordering Using Rules

In the final step, the business operations manager correlates and reconciles the sales demand forecasted from step one with the supply forecast in step two and then get approval to order components and build products based on strict business rules.

One business rule could be that the company will not increase the inventory of an old product that is to be replaced by a newer product within a six-month window. A second rule could be that the company will throttle back the production volume of products with low yields until these yields are above a certain level. Yet another rule could be to carry excess inventory only on new products or those that have a long, active sales life (*long tails*). There may also be business rules specified by your manufacturer on how much they can produce each week, which sets a schedule for placing orders. Every company will have its own set of rules based on its situation and manufacturing contracts.

Forecasts made with bad data are invariably bad. Similarly, orders placed without good business rules result in bad outcomes.

If you are selling products such as software, you do not carry inventory, but you will still need demand forecasting to predict your future revenue. Thus, even with such product sales, a detailed understanding of channel dynamics matters, and one still needs Step 1 of the above process.

Forecast Linearity and Ownership

Linearity of sales orders and ownership of the demand-forecast process can a have major impact on a company's financials.

As often as possible, the sales team should secure orders that can be fulfilled uniformly (linearly) over the quarter. If the demand forecast is such that most sales orders are only fulfilled in the last few weeks of the quarter, it causes two problems. First, it puts tremendous pressure on the sales team to make the quarterly numbers and amplifies the risk of not achieving revenue targets—because any slip in getting an order means you do not make your numbers. Second, to satisfy the potential higher demand at the end of the quarter, the supply team will have to either build higher inventory ahead of time or secure high production capacity at the end of the quarter that they may not use—both having cost impacts.

Ownership of the demand forecast is equally critical. Clearly, the demand-forecasting process is a joint effort by sales, business, and supply chain. But who is the owner? In chapter four on culture, I stated that there can be only one owner for each major deliverable. If there is no clear owner, each group (sales, supply, business owner) is likely to develop an independent forecasting model that is unsynchronized with the others. Multiple unsynchronized forecasts result in conflicting product-build signals—increasing the likelihood of high inventory and concomitant cash burn.

I have seen this chaos twice in my career, both at major companies, and the results were catastrophic—hundreds of millions to billions of dollars of loss due to the build-up of high inventory and subsequent write-offs. The only way to avoid this loss is to have one forecast for the entire company, with clear accountability when it comes to who decides what to build.

I strongly believe that the group responsible for the demand forecast should also own the inventory, to avoid over-forecasting and building inventory. This group should also have the authority (within guidelines and rules) to price products to move excess inventory, or else they have been assigned accountability without authority. Thus, I vote for sales or a business unit owning demand forecasting and inventory depletion. This ownership and authority issue is a hotly debated topic in many companies.

Only in one company in my career, Sony-Ericsson, did I find this responsibility well-managed, through a Japanese process called *seihan*. Our CEO grew weary of the tension between the sales and supply departments. Sales always complained they did not have the right product mix to sell, and supply complained that sales never gave them good forecasts and they always had to guess. So, the CEO decided that going forward, we would build whatever sales wanted, but then they would own the inventory. He joked that if sales did not sell the inventory of components by Christmas each year, their annual bonus would be paid using the bucketful of leftover components and not cash. Interestingly, we never had an issue after this assignment of responsibility.

Revenue Recognition – Sell-In Versus Sell-Through

Your company can choose to recognize revenue when it sells-in products to the channel or when its channels sell-through products. The decision has impacts to consider.

With sell-in revenue recognition, a company may sell products (hardware) to a distributor and recognize revenue. However, the distributor will typically not carry risk and will have the right to return the product if they cannot sell it. Therefore, it is important to monitor the distributor's inventory and aging of this inventory because the company has recognized the revenue for the products it has sold-in to the channel and will have to reverse this revenue later if products that have not sold-through are returned. This problem gets more complicated when a new product with better specifications is launched. The old product's appeal is diminished and may result in high returns, or the company having to reprice the old inventory and pay distributors for the difference in price.

On the other hand, a company can choose sell-through accounting.

For an example of sell-through revenue recognition, assume a company that is selling software using the channel model shown in Figure 11. A Tier 2 supplier sells software to a Tier 1 customer. When the Tier 1 incorporates this software into its product and ships their product to an OEM, they record this as a one-copy use of the software. The Tier 1 customer records the total copies of software it has used based on the number of units they ship to the OEM, and they report this number to the Tier 2 (your company). Your company then recognizes the price per copy times the number of copies used as the revenue. In this case, there is no returning of products. However, it is important to understand the channel inventory, your customer's product sell-through, and their customer's product sell-out in order to enable you to forecast revenue for the next period. I would like to point out that selling software has certain defined rules for how revenue can be recognized, but we will not go into this complexity here.

Channel Incentives – Reward or Entitlement

Your products should constantly be moving through the channel, pref-erably through natural demand. This is like a pipe carrying water. If there is a clog, everything gets backed up and creates a mess. The big-ger the clog, the longer it takes to clean.

Companies typically use price moves and incentives or market-ing funds to help keep the channel sales flowing. Incentives or mar-keting funds are also used to place and promote the product, support co-advertising with customers, and facilitate sell-in, sell-through, and sell-out of the product. Both price moves and incentives should be used wisely.

Price moves are most effective when planned and proactive. Reac-tive price moves are a fast-follower tactic that has already ceded ground to the first mover.

When channels are stuffed to meet revenue targets that do not follow natural demand, the use of incentives typically becomes inefficient and costly. Since there is no demand, the only way to sell-in more products is to provide large incentives to a customer or distributor. These incentives cost the company and dilute gross margin and profits. Further, as mentioned earlier, there is a risk of returns from distributors, which impact revenue in the case of sell-in accounting.

Price moves and incentives are investments that must be measured by returns. There are two ways to accomplish this.

- Method One: Measure the benefit of the incentive spend in a period as a function of revenue realized in that channel in correlated periods. The reason I highlight correlated periods is that sales may be offset in time from the period in which incentives are used. You typically spend money and only see the result of the spend on sales in a later period.

One metric to measure the return on the incentives spend is the *net contribution margin* of the product in that channel. In this context, the net contribution margin is revenue minus the regular cost of goods sold minus operating expenses *minus incentives.*

- Method Two: Measure the stage or "dam" in the channel where the incentive, when applied, has the highest impact to drive revenue by opening the "sluice gates." It is better to incentivize those parts of the channel that are more successful in converting product to revenue than other parts of the channel.

Incentives must be rewards and not entitlements. The difference between a reward and entitlement is akin to *paying for performance* versus *paying to participate.*

As an example, take a company that builds and sells home appliances through a variety of retail channels. If this company allocates its marketing dollars to each retail channel as a percentage of how much each channel is willing to order and stock, I call it an entitlement. That is, this company is giving retailers marketing money not based on what they sell but for being a partner that carries their products. It is paying to participate. This money is wasted if the retailers do not sell the stock. What's worse is that they may come back to the company for more money or rebates to sell what they have not sold. It would be far better if the company rewarded, with incentives, those retail channels that sold their stock every month and ordered more appliances. These rewards could come in two forms: more marketing money to help move products even faster and bonuses to hit targets so the retailer makes more money. This is paying to perform.

I acknowledge that the above methods and metrics are not always easy to implement and track. However, not using metrics at all to gauge incentive-spend efficiency or distributing incentives evenly through the channel suggests inefficiency and a lack of channel management.

Summary: Sales Channels
The South Tower

Sales channels are critical to a company's success. They are your pipes of sustenance. They bring revenue. I have found the following principles useful in building and managing sales channels:

- Maximize your sales channels for *reach* and *coverage* by leveraging your direct-sales team and indirect channels (partners), as force multipliers. Prioritize those channels that optimize your coverage, margin, and conversion rates under a fixed-budget constraint.

- Invest in a high-touch sales force using consultative selling to understand your customers' needs and help them solve problems, which in turn will raise your value to them.

- Always *pay for performance* with structured and fair incentive compensation plans that motivate salespeople to create value for themselves by creating value for the company.

- Do not get stuck on contracts. This delays sales and revenue. Contract closure can be expedited if you have balanced contracts, deal with decision-makers, and avoid stalemates by proactively suggesting solutions for contentious issues.

- Create a *push-pull* sales model in your channel to lower end-to-end resistance to selling your products.

- Manage the channel efficiently via the following methods:

  - Perform accurate demand forecasting using detailed channel knowledge, good data, and analytical models.

  - Try and satisfy the demand for your products and services uniformly over a quarter to lower supply and revenue risk.

  - Be proactive when compared to the competition when it comes to pricing. Have a plan instead of being perpetually reactive.

  - Use metrics-driven incentive deployment—pay to perform instead of paying to participate.

At this point, we have established our foundation, built a strategy and culture, defined and delivered products, and created channels through which to sell our products. All these different elements across a company must be synchronized and made to work reliably and consistently as one unit. This is what our next and final tower is about: execution.

8

The North Tower
Execution Builds
the Discipline of Success

Execution is about doing the little things right consistently, day in and day out.

Execution, representing our castle's North Tower, is not as glamorous as the disciplines of strategy creation or product creation or sales. But this tower is essential, as it protects the access points into and out of the castle.

Gates were vulnerabilities in castles and hence kept to a minimum. The main gate was how most traffic passed in and out of the castle. There was also a secondary gate called the postern that gave defenders a chance to come and go inconspicuously—and to deploy forces if the castle was under attack.

During a siege, the main gate was targeted as a weak point. Therefore, the main gate had to be protected by a heavily fortified tower—the gatehouse, or barbican, which housed guards.

To enter the castle, you had to cross a drawbridge, break down the main door, and then pass through a gatehouse passageway that was filled with obstacles and traps. These traps included portcullises—heavy iron grilles that could be lowered from the ceiling using winches. There could be a series of these devices placed yards apart to trap the enemy in the passageway. The ceilings of the passageway had murder holes through which hot liquids could be poured down on attackers. There were thin slits strategically placed along the stone walls of the passageway called arrow-loops that allowed guards to pick of enemies one by one as they entered the passageway.

The King's Gate at the Caernarfon Castle in North Wales had two drawbridges, five doors, and six portcullises, which made this entry point very unattractive to enemies.[140] The Krak des Chevaliers Castle had an even more intimidating entrance. It featured three consecutive turns, a hairpin bend, and rapid changes in sunlight and darkness to slow down and confuse the enemy.[141] The Mehrangarh Fort built in the fifteenth century sits four hundred feet atop a hill with walls that are one hundred and eighteen-feet high and sixty-nine-feet thick in places. The only way into the fort is a narrow zig-zag passage that passes through seven gates.[142]

Execution, our North Tower, protects the entrance to the castle. When it fails, the castle inevitably falls. The design of this defensive structure had to be intricate and carefully thought through. Every protective mechanism in its defensive structure had to be checked daily to make sure it worked, lest it fail when needed. Execution in a company is no different.

Without proper execution, your company's strategy will be wasted effort. If your gatehouse is breached, it will not matter if the perimeter wall is standing.

Execution is a process built on *details, discipline, and rigor.* It is what delivers the strategy.

You can create a great product, but if you cannot deliver the product on time, or if your sales team does not forecast demand properly, or if your supply chain does not fulfill the demand, or if your salespeople have trouble selling the product, or if your marketing department does not secure product reach and coverage, or if you do not collect money in time, your business will stumble and begin to break. Every aspect of the business must work in unison.

I will diverge from my castle analogy and use a formula one race car example to illustrate this point. The crew chief coordinates how the car will be built and tweaked for race day. Crew members practice pit stops thousands of times to streamline and perfect their roles. The car itself has numerous sensors that are constantly monitoring and sending status reports about critical parts of the car, and these reports are analyzed by the engineering team. The driver communicates with the pit crew and competition manager, who in turn coordinate when the driver comes in for a pit stop. With all the data and communication, there is constant analysis and race-strategy development. Winning the race is about getting everything right, lap after lap.

There are two quotes by Lou Gerstner, who led a remarkable turn-around of IBM in the 1990s, etched in my head:

- "So, execution is really the critical part of a successful strategy. Getting it done, getting it done right, getting it done better than the next person is far more important than dreaming up new visions of the future."[143]
- "People don't do what you expect but what you inspect."[144]

In my experience, execution is driven by a process to get agreement on commitments and then develop a mindset and habit to meet those commitments.

Several years ago, I was appointed to lead a multi-product line business. Our sales were behind the business's targets, and we were two months from the close of the year. We were at a trade show in Las

Vegas, and I had arranged to meet my sales leader after dinner to get his perspective. As we were walking along one of those long corridors at the Venetian, I asked him bluntly why we were behind on the targets. His answer was interesting. He said he had not committed to the targets—his previous boss had. I almost tripped.

How had they set the target? Why hadn't he or anyone else voiced an objection earlier? How was performance managed in this business? This answer, I found, was not unusual—no wonder they did not deliver to expectations. No company or business should be in such a position.

This situation validated, yet again, the model I use to secure excellence in execution.

- Goal setting: Create a credible and committed annual operating plan (AOP) from which department and individual goals are derived.
- Metrics: Set good metrics to assess progress to goals and diagnose execution issues.
- Structured follow-through: Hold weekly and monthly operations reviews focusing on execution status, metrics, and providing direct and timely feedback.
- Operational leadership: Help your team diagnose and solve problems to keep moving forward.
- Performance management: Set goals for employees that are aligned with company goals, along with periodic reviews and coaching.

Goal-Setting – Annual Operating Plan

Execution involves following a structured process to keep the company on track to hit its targets. This effort begins with the creation of an annual operating plan from which you derive what each department must do to realize your company's targets for that year. This plan must be built and approved before the end of each financial year, so the teams start off the new year running and not waiting for approvals. The plan should define the market, the financial goals of the company, and key actions, along with needs, to achieve the goals.

To be more precise, the plan must include:

- Market trends, size, and growth to act as a reference for your plan.

- A top-down (TAM/SAM/SOM) and bottom-up (by each customer or sales channel) analysis of the revenue to be attained. This analysis sets the anchor for the operating plan.

- Major elements of the company's execution plan to attain the targets (i.e., the sales and go-to-market plan).

- A view on key competitors and the potential threats they pose to achieving your targets.

- Product mix and revenue, and gross margin they will generate.

- New products that will be launched, their timing, and impact on the goals.

- Details of all costs (cost of goods sold, operating expenses—research and development, sales, marketing, administration, capital expenses, working capital needs).

- Hiring needs.

- Assumptions on risks such as currency exchange rates, inflation, price erosion, and talent attrition that can impact realization of the targets.

The above data feeds into creating:

- A quarterly view of the income and cash-flow statements.

- A balanced set of risks and opportunities.

- A set of key actions to mitigate risks and capture opportunities.

- Sensitivity or scenario analysis—typically low-end, mid, and high-end scenarios of predicted achievement.

Of course, one cannot plan for every risk and contingency. Many businesses have been impacted by the COVID-19 pandemic since the beginning of 2020. The pandemic could not have been predicted. Every plan has some inherent risk.

The annual operating plan needs to be approved by the board of directors. To facilitate this approval, the data in the annual operating plan should be such that the approver can understand it and come to the same conclusion as the team that prepared the data.

To get approval, the plan must be credible, and facts should line up. For example, take a business that has grown steadily at 7 percent per year for the past three years, in line with the market growth. However, in the coming year, the market is expected to shrink and experience a negative growth of 3 percent due to macroeconomics—and yet, the annual operating plan shows that revenue is going to grow by 20 percent. The approvers are likely to be skeptical about how the company will make such a large share jump in a negative macroeconomic environment. Another common flaw is to assume optimistic revenue growth to fund growing operating expenses.

A credible plan must also be a fair plan to be achievable under reasonable assumptions of the market conditions. For example, expecting significant growth with no investment in products, channels, and people is not fair. Such plans demotivate the teams, as they require them to squeeze water out of a stone.

Plans that are agreed upon foster ownership and accountability. Plans that are dictated or forced upon teams invariably fail.

The creation of a well-aligned plan needs at least one or two rounds of open discussion with the approvers to adjust the plan and reach a consensus. It takes time to get consensus, and I suggest that the annual operating plan be prepared at least four months prior to the end of the year.

Once the annual operating plan is approved, the company or business's management team should communicate it appropriately to their organization, set the metrics that will be tracked, and ask each department to make detailed plans for execution and set appropriately aligned goals.

Metrics: Thermostats, Not Thermometers

Once you have created an annual operating plan, you can monitor whether your execution is on track using metrics. But you need to make sure to choose the right metrics—those that are diagnostic and serve as leading indicators for what is to come. Diagnostic metrics represent business thermostats, helping you regulate and react to a situation. Metrics that are thermometers are not useful because all they do is tell you the temperature, without helping you set or maintain it.

As an illustrative example, I will describe four categories of metrics that I used to build operational excellence in the businesses I led.

- Financial
  - Revenue
  - Gross margin
  - Operating expenses
  - Channel-spend (marketing) return on investment
  - Cash conversion cycle
  - Inventory (levels and inventory turnover)
  - Free cash flow to the firm

- Competitiveness
  - Product competitiveness
  - Customer endorsement
  - Cost improvement
- Operational Effectiveness
  - Demand-forecast accuracy
  - New-product introduction (NPI) delivery accuracy
  - Supply-commit accuracy
  - Field failures, product error reports, and product returns
- Performance Management
  - Goal setting and performance reviews

This is a large set of metrics, fifteen in all, but it provides a comprehensive insight into the operations of a business. Not all these metrics are relevant to every business, and you should create those that are most suitable to your business. Just make them quantitative, easily understood, measurable, and diagnostic—so when things go astray, you can double-click on these metrics and get to the root cause.

In chapter four, under Know Your Numbers, you may recall that I only used five metrics to form the culture of the business. These metrics are a super-set of the fifteen metrics listed above, aligning culture and execution.

Financial

Most of these metrics measure the factors that influence the company's financial foundation, as described in chapter two.

Revenue

When reviewing revenue, I try to understand how and why the

company's revenue is growing or not growing through the following questions:

- What is the order backlog?
- What are the contributions of legacy products and new products, i.e., the product mix?
- Is the customer base growing or shrinking?
- Is the share of addressable business at each customer growing or shrinking?
- What percentage of sales is recurring revenue?
- What are the design wins and the composition of these wins?

Most of these questions are self-explanatory. The answers to these questions are leading indicators of what is to come. For example, the order backlog is a short-term metric and tells one what the next quarter or two will look like. Order backlog refers to confirmed customer orders that you have not fulfilled by shipping product to these customers. In the mobile-phone business, we typically wanted two-thirds or more of our next quarter sales in order backlog thirty days before the start of the quarter because it meant steady sales would continue into the next quarter. If the order backlog was lower, it meant we were in for a rough ride.

A good indicator of future revenue growth comes from design wins. The composition of design wins (share of customer's business, product mix, and revenue type) and their projected lifetime value provide the input for future revenue modeling.

Gross Margin

Gross margin is important for established companies, as it sets what operating expenses you can afford while still being profitable. It is important to track gross margin in two dimensions: the change in gross margin (hopefully upwards) during each period, and how the company is performing compared to its competitors regarding gross margin. Gross margin that is growing will at some point plateau at the desired state. On the other hand, a lower-than-desired gross margin typically occurs when the product costs are high, the product mix is biased toward low-gross-margin products, or the product net pricing (after incentives and discounts) is a problem. Each of these issues points to what needs to be addressed.

Operating Expenses

Operating expenses must track what was budgeted for the quarter and must typically only scale with revenue and gross margin. It is equally important to assess whether the efficiency of the company is improving via an expansion of its capability cube, as we described in chapter four, on culture. This efficiency can be measured by the percentage of operating expenses versus revenue generated. If this number decreases as a percentage of revenue, even incrementally, each year, it helps to improve your business's operating leverage.

Channel-Spend Return on Investment

Channel incentives and marketing spend should spur sales-revenue growth. It is important to understand the *return on investment* (ROI) for this spend in each channel. Without such insight, it is hard to optimize the spend to generate higher revenue and improve channel efficiency. You could be dumping money into low-performing channels that detract from strengthening your productive channels.

Cash Conversion Cycle

This metric measures how efficiently the company is using its pot of cash to run its business in each period. The definition and formula to calculate the cash conversion cycle (CCC) metric is detailed in chapter two. The lower the CCC value, the more efficient the cash usage and the lower the concomitant working capital needs.

Inventory Levels and Inventory Turnover (ITO)

This is only applicable to companies that carry inventory, such as clothing stores, grocery stores, auto spare parts, vehicle dealerships, luxury goods, and electronic devices. Inventory levels determine the absolute amount of inventory you carry. ITO expresses how fast the company sells its inventory—it is sales divided by inventory held in a period.

I used a crude saying with all my teams to bring a point home: "Inventory is like horse manure in a stable. It stinks with time. So, the faster you rake it out, the better."

For efficient cash usage, inventory levels should be low, and ITO should be high. As regards absolute inventory, I recommend segregating this inventory into two separate buckets: the inventory of legacy products whose demand is falling and the inventory of new products that are being actively sold. If the legacy product inventory bucket is large and not selling, it creates a write-off risk. It pays to get very granular with inventory to truly understand what you have and what you can sell and where.

Further, inventory turnover (ITO) is a good measure of sales velocity and demand-forecasting effectiveness.

Free Cash Flow to the Firm (FCFF)

This is the key metric for most if not all established businesses and is usually healthy if all the previous metrics are healthy. It is the measure of how the company is performing to the financial expectation of its investors.

Competitiveness

Product Competitiveness

Each product should be measured against its leading competitor and a challenger using, for example, the following:

- Features
- Performance—preferably with neutral or industry-standard benchmarks
- Compliance with customer and regulatory requirements
- Price
- Solution enablement

These measures can be mapped using graphical methods such as spider charts or heat maps. These maps will highlight the gaps that can hurt competitiveness and, hence, revenue.

Features, performance, compliance with customer and regulatory requirements, and price are self-explanatory. Solution enablement refers to the additional convenience you can create for a customer using your product. It is what enhances your product's appeal.

An excellent example of solution enablement is the file sharing system Dropbox, which I used in writing this book. It was a cinch to install. After this intuitive set-up, an icon appeared on my desktop computer. As I wrote chapters, I would drag and drop these files into the Dropbox folder (icon on my computer). My editors would be notified, and they could review these files which automatically appeared in a folder on their computers. When they made edits, I got a notification and could immediately see the changes they made on the files in my Dropbox folder. It was an amazingly convenient and secure experience.

Thus, solution enablement should focus on two aspects: first, make it simple and very convenient for your customers to use your product, and second, make sure everything works smoothly without glitches.

You don't want your customer to be the first to find out things do not work as they use your product.

Customer Endorsement

This is a measure of satisfaction or product stickiness, as described under chapter five on product creation. One can use Net Promoter Score, user satisfaction surveys, compliance to feature and performance requirements, quality or return rates, and any other quantitative feedback that can help improve customer endorsement of your products.

Cost Improvement

Cost improvement is critical to maintain and improve gross margins. Prices of a product go down with time—this is called price erosion. Costs must go down proportionally to maintain the overall gross margin. This cost reduction can come from design improvements, manufacturing improvements, testing improvements, higher quality, and so on. As such, cost reduction is a collective responsibility of an organization, and each responsible cost-control center must have targets that they should strive to meet. Sustained cost improvement does not happen via the purchasing department tightening the screws on the suppliers. Cost improvement starts with product design and early involvement of all associated cost-control centers in this design phase. I chose to include this metric in the competitiveness category, but it could also be included in operational effectiveness.

Operational Effectiveness

Demand-forecast Accuracy

In chapter seven, on sales channels, we identified demand-forecast accuracy as a critical capability for a company to meet its revenue target and to avoid building excess inventory. One useful measure for demand-forecast accuracy is the *mean absolute percentage error,* or MAPE. This is the moving average of the percentage error between forecasted sales and actual sales in each period. In simpler terms, it is the average error of what you agreed to deliver and what you did deliver in revenue.

MAPE can be used to assess each channel's demand-forecast accuracy and pinpoint where you may have issues. A channel that shows consistently high values of MAPE, or where MAPE varies erratically from period to period, points to a forecasting or performance problem in the region or account and needs further investigation.

NPI Delivery Accuracy

Delivery accuracy, defined in chapter six on product delivery, is the key metric for the on-time introduction of new products. It should be measured for each product-delivery program and across all such programs. This is a quantitative metric. When implemented with rigor, it always delivers to expectations.

Supply-Commit Accuracy

This metric is the counterpart to demand-forecast accuracy. The supply-commit accuracy is how accurately the supply chain secures its targets regarding:

- Product manufacturing-yield improvement
- Manufacturing cycle-time improvement
- Flexibility for handling upsides and downsides in forecasted volume

Each of these measures contributes directly to profit and cash usage. For example, cycle-time improvement means products take less time to produce and this, in turn, means the company can lower its buffer inventory to supply customers. This conserves cash and improves working capital. It also makes customers happier, as they get products in shorter time intervals after they order.

Quality

Quality can be measured by field failures, product errors like software bugs, and product returns. Such failures result in loss of customer confidence, costly failure analysis, and repair and warranty costs. This metric can be lumped in with customer endorsement, but I like to track this metric separately because it has a direct impact on product creation, product delivery, manufacturing, and effectiveness of supplier management, as well as consequent liabilities that the company may have to pay because of field failures. By measuring this independently, the company demonstrates its focus on quality.

Performance Management

Goal setting and Feedback

This metric applies to anyone who manages people. It refers to setting clear, measurable, and attainable goals for each employee, together with periodic progress reviews and coaching of employees to achieve the company's goals. Employees without goals cannot be blamed for not performing, because they have no clear targets. When this happens, company targets are missed frequently and the company begins to falter.

At Ericsson Mobile Phones during the 1990s, we grew rapidly from obscurity to over $5 billion in revenue in less than a decade.[145] Per Larry E. Greiner's seminal work on organizations,[146] we would have been midway into the five phases of business evolution maturity. Outside of engineering and supply chain, we did not have many management processes, including performance management. To this day, I believe an overly engineering-centric organization (inward-looking) and a lack of interlocked goals between the different elements of the business made us miss market opportunities. We lost share, and ultimately, unable to sustain a viable business due to lack of scale, we merged with Sony to form Sony-Ericsson.

At every other business I ran, after this experience, I made sure we had very clear goals and a strong performance-management culture. We hit our targets or came very close to these targets for a combined sixty quarters in a row.

Managers who are not engaged with their employees contribute to poor culture and execution. Managers who set goals, conduct periodic reviews, and give good feedback to employees should be highly valued. The worst managers, meanwhile, are very tough on employees and do not spend time coaching them. And they do not take the review process seriously because they are apathetic to employee development. Managers who do not like setting goals or giving feedback and coaching employees should reconsider their roles.

Structured Follow-Through

Once metrics have been set and assigned to owners, the next step is to institute formal reviews to track progress, assess gaps, and take corrective or remedial action. The format and cadence of these reviews depends on the business. I will share the model I used.

I ran a monthly operational review that spanned a day or two, followed by short weekly one-hour follow-up reviews. The amount of time you spend on these reviews depends on the complexity of the business you run and what you want to get out of the reviews. Every member of my management team was invited, and it was mandatory that they attend because it gave them insight into what each department did, and they got to contribute solutions to company-wide issues. Such cross-functional understanding also helps build consensus and teamwork.

We broke these monthly review meetings into time slots, where each slot was devoted to assessing one business area or function by reviewing: its metrics, the gaps to targets, and what was being done to fix issues in a timely manner. Each time slot was allotted to the person accountable for that business area to present to the rest of the management team.

All material for these monthly reviews should be distributed several days early for attendees to have ample time to read the material before coming to the meeting. It is worthwhile to have a common format and guidelines for each presentation, so no one needs to read hundreds of slides. Keep the meeting focused and succinct. By keeping the material to the point and in an easy-to-read format, the preparer also spends less time preparing the material.

A person with a good understanding of the business is appointed to document action items, which are circulated at the end of the meeting. I stress that it is important that the person who records the actions for later distribution must know the business; otherwise, actions are not well captured. The agenda for such a meeting may look as follows:

Agenda for Monthly Operations Reviews

Operations (Day 1)

- Closure of action items from the last meeting by the head of business
- Financial metrics presented by the CFO
- Product competitiveness, and delivery accuracy presented by each business/product unit leader
- Quality metrics presented by the head of quality
- Supply chain/manufacturing metrics presented by the head of supply chain

- Sales results and inventory-depletion plan presented by the head of sales

- Marketing initiatives plus channel-spend metrics presented by the head of marketing

- Performance-management metrics presented by the head of human resources/talent management

Strategic Items (Day 2)

- Review of pricing models and discount authority levels presented by the CFO and the head of sales for approval by the head of the business

- Technology roadmap presented by the CTO or product-management leads

- Review of manufacturing and supply chain capacity and investment requests presented by the head of supply chain and manufacturing

- Assessment of intellectual property, both internal disclosure and patent-filing status, and external claims/cases, presented by the head of legal

- Risk-management topics and readiness presented by the CFO

- Update on people and culture presented by the head of human resources/talent management

- Threat and opportunity assessment and discussion of new ideas to evolve the business

The monthly operations review serves two purposes. It allows for a regular inspection of internal and external threat assessment via metrics. By reviewing internal metrics, the management team should be able to gauge which part of their castle has developed or is developing a potential weakness, and then revert to detective mode (highlighted in chapter two) to uncover the root cause. The management team must fix this potential weakness before it becomes a threat to the structure of the castle. By reviewing external metrics, the management team can assess where an attack may come from and plan to thwart it. As such, these monthly operations reviews need to be organized to provide the relevant information to assess and correct these threats.

To do this well, presentations must be to the point and enable decision-making. Typically, when people understand their business area, they are precise. It reflects their experience, engagement, and confidence in knowing their numbers.

It is also critical that all actions captured to close gaps are specific and important and are assigned a time frame. Too often, I have seen an endless list of actions that just keep staying on the list. This demonstrates inefficiency and an accountability problem. Therefore, I suggest that the action-item list from the last meeting be the first item on the agenda and led by the head of the business. This adheres to the core principle: expect what you inspect.

In addition to the monthly operations reviews, I recommend a weekly one-hour review where each member of the management team provides the highlights in their area of responsibility and notes any issues that have arisen since the prior week's report. This ought to be a status-update meeting and not a problem-solving meeting. By having this weekly meeting to augment the monthly detailed reviews, the management team can stay on top of the status of the business and issues in an efficient manner.

Operational Leadership: Truffles, Triage, and Temperature

Perfect execution day in and day out is difficult. Businesses experience problems that are unanticipated, serious, and hard to solve. These problems usually do not get solved by committees, lots of meetings, fire drills, table-banging tantrums, or reading the riot act to employees. How these problems are solved provides insight into the execution machine of the company.

The best problem-solvers I have worked with have had five skills that make them excel at this task.

- First, they can sense that a problem is brewing. These problem-solvers have a special sense, much like hogs that can identify truffles three feet underground. This acquired sense is one honed by experience.

- Next, they gather information by asking diagnostic questions and are never satisfied with fluffy answers. If they ask more questions, it means they are dissatisfied with the answers and are probing to find the root cause of the problem. Their analytical engine relies on credible data.

- Using the data, they can triage and identify who to involve in solving the problem. They suggest how to form such a "special-ops team" to chase down the problem.

- They arrange regular follow-ups from the special-ops team leader and give the team time to come up with options and solutions. They understand that rushing the team and setting unrealistic deadlines does not help. They also do not micromanage the team, but rather manage the temperature of the team.

- When the team is stuck, they use three powerful techniques:
  - Teach how to break up a big problem into smaller chunks, which are easier to solve. This technique is a way of systematically building confidence in the team's ability to find a solution.
  - Suggest looking at the problem from a new angle.

- Take responsibility for the hard choices, unburdening the team.

These traits, in short, are operational leadership. Solving hard problems creates stress in a team, which works long hours for weeks to find solutions. The team is invariably tired and edgy. So, it is imperative that the leader brings confidence and calm to the team. The team feeds off what the leader portrays.

I had a well-developed sense for triaging issues but had to learn the other skills by observing those who were good at them. A deputy of mine, who was the chief operating officer in a business I ran, excelled at operational leadership, and he became my model to emulate.

We were working on a complex program to launch a new chipset and software for a new technology standard. This program employed eight hundred engineers for close to three years. Forty weeks from the launch date, which was immovable, I sensed that our project was not on track, even if the data presented showed we were on schedule, because of the answers I got to my questions in a routine project review. I just could not connect the dots.

If we missed our launch, I estimated we would lose over two-thirds of our market share, as every customer was preparing to migrate to this newer technology. That afternoon, I conveyed my reservation to my deputy. He was one who never reacted immediately and was very thoughtful. Two days later, he called me while I was on a business trip in Geneva. "You are right," he said. "I was too close to the fire to see how it had spread."

He went on to analyze what changes were needed and steadfastly brought the project back on track, and we launched on time. He changed the project leadership, entrusting the execution to our most resourceful program manager. Next, he brought in our most experienced technical people to solve all blocking issues along the critical path. This reassignment created holes in other projects, so he rescaled those projects in scope. Lastly, he kept the team calm and guided them every day with logical direction to launch on time despite being so far off target. I got to observe his methods as an apprentice watches a master craftsman at work.

Performance Management – Results Matter

Everyone in a company needs goals and must be measured by those goals. This requires sitting down with each employee, setting goals, getting agreements, and providing them feedback on how they are performing at least twice a year.

Feedback is valuable if it is designed to coach and help someone improve. It is well-received if conveyed properly and the employee respects the manager and wants to learn what is required to grow in their career. I say this because, in all such communication, the transmitter and receiver must be tuned to hear each other. When a manager is both a mentor and a sponsor, the employee gets validation that the manager is there to help them advance in their career. Actions always trump words.

I learned about performance management the hard way. Early in my career, I was promoted to become a general manager rather rapidly based on my technical and operational knowledge. I was inexperienced in general management and did not have the tools or knowledge to build processes like performance management. Those who reported to me were senior in age and experience. They invariably negotiated goals that were qualitative. For example, I would suggest that we hit a certain cost target on our products to secure say 50 percent gross margin as one goal. They would argue that managing cost was not solely in their control and all they could agree to was to try hard—a subjective goal. Therefore, the year-end performance reviews were subjective, contentious, and worthless. There was no accountability for missing targets, only explanations and excuses. I left every year-end review feeling as if I were the one getting reviewed, rather than the goals and targets.

At the same time, I did not get formal reviews from my manager—I was told I was doing a great job and I got great raises. I had no reference for what made a good performance review.

There is nothing to blame for this but my management training and inexperience. To manage my organization, I needed to develop the confidence and ability to set quantitative and measurable targets at the beginning of the year and get consensus through logic and rationale. It took me seven years to hone this ability, aided by talking to mentors and consultants outside my business. By this time, I'd learned to set and present targets cogently and rationally. It is hard to argue with logic. I was also well-versed on the business and, hence, better equipped to manage objections.

From that point, I set no more than five quantitative, measurable targets for each member of my team, followed by two performance reviews and a career-mentoring session. I delivered this feedback with written performance reviews and one-on-one mentoring sessions. By making goals quantitative and agreeing on achievement targets at the beginning of the year, I made sure that each member of my team knew what to expect. The results are what they are. The investment of my time to help them grow in their careers was usually well-received.

Performance reviews are serious and must be taken as such. I will provide two contrasting performance reviews, one of which is indifferent and one of which is recommended.

When I read manager reviews of their employees that are terse and say, "Sam had a good year and met my expectations but can improve in product knowledge," it tells me that the manager did not set clear goals and does not care to provide reviews. Such managers are ineffective and do not appear to be invested in their employees' success. They consider reviews a waste of their precious time.

Contrast this with a manager who writes the following review.

Performance Goals

Sam met or exceeded his performance goals for the year:

- *Exceeded his annual revenue goal of $30M by 5 percent.*

- *Secured five new design wins with a lifetime revenue of $45 million versus a target of $25 million, winning three new logos in his territory.*

- *Met his demand-forecast accuracy target of 95 percent over the year. He missed one quarter on account of his customer's factory shutdown due to a labor issue.*

I am recommending Sam for a promotion in the next cycle due to his consistent performance over the past two years in exceeding his targets.

Career Growth

Based on our discussion, we have jointly identified that Sam would like to grow his knowledge in financial modeling of business cases and be more effective in negotiating contracts.

I recommend that he attend two in-house training programs to acquire a foundation in these areas. We have jointly identified a mentor so he can have a discussion partner after he completes the training programs.

This review says the manager set goals, knows exactly what this employee did during the review period, and has a plan to help his employee grow. The employee also knows his manager is investing time in him.

In addition to performance reviews, I try to provide immediate, direct feedback during operations reviews, with regular follow-up on action items to assist, as needed, to bring closure to issues.

Direct questions and feedback are impactful when delivered properly—they bring clarity to what you are asking for and what you want accomplished. However, you need to be sensitive when it comes to how direct feedback is delivered, as people react very differently. I have chosen two anonymous examples from my journey.

At one management meeting, I pointed out that key revenue-generating products from my division were very hard to locate on the company website. The marketing department disagreed with my assertion and did nothing. So, at the next management meeting, I asked the head of marketing to bring up the website and then asked him to find my products. He struggled. I had made my point. If we could not locate our products, how would our customers? Shortly thereafter, the website got fixed.

We had a supply chain problem at a semiconductor company I consulted for. The forecasting and ordering model invariably led to excess inventory. The issue was two-fold: this company used incomplete and inaccurate data to forecast, and its senior management had a propensity to interfere and override the forecasts—these management adjustments were called "judgment." The template we were using to create forecasts was useful for high-level financial tracking, but not detailed operations. Why had no one challenged this before? At the next operations meeting, I gave feedback to modify the forecasting template and asked senior management not to provide their judgment. Our excess inventory problem went away. Three operations managers for different business lines received this feedback—two were appreciative and one displeased. The offended receiver in this case felt his competence was being questioned.

To avoid such personality conflicts, make it clear that you are addressing the problem and not the person responsible. It could well be that the person responsible is the problem, but that should be handled in a different forum.

Finally, keep an open-door policy, allowing anyone on your team to approach you to get advice on solving problems. I asked that I be among the first to hear bad news, so I was informed, not necessarily to solve the issues, as my team did that most of the time. You cannot solve things you do not know about.

I recall an incident in 1999, when we were ready to launch the world's smallest digital phone with a North American operator. It was an important launch, and we had a standing call with an executive vice president from the customer side every Friday. On a Thursday, a week before the launch, my deputy informed me that our quality department had assessed that one component on the phone was susceptible to failure, possibly over time. They could not conclusively prove this issue and asked that I make a call on it. I asked my deputy what he would do. He was not comfortable with the launch. That evening, after I reviewed all the engineering data, I reached the same conclusion. It would take us two weeks to make the fix and to repair phones we had already built. The next day at our regular Friday call with the executive vice president, I informed him of the issue. He was unhappy that the launch would be delayed but agreed with our decision. We made the fix and launched the phone in two weeks. I am glad this problem got to me, and that we made the right call.

I typically work late into the evening. Employees often drop by my office to chat after 6 p.m. This is something I would never trade because I learn so much and am able to connect with employees on a personal level. I learn about what is happening in the organization, about employees' concerns and feedback. On more than one occasion, these informal open-door chats have allowed me to intervene and solve problems that I would never have known about until they hit us. I also get valuable feedback—a senior financial controller from a military background once told me, "You are a smart GM who thinks two steps ahead, but often, we do not know where you are going. Stop and look behind you to see if your team is there with you. It is unwise to try to cross the bridge into unknown territory without your army." Wow! There is nothing better than getting such direct feedback in private.

Summary: Execution
The North Tower

Execution is about getting things done to meet or exceed targets, which can be achieved using the following guidelines:

- Create a credible annual operating plan (AOP).

- Create department and individual employee goals and plans that correlate to the AOP. Goals and targets need to be agreed-upon, clear, realistic, and measurable.

- Use metrics to track progress to goals and diagnose issues before they become major problems.

- Run mandatory monthly operations meetings where the entire management team is present, augmented by weekly status updates, to review progress.

- Ensure that these meetings are focused and structured and not large, confusing dumps of data that are costly in time to prepare, read, and make sense of. Meetings must provide clarity on issues and enable decision-making.

- Correct issues identified in these reviews immediately, before they get too large.

- Provide timely feedback and reinforce clarity of responsibility to avoid the blame game.

- Ensure each member of your immediate team has at least two performance reviews a year to receive formal, relatable feedback, as well as at least one coaching session to identify what is needed to grow in their career. When a manager opens opportunity doors for employees by being a sponsor, it validates the value of mentorship.

- Ask to be the first to hear bad news and be accessible.

When this structure is cascaded throughout the company, you will find it creates engagement and accountability.

Our castle is almost complete. The last remaining step is to add the roof, which should protect the inhabitants against nature's elements and enemy arrows.

9

The Castle Roof

Four Factors to
Create Stakeholder Confidence

So far, we have addressed how to build a strong financial foundation, a strategy that frames the castle, culture as a central defining feature, and the four towers, which are product creation, product delivery, sales channels, and execution. In this penultimate chapter, we discuss building stakeholder confidence, which is akin to laying the castle roof.

Roofs were a significant component of any medieval castle. They were aesthetic, as well as functional and protective structures. These roofs could be flat, dome shaped, gabled, conical, or have other shapes. The roof over the keep or donjon shielded inhabitants from nature's elements and kept food and supplies dry. Often the keep had many floors, and each floor was separated by a sturdy inner roof. In addition, the main roof served as further protection from enemy arrows and other projectiles, in case of an attack.

Some roofs are intriguing, like the one at the Himeji Castle in Japan. Its closely locked and superposed gabled roofs make every façade of the keep look different.[147] This would puzzle an enemy trying to decipher how many stories a keep had, what its internal layout was, and what other structures it could it be connected to—information that was vital in planning how to seize the keep should they be able to enter it.

The construction of the roof was involved. Castle roofs were usually framed with timber and covered with different materials—thatch, wooden shingles, slate, flag stone, fired clay tiles, stone, and even lead.[148] The material used in the construction of the roof determined its ability to last and protect the inhabitants and supplies. Thatch and wooden roofs were cheap. They could be constructed quickly but burned easily, and they were found only on the earliest of castles. Stone and lead roofs were more robust and weathered well. Lead was expensive but withstood wind, water, and flaming arrows well. Stone roofs were the most resilient but also the most elaborate to construct.

The basic support structures to construct a roof were pillars and corbels.[149] A corbel is a structure that protrudes out of a wall and can be used as a support structure. Corbels placed on the internal walls supported thick wooden beams that spanned a room. Then other wooden beams or slats were placed across the supporting beams as a cover. This cover was then lined with the roofing material.

Vaulted stone ceilings and roofs were built using arches supported by corbels or pillars built up from the foundation. The arches helped distribute the stress induced by the heavy load of a roof stone onto the corbels and pillars. Arches were made to crisscross to increase strength and support elaborate stone roofs.

Just as a roof shelters a castle's inhabitants and supplies, there are three stakeholders that shelter and shield companies during stormy times: the investors (both equity and debt), customers, and employees. Each of these stakeholders wants to see the company do well because they are invested in it. If the company does poorly, they are impacted. And if it does well, they gain.

Every company must earn the confidence of this group of

stakeholders, which I call building the "triangle of trust." These stake-holders determine the future of the company. All three stakeholders are crucial and intertwined. Investors give you money to do good things. Without employees, you do not have the capability to do the good things. And without customers, no one is paying you, so you cannot continue to do good things.

Recall my example at EMP. When I joined the business, it was in a dire situation. Had the investors, customers, and employees abandoned EMP, none of our plans would have mattered. Instead, investors (our parent company) continued to fund us, customers gave us time to make our turnaround, and employees made the turnaround happen. Gaining and maintaining this confidence from the stakeholders does not happen automatically. It relies on certain factors just as the construction of the roof depends on pillars/corbels, beams, arches, and roof material. In the context of a company, these factors are:

- Financial health
- Reliable execution
- Innovation
- Engagement

These four factors are dependent on all the other castle elements. In a sense, our castle needs to have the structural integrity to bear the requirements of the roof.

Financial Health – A Matter of Faith

Companies raise money from various sources, but mostly from private equity, venture capital, and capital markets in the form of equity (shares) and/or debt (bonds). In this book, we have focused on established companies and, hence, will only consider investors who have bought shares or invested in bonds that a company has offered.

Investors provide money based on research and confidence that the company can provide a good return on their investment. If the company does well and grows in revenue and profit (free cash flow to the firm), then it is likely that its enterprise value or market capitalization rises. This makes the share price rise and makes equity shareholders happy. The company's positive cash flow allows it to service its debt (pay interest), and with time, the company can pay off the bonds (debt), so bondholders are satisfied.

When the company loses money and does not grow its enterprise value, or when its market capitalization drops, it may struggle to generate cash to meet its debt obligations. Investors walk away from such companies. The last thing investors want to see is the company going bankrupt and being put into receivership. The best way to secure investor confidence is to grow and generate free cash flow that drives enterprise value or market capitalization.

In some cases, investors back a company with potential. But the company must execute to show it deserves their continued confidence—it is a matter of faith and repaying that faith.

Customers also like to work with financially healthy companies. Such companies can invest in innovation, product roadmaps, operations, and channels to grow. A company that is bleeding cash and not growing is concerning, and customers will worry that the company could go bankrupt or be sold to a hostile entity. Financially unhealthy companies are a risky bet for customers, irrespective of how good their technology or other attributes may be.

One example is Nortel, the one-time Canadian Telecom giant. Nortel competed head-to-head with Ericsson, Nokia, Alcatel, and Lucent. At its peak in 2000, Nortel generated $30 billion in annual revenue and employed more than ninety thousand people. Yet Nortel declared bankruptcy in 2009.[150] A detailed report is available on the website of the Telfer School of Management at the University of Ottawa.[151] There were three main reasons for the demise of Nortel: bad management decisions, a changing market, and the eroding confidence of its clients. The company focused on growth versus cash flow and in the process overspent and had bad financial performance. It did not invest in building wireless technology to keep up with the market and competitors took advantage. Finally, it could not deliver competitively or on its promises, upsetting customers.[152] Its triangle of trust was broken beyond repair.

Employees work primarily for compensation that pays bills and provides financial security for their future, but another important factor is whether the job offers exciting challenges. In highly competitive markets, talent is valued, and this raises the bar on salaries, benefits, and incentives such as stock options. A company that is growing and making money has an easier time attracting top talent. First, such a company is probably building exciting products that are in high demand, and this offers top talent an opportunity to work on these products and contribute. Second, the company can offer attractive compensation packages. Third, the company's rising market capitalization means the shares appreciate, and employees who get stock options benefit. On the other hand, a company that is in a negative spiral not only finds it difficult to hire new talent but struggles to retain its current talent. No one feels secure in a company whose financial health is a mess and whose future is uncertain.

For these reasons, I rank a company's financial health and growth as the most important factor for stakeholder confidence.

Reliability – Trust Is Earned

Reliability is the ability to deliver on one's promises. It represents operational excellence in execution.

Investors measure reliability by a company's ability to achieve its quarterly targets. If the company falters and misses its numbers for consecutive quarters, confidence begins to wane, and investors are apt to sell their shares or avoid investing further unless they believe there is additional value in the company that will be realized.

For customers, reliability means the ability of the company to deliver products on time, to the promised specifications, and with high quality. When products are late (especially unpredictably late), lack features that were promised, and have poor quality or supply shortages, it creates significant losses for customers. To give you an idea of the magnitude of such problems, the auto industry suffered a $110 billion loss due to chip shortages in 2021.[153] This is a large number, but it's not surprising when you learn that modern cars have several hundred chips each and millions of lines of software. Cars are computers on wheels.

In 2010, EA Sports had planned to launch their highly anticipated NBA Elite 11 video game for the PS3 and Xbox 360 game consoles. However, due to issues, they kept delaying the release of the game,[154] and their competitor 2K Sports released NBA 2K11, which went on to become arguably the best basketball video game on the market.[155] I know this story only because my son, an avid gamer, pre-ordered NBA Elite 11 and was refunded his money due to the delays. The NBA 2K series of releases became a monopoly for the next five years and still commands a very loyal and large clientele.

Reliability is about securing trust and confidence. When trust breaks down, it causes long-term damage to the relationship, even if the supplier compensates the customer. Trust is a funny thing; you can go years being an excellent supplier and then have an issue, and trust invariably gets reset. I liken this to squeezing lime juice into milk. The milk curdles and cannot become milk again.

In a high-school American-football team, a player keeps pestering the coach for playing time. Yet, every time the player is put into the game, he fumbles the ball, picks up penalties, fails to tackle opponents, and drops easy passes. This creates a confidence issue with his team-mates and coach, making it less likely that the player will continue getting game time. If the player does get more game time, teammates will avoid passing him the ball. In this example, the player is the supplier, and the coach and team are the customer.

Just as employees are asked to deliver, management must also deliver on their promises. A company could lose money despite good product creation because the management did not invest in product delivery, marketing, and sales channels, or exhibited poor governance, leading to execution issues and poor results. This results in lost employee bonuses, withering stock value, and, in the worst case, layoffs. It is hard for employees facing such a scenario to maintain trust, and the top employees are liable to be the first to leave as such signs of trouble emerge.

Reliability is the cornerstone for building trust and confidence among stakeholders. It essentially means you consistently do what you say you will do.

Innovation – Building Excitement and Moats

Innovation brings advantages that can create a better future for companies. Companies that innovate can change the game, bring disruptions, and extend their lead over their competitors. Constant innovation reinforces that the company has a culture of challenging the status quo, regularly inventing something new. It underscores the company's ability to remain a leader by predicting, intersecting, or creating new market trends. Innovations add that extra magic to building confidence among stakeholders.

Between 1998 and 2010, Apple launched a wave of innovative products: iMac, iPod, iTunes, iPhone, iStore, and iPad. Those innovations turned a languishing company into one of the top five brands in the world. The leading companies on the S&P 500 index as of July 2020 were Apple, Microsoft, Amazon, Facebook, and Alphabet (Google).[156] Each one of these is a high-tech company that has grown by innovation in products and business models. Interestingly, Microsoft, Apple, Amazon, and Google all featured in the top fifteen companies with the most granted patents in 2019, validating their innovation prowess.[157]

Warren Buffett is credited with coining the term *economic moat*, which refers to the ability of a business or company to maintain an advantage over its competitors to protect its long-term profits and market share.[158] Moats protect castles. The width and depth of this moat is, in my view, created by sustained innovation and execution. Investors value innovation as an important investment factor, as they believe innovative companies are more resistant to attack from competitors.

Innovation can disrupt industries.

Clayton Christensen writes about disruptive innovation in his thought-provoking book *The Innovator's Dilemma: When New Technologies Cause Great Firms to Fail.*[159] A compelling point he makes is that, often, a disruptive innovation comes from the low end of the market, making it accessible to a large population of consumers who previously had no access because of a price barrier. When innovation drops the price barrier, it drives wider-spread acceptance. Cellphones and mini-steel mills are two examples he provides. Mini-steel mills rose by being able to process scrap metal instead of raw iron ore to produce low-cost steel products.

In 2007, I attended a company management conference where a professor from Harvard Business School coached us on change management. I recall a question posed to him regarding what constituted Harvard's biggest threat. The professor said University of Phoenix—an online educational program. Today, there are so many online educational programs and resources that many students prefer these to sitting in a classroom. Furthermore, during the COVID-19 pandemic

(2019–2021), classes were primarily offered online, via Zoom or similar platforms. This trend begged the questions: how will we learn over the next decade, and what disruptions or opportunities will it bring to global education?

Customers like innovation because it adds a competitive dimension to their products that adds value and brings them success.

In the early 2000s, Motorola's cellphone division was losing money and not growing. Then, they launched the iconic Razr in 2004. It was a best-seller—the thinnest clamshell phone.[160] While I applaud the engineers and industrial designers for conceiving this product, I doubt whether this slim phone would have been possible had Foxconn not been able to produce the keypad from a single laser-etched metal wafer. This manufacturing innovation enabled the iconic phone that revived a flagging company.

Thinking into the future, imagine how self-repairing concrete will transform the construction industry. Concrete is the second most-consumed substance in the world after water.[161] Concrete shrinks when it hardens, and then cracks. Innovations are underway that add certain materials, dormant bacteria, and capsules containing liquids to concrete. When the concrete cracks, so do the capsules, releasing the liquids, which interact with other added materials or dormant bacteria to create compounds that plug the cracks. Won't construction companies just love this innovation?

Employees also like working for innovative companies because they get to work on new technologies, solve challenging problems, learn, and grow.

People often ask me which company and department, throughout my long career, I most enjoyed working at and why. I have enjoyed every one of the companies and departments at which I worked, but none more so than Ericsson Research. During my tenure, we went through two recessions, and during each, the company decided to double down and invest in R&D instead of cutting costs—an engineer's paradise. Management's logic was to emerge from the recession stronger, and we did. During this time, our team of engineers pioneered core technology for 2G, 3G, and 4G cellular products, invented Bluetooth, and devised a mobile-satellite system that provides maritime wireless connectivity in Southeast Asia, in addition to many other inventions.

A tough week went as follows: A product line manager urgently approached my team and said he needed to securely load software from a remote PC into phones for a customer or we would have to pay $1 million per week in penalties. It meant we had to develop and implement a special algorithm in a very short time. It was 1994, and I wondered who had agreed to such a work order. Nevertheless, we had a week to invent and implement the solution. The solution was complex, as it required two remote systems to authenticate each other, exchange secret keys, encrypt and transfer the software image, and load it into the phone. And we had to implement the code in a language we were unfamiliar with. Our security expert defined the algorithms. Our software expert learned the language and coded the solution. Our system people verified the solution. It worked, and we did not pay the penalty.

Every week, we had a new set of challenges solving hard technical problems. We tried, failed, and tried again until we had solutions—that is how research goes. We not only got to solve hard system problems with mathematical algorithms, but we had to make our solutions work in products that were sold on the market, bridging theory and practice. This work by twenty research engineers resulted in more than one thousand and five hundred issued patents that generated billions of dollars of licensing revenue for the company. Individuals from this group won the inventor of the year award for ten successive years—a streak that no other team in the company has replicated. And we did not lose a member of our core team for fifteen years. We were a family.

Finally, innovation should not be restricted to technology and products. To stay ahead of the competition, a company should constantly look for new and smarter ways of working in every facet of its operations.

For instance, consider artificial intelligence (AI), which has widespread uses can be leveraged by the human resources department for recruiting and training. As soon as a new job is opened, AI engines can query resumes from a database and alert candidates—this is push versus pull job sourcing. AI-based virtual reality training creates real-life settings and work challenges and allows employees to solve these challenges without having real physical equipment or causing any harm through error. An example is learning to disarm a bomb or fix a high voltage circuit without fear of electrocution.

For a company to protect its future, innovation must be fostered by management as a key ingredient for success through long-term vision, steady funding, encouragement, and recognition of the contributions of innovation.

Engagement – Mutual Reliance

The last of the four factors is engagement. The company needs to be engaged with its stakeholders to provide updates on the company and to answer questions. When stakeholders are informed about the company, there is less uncertainty. Naturally, all public disclosure must be within the legal guidelines to ensure that one does not violate selective disclosure rules.

Companies typically meet with investors and analysts to provide updates on their latest-announced results and answer questions that investors have on these results, as well as questions on topics that need clarification. For example, investors and analysts might need clarity on the business model or product roadmap. Investors will also inquire about technology trends and expect that your company has a strong grasp of these trends and what the competition is doing. Analysts conduct research and write reports that investors study before investing, meaning it is essential that these analysts have a good understanding of your business so they can represent it in the right light. This does not happen without strong engagement with the appropriate industry- and financial-analyst communities.

Companies need to have regular contact with all levels of their customers' management. Sometimes, the company may need to talk to the customer's customer without causing any conflict. The data shared with customers is more detailed than that shared with analysts, as it is also provided under confidential non-disclosure agreements. Customers need to be able to provide feedback on their experience using the product, on its quality and reliability, and on the support they are getting. The company must respond and be fast about solving issues. The fastest way to destroy trust is to be unresponsive. Furthermore, the company must keep customers regularly updated on the company products, roadmaps, innovations, and how they can create better solutions for the customer. When this engagement is tightly coupled and both parties exchange information as freely as possible to find mutually beneficial solutions, the relationship is a partnership and likely solid. When it is one-sided, it shows that the customer has not yet embraced the supplier as a total partner. This company must find out why this is the case and address the issues to foster a closer partnership.

I am reminded of one of our major suppliers who was critical to our business. At our peak, we generated hundreds of millions of dollars in annual sales for this supplier. The head of that business should have engaged actively to grow the relationship with us. Yet every telephone discussion with him was difficult and unaccommodating. I think he took our business for granted, since it would have been very hard for us to switch this supplier's components out of our products. But he forced our hand, and our entire company invested enormous time to find an alternative. Such was my employees' resolve. Surprisingly, he felt betrayed when we switched to another competent supplier.

It is equally important to engage with employees meaningfully. I stressed this in chapters four and eight with regard to building culture and execution. Management must engage with employees to share the vision and strategy, get alignment, provide and receive feedback, and share success stories to validate the strategy. Engaged employees are more able to help a company because they understand what is going on and what is needed from them to help. Engagement drives a heightened sense of ownership of success and failure. I strongly believe that employees work for people they trust and respect just as much as for the company's brand name.

Financial health brings belief and faith. Reliability builds trust. Innovation brings excitement. And engagement eliminates uncertainty and builds reliance for stakeholders.

If these four factors are properly constructed, the roof of your castle will offer you more protection against risk, sheltering your company from nature's elements and projectiles during enemy attacks.

Summary: Stakeholder Confidence
The Castle Roof

Stakeholder confidence refers to the confidence the company or business instills in its investors, its customers, and its employees, and the corresponding belief/faith, trust, excitement, and reliance that they have in the company. There are four factors that drive this symbiosis:

- Sound financial health and steady performance in terms of revenue and free-cash-flow growth.

- Reliable execution of promises and commitments to the company's stakeholders.

- Innovation in every area of your business to widen your economic moat and bring value to the company's stakeholders (innovation needs a long-term vision, steady funding, encouragement, and recognition of its contributions by management).

- Engagement with the company's stakeholders, regularly providing information, eliminating uncertainty, and building mutual reliance.

We have now built our castle with a framework of eight elements. Within that framework, I have described a set of principles and recipes (models) to build the elements and interlink them. This framework, when all the elements work together, will build resilience in your business.

This is just the beginning. I hope you will enhance this framework and build an epic castle that will serve you and your stakeholders well. Before you begin to do that, I want to introduce you to one last chapter that focuses on personal growth.

Conclusion

Seven Beliefs to Take on Your Career Journey

In the preceding nine chapters, I have described how to build a strong business, incorporating interlinked elements in the form of an analogous castle. I focused on the structure of the castle and how it is built, not the person inside and how that person is built.

As you build your castle, and master each of the eight elements, you should also shape yourself to run the castle.

Personal growth is a lifelong project and a testament to your work ethic, humility, character, and determination. My journey takes me back to humble beginnings. I entered the United States of America in December 1984 to begin my PhD studies with about $100 in my pocket—not too different from many immigrants.

Even with that small amount of money, I felt fortunate in many ways.

Until my stipend kicked in from my scholarship award to cover expenses, I scraped by on $1 lunches from 7-Eleven and slices of fruit cake from my aunt. I would spend 50 cents to catch a bus that would take me three miles away from the house where I was staying, and I would walk the rest of the way. Most days, people would feel sorry for this young student walking, and they would give me a ride. Things fell into place after that. But even as my circumstances improved, I remained hungry.

I never imagined that thirty-five years later, I would be standing on the floor of the NASDAQ at a bell-ringing ceremony, clapping as confetti rained down, my image broadcast on the facade of the NASDAQ building in Times Square. Nor did I ever expect that I would be the first foreign-born chief technology officer of a major mobile-phone company or be selected for any of the leadership roles I have held. Did I have a career plan? No, I did not. I just seized the opportunities I was given, and through this journey over the years, I developed a set of beliefs that I use to advise my mentees and children.

The Seven Beliefs

Each of these beliefs is personal, as much as each person's career journey is. I will leave you with some stories of my career journey to emphasize why these seven beliefs matter to me.

- Dream with conviction.
- Leave your comfort zone.
- Learn from success and failure.
- Deal with adversity.
- Get battle tested.
- Be curious.
- Stay true.

Dream with Conviction

When I first became captivated by mobile phones in the early 1980s and decided to pursue a PhD and career in this area, many a well-wisher advised me that my choice would lead to an uncertain path. They worried that I was severely limiting my future opportunities. A famous consulting company estimated that the market was small, with a million mobile phones being sold by the year 2000. Mobile-phone products in the early 1980s were big, bulky, and needed to be strapped on to humans as backpacks. As such, many did not see their potential. I saw the situation differently—I felt these devices would evolve, as all technology does, and become an indispensable tool for human communications. I am glad I had the conviction to proceed as I did, backed by my MSc and PhD supervisors.

Leave Your Comfort Zone

After I graduated, I began a career in research and got to work beside incredibly talented people who pioneered, innovated, and contributed to building many systems that included the 2G, 3G, and 4G cellular technologies, Bluetooth, and the ACeS mobile-satellite system. Life as a researcher was good, but I did not know how to build the products I researched. As opportunities presented themselves, I volunteered and moved into product development. The first move is the hardest, as it takes a big adjustment to step out of one's comfort zone. You must recalibrate your mindset and rebuild your knowledge base. You need to get used to being the runt in the litter for a while. While initially rough, you soon learn to adapt and build your formula to deal with change. After this initial move, I regularly rotated through different operational areas of a business. Each time, I went through the anxiety of knowing less initially but learning more with time. The breadth and depth of this learning was irreplaceable.

Learn from Success and Failure

As I gained experience, I got opportunities to run businesses and had many successes and some failures. While the memories of success are confidence-boosting, the bitter lessons of failure are enlightening, should you wish to confront and reflect on them. Hindsight is always 20/20 and gives you a perspective of what actions you could have taken to have averted failure. More importantly, I found that success and failure calibrate one's approach, judgment, and decision-making in business.

In my first general manager role at Ericsson, our business grew impressively. After three years of success, we got arrogant. This led to bad decisions on excessive hiring and installing factory capacity for sales that would never materialize. Our costs grew on the back of hubris and imaginary visions of future revenue. I knew we were in trouble but did not speak up at management meetings. I did not have the confidence and did not want to disagree—I wanted to fit in with the pack. Little did I know that it was my voice that was highly respected by the team. That year, we lost over half a billion dollars. This loss was within 2 percent of my prediction. I stepped down from my role to clean up the mess, which took a whole year. Since that disaster, I have never been afraid to voice my reservations on decisions that I felt would lead to a bad outcome.

Deal with Adversity

To use a baseball term, you will face many curveballs in your life. Getting rejected for the job you were perfect for, being overlooked for a promotion despite excelling and delivering on all your commitments, dealing with bias or unprofessional behavior, coming up with a great idea only to have someone else steal it and get credit, or making a major error on a project you were entrusted to deliver are some examples of challenges people face or have faced at work.

Curveballs can embarrass you, freeze you in place, or make you look foolish. They may get you out, but it is important to focus on your next inning and your next at-bat. The only way to deal with setbacks is to look forward, not back. My wife of thirty years wisely told me that nothing in life goes only uphill; at some point, it must go in your favor. Your attitude when facing adversity matters. It is difficult to embrace and overcome adversity, but the way you handle it builds character. When faced with adversity, deal with it or walk away from it, but never let it swallow you.

I remember the wisdom in the words of a professor friend of mine when dealing with disappointment. He told me: "When your plate is full of sandwiches, it is okay if someone takes a couple. You need to get upset if you only had one sandwich on your plate and someone took it." I translated this as: in life you are going to create and get many opportunities; chase them, and don't dwell on what you lost.

However, there were times when I struggled at work dealing with difficult situations and hard problems, but hanging in there taught me about myself and the weaknesses I had to overcome, and when I did, success came. I have also walked away from jobs that rewarded me handsomely when I felt that I could not be successful in my environment despite the best I could give. Never trade your reputation for money.

Get Battle-Tested

I loved cricket more than any sport I played, and I learned many lessons from it. No amount of practice mattered as much as results in an actual game. Time in the middle, playing the game against formidable opponents, allows one to get battle-tested and face the pressure to perform when it matters. Business is no different, and my best learning was on the job, getting results.

At GE Corporate Research, our customer Ericsson contracted me to design an algorithm called an equalizer to combat echoes that distorted wireless signals. We had one year to deliver the design. This algorithm had to go into a phone and work in real-life scenarios. This problem had not been solved before, so there was no reference. Unlike grad school, there was no passing grade for hard work or partial success—either we solved the problem and succeeded, or we failed and might not get another contract for design. We did succeed and gave our customer a few algorithms that solved the problem. Our work was appreciated. For me, it was a year of great learning through ideas and experimentation and creation of a process to solve hard problems. It was also the launch of a fantastic career—we continued to get contracts, and a few years later, Ericsson hired me and my entire team from GE. I wonder if this is any different from how cricket players around the world are picked for the prestigious Indian premier league (IPL)—it is based on ability and delivery.

You learn most about the game by being a player on the field and not an analyst of the game. I volunteered for tough jobs to test and grow my ability. Every time I volunteered for a tough job, I took comfort in what a mentor told me early in my career: steel is forged by repeatedly heating, beating, and cooling.

As in cricket, only you need to be the judge of your scorecard.

Be Curious

A high-school teacher of mine, a Jesuit priest, once told me that it is my choice to be ignorant or not. For a long time, I have allocated time every day to learning something new. Fortunately, there are many incredible tools in today's world to assist such learning. In this learning, I have never attempted to become an expert about everything but have focused on getting familiar with as many things as possible that could help me be less ignorant. One tip I learned was to jot down, in a notebook, what was unfamiliar to me in my business and to look up the issues or ask someone to teach me. Learning brings knowledge, and knowledge brings confidence. Knowledge commands respect when used appropriately. I have found that knowledge and a can-do attitude breaks down most barriers that inhibit advancement.

Stay True

Believe in yourself because no one will believe in you more. You will need this belief to act decisively when you lead. Listening and learning are essential, but when you are accountable, you must have the courage and conviction to act on your assessment and not on the opinions of others. You—not the myriad of people who gave you their opinions—will be held accountable for the outcome. Remember, a lot of advice is free—but these advisors do not bear the responsibility of a bad outcome, only you do.

Lastly, as a leader, it is not necessary to say popular things to be liked. If you say something, then show you will do it. For years, I have heard leaders talk about inequity in the workplace. It is the politically right thing to say. Take gender equity for example. Do the same leaders take time to mentor the next generation of female leaders? Have they created opportunities for female leaders? Token representation does not count.

It is important to match your actions to your words or, as they say in America, *walk your talk.*

My Closing Thought

Having exhausted what I can offer from my experience, I would like to leave you with one last piece of advice: believe in yourself, do things you enjoy, work with people you respect, and focus on the bright hope that the future always brings.

Appendix

Cash Flow and Financial Terms

This appendix describes the flow of cash in a company. It is written for those unfamiliar with such cash flow and its associated financial terms. You will find detailed descriptions in most financial textbooks and articles.

Figure 1A (see next page) is an illustration of the journey of cash in a company. The way you read Figure 1A is as follows: gray-colored boxes represent cash inflows, white-colored boxes represent cash outflows or usage of cash, and the dual-color gray-and-white boxes represent situations where that box can consume cash (white) or save or generate cash (gray). The arrows show how cash flows through a company via the various boxes, with each box acting as an inlet or outlet valve. An inlet valve brings cash into the company, and an outlet value consumes cash or takes cash out of the company. The difference between all cash-in minus cash-out represents cash flow.

All companies need cash to operate daily and raise money by issuing *stock* (called *equity*) or *bonds* (called *debt*).

A stock or a share gives the buyer (shareholder) the right to partake in any gains in the company's share price and profits (if the company

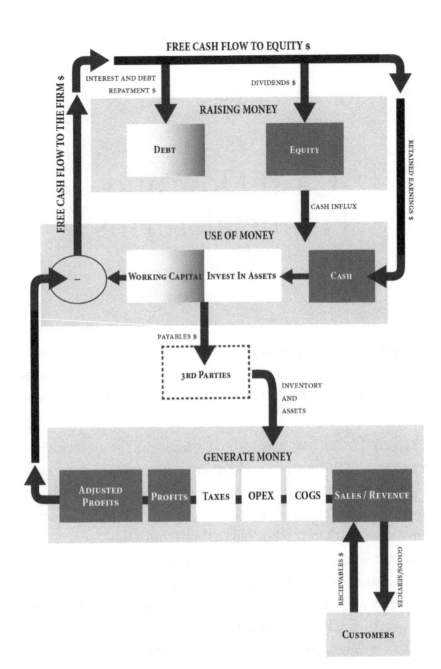

Figure 1A: Journey of Cash in a Business

issues a dividend). If the company does not make a profit or the share price drops, the shareholder does not make money on their investment and can even lose value in their investment. The sum of all shares issued by a company is collectively called equity.

A bond represents a loan that must be paid back. A company sells bonds to buyers (creditors). The company then pays interest on the bonds, at regular intervals of time, for a certain number of years, called the term of the bond. If the company is still solvent at the end of the period, it repays the original price of the bond (called the *face value*) to the bondholder or creditor. If the company goes bankrupt, it is put into what is called *receivership*. Its assets are sold, and the proceeds are distributed to bondholders (creditors) in a certain order based on their relative priorities, as defined by contractual terms (*covenants*).

Typically, stocks and bonds are issued in *capital markets*, where investors buy these financial instruments depending on how attractive the company is to them. If the company is risky, investors will expect a higher return on their investment. Return and risk are captured by a formula called the *weighted average cost of capital*, which we labeled as W in this book. The weighted average cost of capital is the proportionally weighted sum of the interest rate on the bonds and the return expected on the equity. For example, if you raised $1 million by issuing $400,000 in bonds (40 percent of total) at an interest rate of 4 percent, and $600,000 (60 percent of total) in equity with an expected rate of return of 8 percent, then your weighted average cost of capital is 40 percent times 4 percent plus 60 percent times 8 percent = 6.4 percent. The interest rate on the bond is called the *cost of debt*, and the return rate expected on the equity is called *cost of equity*.

Once companies have raised cash, they can put it to use. Companies use this cash to buy or lease assets (such as buildings), buy raw materials to create products, buy equipment to manufacture products, pay vendors/suppliers, hire employees, and pay salaries, and spend on travel for business purposes. They may even use the cash to make investments in other companies.

The company maintains a statement called the *balance sheet* that records how the company has used the money it has raised. Essentially, this statement records *assets, liabilities,* and *shareholder equity.* An asset is anything the company owns that can be sold for cash. Liabilities are what the company owes others. Shareholder equity represents the money raised by the company by issuing shares. In any balance sheet, the assets will equal the sum of liabilities and shareholder's equity.

Companies create products, which are sold to realize *revenue.* When companies sell products, they typically get paid only after thirty to ninety days (it could be even longer depending on the customer's negotiation power). This is important to understand. The company can recognize revenue as soon as it sells products, but it does not receive cash until later. This pending receipt of cash for the products sold is called *accounts receivable* (AR).

Companies buy raw materials/components and manufacture products. The cost associated with producing a product is called the *cost of goods sold* (COGS). Companies pay suppliers for these materials and manufacturing services. Typically, companies negotiate to pay as late as possible. These pending payments that are owed to suppliers are called *accounts payable* (AP).

When you subtract the cost of goods sold from revenue, the company realizes a *gross margin* (GM). This gross margin is also called *gross profit.* Companies have operating expenses such as salaries for employees, rent for office space, utilities, equipment used by employees (computers, telephones, engineering equipment), travel, food, etc. The company subtracts its *operating expenses* (OPEX) from this gross margin to realize an *operating profit or operating income.*

From this operating income, the company pays taxes to the government. What is left after all these transactions is *profit* in Figure 1A. This profit (positive or negative) results from the daily workings of the company, or *operations.*

The calculation of profit from operations needs to be adjusted because it contains some *non-cash items*. The biggest item is typically depreciation and amortization. When a company buys an asset, such as engineering equipment, it pays cash, and this is called a capital expense (CAPEX). This CAPEX is then depreciated in equal chunks over a period (e.g., five years). Depreciation and amortization are included in operating expenses (OPEX). Because this inclusion is not real cash but an accounting treatment, all non-cash items need to be added back to the profit from operations to calculate true cash flow. Recall that OPEX (which includes depreciation and amortization) is subtractive to profit. Thus, to remove this dilutive effect of depreciation and amortization on the cash flow, it must be added back. The resultant value is called the *adjusted profit* in Figure 1A.

For completeness, there are two other non-cash items, and those are stock-based compensation and deferred taxes. Stock-based compensation is compensation provided to employees as incentives. This is not paid out until some future date. As such, it is a non-cash item.

Taxes need to be paid on cash received by the company. Recall that the company can recognize revenue in a period but may collect the associated cash later. Because the financial reporting period for a company is fixed, there may be a gap between when it recognizes its revenue and cash received. As such, its tax payment in a period may fluctuate depending on cash collected. This tax adjustment falls into a bucket called deferred tax.

Finally, the company needs a pot of cash to fund its day-to-day operations because it must buy raw material, build products, pay employees and suppliers, hold products in storage (inventory), pay taxes, and so on, until it can sell products and collect cash from the sale. This pot of cash is called *working capital*. If working capital usage increases from the prior period, you need more cash (a positive number). If it decreases, you need less cash (a negative number).

The company can also use cash to make investments in assets such as equipment (CAPEX).

The changes in working capital and investment in assets are subtracted from the adjusted profit. The cash that remains is *free cash flow to the firm (FCFF)*, as shown in Figure 1A.

There are two important cash flows from an operational perspective:

- FCFF: Free cash flow to the firm
- FCFE: Free cash flow to equity.

Free cash flow to the firm (FCFF) defines how much cash is generated from the operations of the company after paying taxes. This calculation specifically excludes interest payments on the debt as well as any repayment of the debt.

Free cash flow to equity (FCFE) defines the cash that remains after paying interest on debt and any repayment of debt. From this remaining cash, namely FCFE, the company can choose to pay dividends to shareholders. The cash that remains is called *retained earnings*. Hence, retained earnings is cash generated by company operations minus all interest payments to creditors and dividend payments to shareholders.

This completes the cycle of how cash flows in a company.

The more retained earnings generated, the healthier the company. However, it is also important to understand how the company invests and spends its retained earnings to generate even more profits and cash.

My recommendation to all business leaders is to focus on both these free-cash-flow measures and maximize them in accordance with the Golden Rule (as covered in chapter one).

Acknowledgments

Over my thirty-year career, I have worked and interacted with exceptional people who have taught me much and helped me build my knowledge of running businesses. While I have many to thank for my learning, I would especially like to thank the following people:

Most education begins at home, and both my parents laid a solid foundation. My father, Group Captain S. C. Keshu, a retired Indian Air Force officer, was a pioneer of India's jet-aircraft industry and the managing director of a large, state-owned aircraft company. He taught me my earliest lessons in management and leadership—which I did not appreciate until I was put to the test. My mother, Shanthi Keshu, taught me financial prudence and to never be satisfied with the status quo.

Professor David E. Dodds and Professor Someshwar Gupta were my MSc and PhD thesis advisors, respectively. They coached me to think independently and develop my intuition, and they encouraged me to pursue the field I chose with conviction.

Don Puckette took an unknown bet on me and gave me my first job at GE Corporate Research. He mentored me to build and manage my first high-performance team, which was later acquired by Ericsson. He launched my career, for which I am eternally grateful.

Dr. Nils Rydbeck, CTO of Ericsson Mobile Phones, for whom I worked for twelve years, has been a role model, as he was not only an outstanding engineer but a visionary who led by example. He rotated me through every aspect of the business to get a firsthand understanding of how a complex machine is run. He made me think with a

360-degree view. He taught me how to deconstruct a difficult problem and solve it in parts to achieve the whole result. And he taught me to learn by keeping an open mind. If I am considered a good engineer and operational leader today, it is because of him.

Katsumi Ihara, president of Sony-Ericsson, who led its turnaround, taught me about strategy, product creation, and most of all, *genba genbutsu*—"go see for yourself." Ihara-san taught me that it is more productive to create a frame and teach your students to paint the picture you want in that frame than it is to paint every picture yourself. His philosophy has guided me immensely for the past eighteen years.

As I contemplated writing this book, I got strong encouragement and help from the following people.

My deep thanks to Professor Vijay Mahajan, the John P. Harbin Centennial Chair in Business at McCombs School of Business, University of Texas at Austin, who encouraged me to write this book and supported me with valuable advice along the way.

I was privileged to have Professor Venkatesh Narayanamurti, the Benjamin Peirce Research Professor of Technology and Public Policy at Harvard Kennedy School and the Founding Dean of Harvard's School of Engineering and Applied Science, review this book and encourage me to publish it.

While I did the writing, this book would not have reached its current form but for Paul Whitlach, Dan Good, Sara Litchfield, Shelley Holloway, and Gregory Brown.

Paul is a renowned executive editor whose substance edits made me rethink and refine parts of my book, plugging gaps, adding examples, and sewing a more connective thread through the chapters.

Dan is a former news editor who has worked for outlets like ABC and NBC News. Collaborating with him as my structural editor was very rewarding—I could not have asked for a better collaborator.

Sara is an author, explorer, and former accountant. Sara's informed read, thoughtful advice, and content edits fine-tuned the book.

Shelley is an accomplished editor and proofreader. Shelley's meticulous copy edits improved the clarity and correctness of my writing.

Gregory Brown is an acclaimed copy editor who added the finishing touches to my book.

Dilip Keshu (CEO of Born Group), my younger brother, and my colleagues Kaivan Karimi, Polly Coons, Sandra Ironside, Rajeev Kathuria, Scott MacMillan, Guy Miasnik, and Eileen Pruette read various drafts of the manuscript and made excellent suggestions for improvements that I incorporated.

I am grateful to my agent Esther Fedorkevich, managing editor Tori Thacher, and the entire Fedd Books team for making this publication a reality after two years of invested effort.

Thanks to Hank Musolf for his detailed fact check of the manuscript and Mathew Leish for his legal review.

Thank you, Sofia Maria Paz, for transforming my raw PowerPoint drawings into professional illustrations.

Without the encouragement and endorsement from all my reviewers, I would not have ventured to publish this book. A heartfelt thanks to all of them.

Sabitha, Mekala, and Sameer, thank you for your patience as I have been lost in this book for over two years. More importantly, thank you for your insights through our discussions of various examples, which helped improve the book immensely. You are the lights of my life and the wind beneath my wings.

Finally, I want to recognize Nobuyuki Idei, Former Chairman and CEO of Sony who I worked for and was the first to endorse my book with these supporting words:

When you combine decades of successful product creation and business transformation experience, you get a book such as this. This carefully crafted book, filled with analogies and examples, is a must-read for every professional who aspires to grow in a company. A priceless collection of insights and practical models to use in running a business.

Sadly, Idei-san passed away on June 6, 2022.

Endnotes

Introduction

1 Guy Hall, "The first cell phone and the origins of modern mobile," Ting Blog, August 24, 2021, https://ting.blog/the-first-cell-phone/.

2 Donald Sull, "Why Good Companies Go Bad," *Harvard Business Review* (July–August 1999), https://hbr.org/1999/07/why-good-companies-go-bad.

3 Becky Kane, "The Science of Analysis Paralysis," Ambition and Balance by Doist, https://blog.doist.com/analysis-paralysis-productivity/.

4 Carmel Lobello, "Carigslist took nearly 1 billion a year away from dying newspapers," The Week, January 11, https://theweek.com/articles/461056/craigslist-took-nearly-1-billion-year-away-from-dying-newspapers#:~:text=%22Your%20average%20newspaper%20in%20the,the%20death%20of%20newspapers..%222015,

5 Michael T. Deane, "Top 6 Reasons New Businesses Fail," Investopedia, February 28, 2020, https://www.investopedia.com/financial-edge/1010/top-6-reasons-new-businesses-fail.aspx#.

6 Chad Otar, "What Percentage OF Small Businesses Fail – And How can You Avoid Being One of Them?", Forbes, Oct 25, 2018, https://www.forbes.com/sites/forbesfinancecouncil/2018/10/25/what-percentage-of-small-businesses-fail-and-how-can-you-avoid-being-one-of-them/?sh=25fd7fbd43b5.

Chapter 1

7 Exploring Castles, 2022 E Morris & Exploring Castles, https://www.exploringcastles.com/castle_designs/motte_and_bailey/.

8 15 Historic Forts from India, Heritage Daily, https://www.heritagedaily.com/2017/05/15-historic-forts-from-india/114819.

9 Amber Fort Guide, Asia Highlights, https://www.asiahighlights.com/india/amber-fort-guide.

10 "What is the cost of obtaining a U.S. patent," University of Louisiana at Lafayette, University Research, accessed June 10, 2022, https://vpresearch.louisiana.edu/faq/what-cost-obtaining-u-s-patent/176#:~:text=The%20full%20cost%20of%20obtaining,USPTO%3B%20filing%20fees%2C%20etc.

11 "How to account for a Patent," Accounting Tools, Accounting CPE Courses and Books, May 19, 2022, https://www.accountingtools.com/articles/how-do-i-account-for-a-patent.html.

Chapter 2

12 David Ross, Editor, "Lindisfarne Castle," Britain Express, https://www.britainexpress.com/counties/northumbria/castles/lindisfarne-castle.htm.

13 Alison Gardner, "From Rubble to Restoration," Oman's Heritage Forts and Castles, Travel with a Challenge, accessed March 20, 2022, https://www.travelwithachallenge.com/?page_id=3819.

14 "Krak des Chevaliers,", Wikipedia referenced Feb 28, 2022, https://en.wikipedia.org/wiki/Krak_des_Chevaliers.

15 Peter Stamper, "Krak des Chevaliers," HistoryHit May 18, 2021, https://www.historyhit.com/locations/krak-des-chevaliers/.

16 Mihail Ghelbur, "Do Castles Have Foundations? In The Castles features and design, https://castletourist.com/do-castles-have-foundations/.

17 Castle Architecture - Walls, Castle and Manor Houses around the World, C&MH 2010-2014, https://www.castlesandmanorhouses.com/.

18 "Burdock Piling," Wikipedia, Accessed April 1, 2022, https://en.wikipedia.org/wiki/Burdock_piling#:~:text=It%20was%20used%20to%20build,are%20filled%20in%20with%20pebbles.

19 How to build a medieval castle: 9 top tips", History Extra, Office Website for the History Magazine and BBC History Revealed, May 26, 2021, https://www.historyextra.com/period/medieval/medieval-castle-how-were-they-built/.

20 Scott T. Taylor II, "Adair, Paul Neal [Red] (1915–2004)," Texas State Historical Association (TSHA) Handbook of Texas, accessed August 6, 2021, https://www.tshaonline.org/handbook/entries/adair-paul-neal-red.

21 Michael Flint, "Cash Flow: The Reason 82% of Small Businesses Fail," Preferred CFO, June 8, 2020, https://www.preferredcfo.com/cash-flow-reason-small-businesses-fail/.

22 MoloLamken LLP, "What's Channel Stuffing and Is it a Crime," 2018, https://www.mololamken.com/knowledge-Whats-Channel-Stuffing-and-Is-It-a-Crime#:~:text=Channel%2Dstuffing%20is%20a%20means,%2C%20in%20fact%2C%20it%20is.

23 GoCardless, "What is invoice factoring and how does it work," August 2020, https://gocardless.com/en-us/guides/posts/what-is-invoice-factoring/.

24 Parsa Saljoughian, "Operating Expense Benchmarks for SaaS Startups (S&M, R&D, G&A), Medium.com, Parsa VC, December 4, 2019, https://medium.com/parsa-vc/operating-expense-benchmarks-for-saas-startups-e49697abf3ed.

25 Rosemary Carlson, "How to Calculate the Cash Conversion Cycle," The balance small business, September 5, https://www.thebalancesmb.com/calculate-cash-conversion-cycle-3931152019.

26 Terry Collins, "COVID-19 impact: Work from home more appealing than return to 'business as usual,' Harvard survey shows," *USA Today*, updated March 25, 2021, https://www.usatoday.com/story/tech/2021/03/25/covid-remote-work-office-return-survey-zoom-meeting-fatigue/6989446002/.

Chapter 3

27 "Great Wall of China," Editors of the Encyclopedia Britannica, Accessed March 26, 2022, https://www.britannica.com/topic/Great-Wall-of-China.

28 Rashmi S., "Kumbalgarh Fort Rajasthan – story of an invincible fort," Blog, Beyonder Travel, Accessed March 26, 2022, https://beyonder.travel/india/west-central-india/kumbhalgarh-fort/.

29 "8 Oldest Castles in the World", Oldest.org, https://www.oldest.org/structures/castles/.

30 Juliana LaBianca, "17 Wild Secrets Yo Never Knew About Windsor Castle", Readers Digest, Jan 4, 2022, https://www.rd.com/list/secrets-windsor-castle/#:~:text=Windsor%20Castle%20is%20officially%20one,are%20visible%20from%20every%20approach.

31 Harish Satwani, "18ᵗʰ Century Tunnel at Amber Fort- A Secret," Jaipur City Blog, April 6, 2017, https://www.jaipurcityblog.com/18th-century-tunnel-at-amber-fort-a-secret/#:~:text=Amer%20fort%20has%20a%20secret,not%20open%20for%20some%20reasons.

32 Sun Tzu, "The Art of War," North Chelmsford, MA: Courier Corporation, 2012.

33 "Wayne Gretzky takes part in BlackBerry Passport smartphone launch," *CityNews*, September 24, 2014, https://toronto.citynews.ca/2014/09/24/wayne-gretzky-takes-part-in-blackberry-passport-smartphone-launch/.

34 Stephen Edelstein, "The Ford GT Has More Lines of Code Than A Boeing Passenger Jet," *Motor Authority*, May 14, 2015, https://www.motorauthority.com/news/1098308_the-ford-gt-has-more-lines-of-code-than-a-boeing-passenger-jet.

35 Greg Neuman, "More Auto Computers Means More Complicated, Costly and Longer Repairs," *CEI Network*, August 18, 2016, https://www.ceinetwork.com/cei-blog/auto-computers-means-complicated-costly-longer-repairs/.

36 Eric Walz, "BlackBerry Reaches Deal to Supply Jaguar Land Rover with Automotive Technology," Future Car, March 22, 2018, https://www.futurecar.com/2068/BlackBerry-Reaches-Deal-to-Supply-Jaguar-Land-Rover-with-Automotive-Technology.

37 "Cloud Access Secuity Brokers (CASBs)," Gartner Glossary, https://www.gartner.com/en/information-technology/glossary/cloud-access-security-brokers-casbs#:~:text=Cloud%20access%20security%20brokers%20(CASBs)%20are%20on%2Dpremises%2C,cloud%2Dbased%20resources%20are%20accessed.

38 Joseph Carlsmith, "How Much Computational Power Does It Take to Match the Human Brain," *Open Philanthropy*, September 11, 2020, https://www.openphilanthropy.org/brain-computation-report.

39 Elizabeth Jackson, "History of food delivery and ho its changed," Thistle thoughts, https://www.thistle.co/learn/thistle-thoughts/history-of-food-delivery-and-how-its-changed#:~:text=1995%3A%20World%20Wide%20Waiter%20goes,offered%20home%20or%20office%20delivery.

40 Zahava Dalin-Kaptzan, "Food Delivery: Industry Trends for 2022 and beyond," Bringg, https://www.bringg.com/blog/delivery/food-delivery-industry-trends/.

41 Statista, "Online food delivery market size worldwide from 2019-2023," May 2020, https://www.statista.com/statistics/1170631/online-food-delivery-market-size-worldwide/#:~:text=The%20market%20size%20of%20the,the%20measures%20to%20contain%20it.

42 Joe Thompson, "A Concise History of the Quartz Watch Revolution," Bloomberg, November 16, 2017, https://www.bloomberg.com/news/articles/2017-11-16/a-concise-history-of-the-quartz-watch-revolution.

43 Norma Buchanan, "The American Time Guide to Quartz Watches," Capetown Diamond, accessed August 6, 2021, http://www.capetowncorp.com/whatsnew/quartz.html.

44 Adi Robertson, "The Last Scan," *The Verge*, February 6, 2018, https://www.theverge.com/2018/2/6/16973914/tvs-crt-restoration-led-gaming-vintage.

45 Renee Mauborgne and W. Chan Kim, "Blue Ocean Strategy," Harvard Business Review Press, 2004, 2015 (expanded edition).

46 "TikTok Statistics" – Updated March 2022, Wallaroo, March 8, 2022, https://wallaroomedia.com/blog/social-media/tiktokstatistics/#:~:text=U.S.%20Audience%20E2%80%93%20As%20we%20mentioned,between%20the%20ages%2025-44.

47 Lauren Thomas, "Peloton says recent spike in Covid-19 cases, lockdowns are boosting sales," *CNBC*, updated November 5, 2020, https://www.cnbc.com/2020/11/05/peloton-says-recent-spike-in-covid-19-cases-lockdowns-boosting-sales.html.

48 Maghan Mcdowell, "Farfetch revenue rises 35 percent to $2.3 billion," Vogue Business, 25 Feb, 2022, https://www.voguebusiness.com/companies/farfetch-revenue-rises-35-per-cent#:~:text=Farfetch%20said%20revenue%20rose%2035,White%20parent%20New%20Guards%20Group.

49 FarFetch Website, March 4, 2022, https://www.farfetchinvestors.com/home/default.aspx.

50 Suzanne Rowan Kelleher, "A Budget Hotel Chain That You've Never Heard Of Is Exploding in the United States," Forbes, Oct 24, 2019, https://www.forbes.com/sites/suzannerowankelleher/2019/10/24/a-budget-hotel-chain-that-youve-never-heard-of-is-exploding-in-the-united-states/?sh=4c4d12d05259.

51 "The Ten Biggest Hotel Chains in the World," The Business Standard, March 4, 2022, https://www.tbsnews.net/features/explorer/10-biggest-hotel-chains-world-303262.

52 Ritesh Pathak, "The Success Story of OYO," Analytic Steps, Dec 7, 2021, https://www.analyticssteps.com/blogs/success-story-oyo-rooms.

53 S. O'Dea, "Smartphones sales worldwide 2007-2021," Statista, March 31, 2021, https://www.statista.com/statistics/263437/global-smartphone-sales-to-end-users-since-2007/.

54 Carl Franzen, "The History of the Walkman: 35 Years of Iconic Music Players," *The Verge*, July 1, 2014.

55 Clancy Morgan, Irene Ana Kim, and Lisa Eadicicco, "The Rise and Fall of the iPOD," *Insider*, Nov 17, 2020.

56 Tom Eisenmann, "Why Start-ups Fail," *Harvard Business Review* (May–June 2021), https://hbr.org/2021/05/why-start-ups-fail.

57 Jesus Diaz, "One of the decade's most hyped robots send its farewell message," *Fast Company*, March 6, 2019, https://www.fastcompany.com/90315692/one-of-the-decades-most-hyped-robots-sends-its-farewell-message.

58 William Gallagher, "Newton launched August 2, 1993 setting the stage for what would become the iPad and iPhone," Apple Insider, August 2, 2018, https://appleinsider.com/articles/18/08/02/newton-launched-august-2-1993-setting-the-stage-for-what-would-become-the-ipad-and-iphone.

59 "Apple Launches iPad," Apple Newsroom, January 27, 2010, https://www.apple.com/newsroom/2010/01/27Apple-Launches-iPad/.

60 "The Story of One of the Most Memorable Marketing Blunders Ever," The Coca-Cola Company, accessed August 7, 2021, https://www.coca-colacompany.com/company/history/the-story-of-one-of-the-most-memorable-marketing-blunders-ever.

61 "A Robotic Dog's Mortality," *The New York Times*, June 17, 2015, https://www.nytimes.com/2015/06/18/technology/robotica-sony-aibo-robotic-dog-mortality.html.

62 Annie Nova, "10 unlikely products that made millions of dollars," *CNBC*, updated December 11, 2017, https://www.cnbc.com/2017/12/11/10-unlikely-products-that-made-millions-of-dollars.html.

63 "Over a Billion Mobile Phones Sold in 2007," *TechCrunch*, February 27, 2008, https://techcrunch.com/2008/02/27/over-a-billion-mobile-phones-sold-in-2007/.

64 Richard Cuthbertson et al., "Apple and Nokia: The Transformation from Product to Services" Essay. In *Innovating in a Service-Driven Economy: Insights, Application and Practice* (Palgrave Macmillan, 2015), https://www.doi.org/10.1057/9781137409034_9.

65 Fred Vogelstein, "The Day Google Had to 'Start Over' on Android," *The Atlantic*, December 18, 2013, https://www.theatlantic.com/technology/archive/2013/12/the-day-google-had-to-start-over-on-android/282479/.

66 Eric Zeman, "Android Dominates Smartphone Market With 85% Share," *EE Times*, August 15, 2014, https://www.eetimes.com/android-dominates-smartphone-market-with-85-share/#.

67 Matt Rosoff, "Former Microsoft Zune Boss Explains Why it Flopped," *Business Insider,* May 11, 2012, https://www.businessinsider.com/robbie-bach-explains-why-the-zune-flopped-2012-5.

68 Rodora Garcia, "MeeGo Operating System: Everything You Have to Know," Cellular News, March 18, 2020, https://cellularnews.com/mobile-operating-systems/meego-operating-system-everything-you-have-to-know/.

69 Ed Bott, "Microsoft 365 (formerly Office 365) for business: Everything you need to know," ZD Net, April 28, 2020, https://www.zdnet.com/article/microsoft-office-365-for-business-everything-you-need-to-know/.

70 Thomas Aslop, "PC Graphics processing unit (GPU) shipment share worldwide from 2nd quarter 2009 to 3rd quarter 2021 by vendor," *Statista,* November 2021, https://www.statista.com/statistics/754557/worldwide-gpu-shipments-market-share-by-vendor/.

71 "F-16 Fighting Falcon," Lockheed Martin, accessed August 7, 2021, https://www.lockheedmartin.com/en-us/products/f-16.html.

72 Yen Nee Lee, "2 charts show how much the world depends on Taiwan for semiconductors," *CNBC*, March 15, 2021, https://www.cnbc.com/2021/03/16/2-charts-show-how-much-the-world-depends-on-taiwan-for-semiconductors.html.

73 Govinda Bhutada, The Top 10 Semiconductor Companies by Market Share," Visual Capitalist, December 14, 2021, https://www.visualcapitalist.com/top-10-semiconductor-companies-by-market-share/.

74 "Revenue of Costco Worldwide from 2017-2021, by region," Statista, Feb 11, 2002, https://www.statista.com/statistics/1109288/global-revenue-of-costco-by-region/.

75 "History," Lululemon, accessed August 7, 2021, https://info.lululemon.com/about/our-story/history.

76 Brand Minds, "Why Did Kodak Fail and What Can You Learn from its Demise?", December 14, 2018, https://brand-minds.medium.com/why-did-kodak-fail-and-what-can-you-learn-from-its-failure-70b92793493c

Chapter 4

77 "donjon," Merriam-Webster, accessed August 6, 2021, https://www.merriam-webster.com/dictionary/donjon.

78 "Chateau de Vincennes Donjon – near Paris," Travel France Online, Accessed March 30, 2022https://www.travelfranceonline.com/chateau-de-vincennes-donjon-near-paris/#:~:text=The%20Donjon%20de%20Vincennes%20is,jail%20at%20the%20French%20Revolution.

79 "The Castle Keep," Ancientfortresses.org, October 2021, http://www.ancientfortresses.org/castle-keep.htm.

80 "Keep,", Wikipedia, accessed March 21, 2022, https://en.wikipedia.org/wiki/Keep.

81 Kidadl Team, "Fascinating Himeji Castle Facts: The Japanese Castle Complex," March 3, 2022, https://kidadl.com/fun-facts/fascinating-himeji-castle-facts-the-japanese-castle-complex.

82 "Himeji Castle," Wikipedia, accessed March 26, 2022, https://en.wikipedia.org/wiki/Himeji_Castle.

83 Gokhan Guley and Tracy Reznik, "Culture Eats Strategy for Breakfast and Transformation for Lunch," *The Jabian Journal* (Fall 2019), https://journal.jabian.com/culture-eats-strategy-for-breakfast-and-transformation-for-lunch/.

84 Lawrence Bossidy and Ram Charan, *Execution: The Discipline of Getting Things Done*. Crown Business (New York, NY: Random House, 2002).

85 Evan Andrews, "What Was the Gordian Knot?" History, updated August 29, 2018, https://www.history.com/news/what-was-the-gordian-knot.

86 Linus Torvalds, "Message to linux-kernel mailing list," August 25, 2000, https://lkml.org/lkml/2000/8/25/132.

87 Diane Hamilton, "Measuring Perception At Work Involves IQ, EQ And CQ," *Forbes*, December 2019, https://www.forbes.com/sites/forbescoachescouncil/2019/12/04/measuring-perception-at-work-involves-iq-eq-and-cq/?sh=73f33ee55226.

88 Clark. J. Wyatt, "From Janitor to CEO: The Ultimate Rags to Riches Story," *Business Barrage*, October 10, 2019, https://businessbarrage.com/2019/10/10/from-janitor-to-ceo-the-ultimate-rags-to-riches-story/.

89 Joel Arthur Barker, *Paradigms: Business of Discovering the Future* (New York, NY: Harper Collins, 1993).

90 *Invictus*, dir. Clint Eastwood, Warner Bros. Pictures, 133 mins. (2009).

91 Christopher Chabris and Daniel Simons, "The Invisible Gorilla: And Other Ways Our Intuitions Deceive Us, Crown, 2010.

Chapter 5

92 Medieval Chronicles, https://www.medievalchronicles.com/medieval-castles/medieval-castle-parts/murder-holes/.

93 Sony Ericsson Net Sales 2002-2011, Statista Research Department, Jan 19, 2012.

94 "Leading carbonated soft drink (CSD) companies in the United States in 2020, based on volume share, " Statista, July 2021, https://www.statista.com/statistics/225504/leading-carbonated-soft-drink-companies-in-the-us/.

95 José Adorno, "IDC: Apple dominates tablet market in Q1 2021 with 31.7% market share," *9to5Mac*, May 1, 2021, https://9to5mac.com/2021/05/01/idc-apple-tablet-market-ipad/.

96 Hayley Peterson, "Keurig's at-home soda machine was doomed from the start," *Insider*, June 7, 2016, https://www.businessinsider.com/why-keurig-kold-failed-2016-6.

97 Jackie Dove and Kevin Parrish, "Apple Maps vs. Google Maps: Which one is best for you?" Digitaltrends, March 9, 2021, https://www.digitaltrends.com/mobile/apple-maps-vs-google-maps/.

98 "Top 5 Reasons to Drive Electric," Drive Clean, California Air Resources Board, ca.gov, 2021, https://driveclean.ca.gov/top-reasons.

99 Ben Preston and Jeff S. Bartlett, "Automakers Are Adding Electric Vehicles to Their Lineup. Here's What's Coming, Consumer Reports, March 7, 2022, https://www.consumerreports.org/hybrids-evs/why-electric-cars-may-soon-flood-the-us-market.

100 Wolf Richter, "Tesla's Market Cap (Gigantic) v. Next 10 Automakers v. Tesla's Global Market Share (Miniscule)," October 26, 2021, https://wolfstreet.com/2021/10/26/teslas-market-cap-gigantic-v-next-10-automakers-v-teslas-global-market-share-minuscule/.

101 C.E. (Sandy) Thomas, "Fuel Cell and Battery Electric Vehicles Compared," White Paper, H_2Gen Innovations Inc., Alexandra Virginia 22304, https://citeseerx.ist.psu.edu/viewdoc/download?doi=10.1.1.453.7691&rep=rep1&type=pdf.

102 Abhishek Mehra, Balaji P, Saurabh Ranadive, Sarang Bhutada, "Southest Airlines – Just Plane Smart," Harvard Business School- Case Study Summary, Slideshare, Aug 6, 2009, https://www.slideshare.net/sarangbhutada/southwest-airlines-case-study.

103 Southwest Media Web Page, Southwest Corporate Fact Sheet, https://www.swamedia.com/pages/corporate-fact-sheet.

104 The Investopedia Team, "Companies and Products With Outstanding Brand Equity," Reviewed by Somer Anderson, Fact Checked by Suzanne Kvilhauf, December 21, 2021, https://www.investopedia.com/ask/answers/020915/what-are-some-examples-companies-or-products-have-outstanding-brand-equity.asp.

105 Milica Stojanovic, "15 Starbuck Statistics for True Coffee Lovers," Comfy Living, Feb 16, 2022, https://comfyliving.net/starbucks-statistics/.

106 "How often does the average customer visit?", Food News, 2021, Accessed March 15, 2022, https://www.foodnewsnews.com/starbucks/how-often-does-the-average-starbucks-customer-visit/.

107 Bain & Company, "Measuring Your Net Promoters Score," Net Promoter System, https://www.netpromotersystem.com/about/measuring-your-net-promoter-score/.

108 "Samsung Net Promoter Score 2021 Benchmarks," Customer Guru, accessed July 7, 2021, https://customer.guru/net-promoter-score/samsung.

109 "Net Promoter Score Benchmarks for Top Brands," Customer Guru, accessed July 7, 2021, https://customer.guru/net-promoter-score/top-brands.

110 By Abigail, "What is Brand Equity," The Branding Journal, December 8, 2021, https://www.thebrandingjournal.com/2021/02/brand-equity/.

Chapter 6

111 Tuan C. Nguyen, "Who Invented Bluetooth?" *ThoughtCo*, updated February 13, 2021, https://www.thoughtco.com/who-invented-bluetooth-4038864.

112 Jethro Mullen and Mark Thompson, "Samsung takes $10 billion hit to end Galaxy Note 7 fiasco," CNN Business, October 11, 2016, https://money.cnn.com/2016/10/11/technology/samsung-galaxy-note-7-what-next/.

113 Hayley Tsukayama, "How Samsung moved beyond its exploding phones," Washington Post, February 23, 2018, https://www.washingtonpost.com/business/how-samsung-moved-beyond-its-exploding-phones/2018/02/23/5675632c-182f-11e8-b681-2d4d462a1921_story.html.

114 Jordan Novet, "Intel chip shortage is pulling down PC makers' revenue expectations," CNBC, Nov 27, 2019, https://www.cnbc.com/2019/11/27/intel-chip-shortage-pulls-down-pc-makers-revenue-expectations.html.

115 Leo Sun, "4 Red Flags for Intel's Future," *The Motley Fool*, December 13, 2021, https://www.fool.com/investing/2021/12/13/4-red-flags-for-intels-future/.

116 Leo Sun, "Will Intel's "Accelerated" Chipmaking Plans Spell trouble for TSMC?" *The Motley Fool*, August 23, 2021, https://www.fool.com/investing/2021/08/03/will-intel-accelerated-chipmaking-plans-spell-tsmc/.

117 Chaim Gartenberg, "The Summer Intel Fell Behind", July 29, 2021, The Verge, https://www.theverge.com/22597713/intel-7nm-delay-summer-2020-apple-arm-switch-roadmap-gelsinger-ceo

118 Dean Takahashi, "Intel aims to regain chip manufacturing leadership by 2025," VentureBeat, July 26, 2021, https://venturebeat.com/2021/07/26/intel-aims-to-regain-chip-manufacturing-leadership-by-2025/.

119 Michael Treacy and Fred Wiersema, *The Discipline of Market Leaders: Choose Your Customers, Narrow Your Focus, Dominate Your Market* (New York, NY: Basic Books, 1997).

120 David Chancellor, "Case Study: Four companies that failed spectacularly, and the lessons of their demise," CMI. September 17, 2015, https://www.managers.org.uk/knowledge-and-insights/case-study/four-companies-that-failed-spectacularly-and-the-lessons-of-their-premature-demise/.

121 Will Kenton, "Walmart Effect", Investopedia, December 30, 2020, https://www.investopedia.com/terms/w/walmart-effect.asp.

122 Alex Osterwalder, Yves Pigneur, Fredric Etiembe, Alan Smith, "The Invincible Company: How to Constantly reinvent Your Organization with Inspiration from the World's Best Business Models," Wiley, April 14, 2002.

123 Renee Bailey, "How Has MacDonald's Been Successful for So Long," Franchise Direct, March 30, 2020, https://www.franchisedirect.com/information/markettrendsfactsaboutfranchising/thesuccessofmcdonalds/8/1111/.

124 Karthick Nambi, "How the Taj Mahal ruined Shah Jahan and led to the colonization of India," *Medium*, March 31, 2020, https://medium.com/lessons-from-history/how-taj-mahal-ruined-shah-jahan-and-let-to-the-colonization-of-india-e3c6084bbf07.

Chapter 7

125 Simon Thurley, "Where there's a well," Financial Times, September 7, 2012, https://www.ft.com/content/8eae39b8-f1fb-11e1-8973-00144feabdc0.

126 "Castle Well," Wikipedia, Extracted March 15, 2022, https://en.wikipedia.org/wiki/Castle_well#:~:text=Many%20of%20the%20deepest%20castle,into%20basalt%20in%20the%20world.

127 Teacher's Kit Warkworth Castle, English Heritage Education, Page 4, Silo. Tips, https://silo.tips/download/history-warkworth-castle-historical-description-the-early-castle-the-percys-of-n.

128 "About Us," Samsara, accessed August 7, 2021, https://www.samsara.com/company/about.

129 "How Samsara hit $243.0M in Revenue with 15K Customers in 2019," Latka, accessed August 7, 2021, https://getlatka.com/companies/samsara.

130 Yuliya Chernova, "Samsara Raising Money at $6 Billion Valuation," *The Wall Street Journal*, September 9, 2019, https://www.wsj.com/articles/samsara-raising-money-at-6-billion-valuation-11568060581.

131 Katie Roof, "Cloud Tech Firms Samara to File as Soon as March for IPO," Bloomberg, updated February 11, 2021, https://www.bloomberg.com/news/articles/2021-02-11/cloud-tech-firm-samsara-is-said-to-file-as-soon-as-march-for-ipo.

132 Roger Fisher, William L. Ury, and Bruce Patton, *Getting to Yes: Negotiating Agreement Without Giving In* (New York, NY: Penguin Books, 2011).

133 "Push-pull strategy," Wikipedia (referenced Feb 28, 2022), https://en.wikipedia.org/wiki/Push%E2%80%93pull_strategy.

134 Peter, J. Paul, James H Donnelly, "A Preface to Marketing Management," McGraw-Hill Professional, 2002, ISBN 978-0-07-246658-4.

135 Prabhakar Alok, "All About BANT," Ampliz, accessed August 6, 2021, https://www.ampliz.com/resources/bant/.

136 "N.E.A.T Selling™," The Harris Consulting Group, accessed August 6, 2021, https://theharrisconsultinggroup.com/neat-selling/.

137 Bass, Frank M., (1969): "A new product growth for model consumer durables," Management Science, Vol. 15, No. 5, 215-227.

138 Bass, Frank M, Krishnan T, Jain D (1994): "Why the Bass model fits without decision variables," Marketing Science, Vol. 13, No. 3.

139 https://www.itl.nist.gov> pmc > section4 > pmc435.

Chapter 8

140 "Castle Gatehouse: The Strongest Part of any Medieval Castle," Exploring Castles, https://www.exploring-castles.com/castle_designs/gatehouse/.

141 "The Krak des Chevaliers: A tough Nut to Krak," Beyond Bones, January 14, 2018, https://blog.hmns.org/2018/01/the-krak-des-chevaliers-a-tough-nut-to-krak/.

142 Rob Carney, "World's Strongest Castles," Architecture of Cities, May 7, 2020, https://architectureofcities.com/castles.

143 Louis V. Gestner, *Who Says Elephants Can't Dance?* (New York, NY: Harper Business, 2002).

144 *How Lou Gerstner Got IBM To Dance*, Forbes, Nov 11, 2002.

145 Ericsson Annual Reports 1997-1999.

146 Larry E. Greiner, "Evolution and Revolution as Organizations Grow," *Harvard Business Review* (May–June 1998), https://hbr.org/1998/05/evolution-and-revolution-as-organizations-grow.

Chapter 9

147 Dr. Adriana Piccinini Higashino, "Himeji Castle: Design and Meaning of Its Roofs," Architectural Department, Akashi National College of Technology, 679-3 Nishioka, Uozumi-cho, Akashi-shi, Hyogo-ken, 674-850 Japan, https://earoph.org/wp-content/uploads/2020/08/1-3.pdf.

148 Marvin Hull, "Castles of Britain, Roofs," Castle Learning Center, 1995-2019 Castles Unlimited, http://www.castles-of-britain.com/roofs.htm.

149 Shadiversity, "How castles were built/constructed in the medieval period?" YouTube, July 27, 2018, https://www.youtube.com/watch?v=pu3O70GeQFY.

150 "TIMELINE: Key dates in the history of Nortel," Reuters, January 14, 2009, https://www.reuters.com/article/us-nortel-timeline-sb/timeline-key-dates-in-the-history-of-nortel-idUSTRE50D3N120090115.

151 "Nortel Study," Telfer School of Management, University of Ottawa, March 17, 2014, https://sites.telfer.uottawa.ca/nortelstudy/.

152 David Sali, "Nortel did not need to die: Ten years since the collapse that shook Ottawa's tech sector," Ottawa Business Journal, Jan 14, 2019, https://obj.ca/article/nortel-did-not-need-die-ten-years-collapse-shook-ottawas-tech-sector.

153 Paul E. Eisenstein, "Chip shortages could cost automakers up to $110 billion," NBC News, May 14, 2021, https://www.nbcnews.com/business/autos/chip-shortage-could-cost-automakers-110-billion-n1267342.

154 Jon Robinson, "EA Sports Delays 'NBA Elite 11,'" ESPN, September 28, 2010, http://www.espn.com/espn/thelife/videogames/blog/_/name/thegamer/id/5624302.

155 Sam Westmoreland, "NBA 2K11 and The 50 Greatest Sports Games Ever Made," Bleacher Report, October 21, 2010, https://bleacherreport.com/articles/496802-nba-2k11-and-the-50-greatest-sports-games-ever-made.

156 Sergei Klebnikov, "Apple, Microsoft, Amazon, Google, And Facebook Make Up a Record Chunk Of The S&P 500. Here's Why That Might Be Dangerous," Forbes, July 24, 2020, https://www.forbes.com/sites/sergeiklebnikov/2020/07/24/apple-microsoft-amazon-google-and-facebook-make-up-a-record-chunk-of-the-sp-500-heres-why-that-might-be-dangerous/?sh=4791439b4f6b.

157 Ingrid Lunden, "US patents hit record 333,530 granted in 2019; IBM, Samsung (not the FAANGs) lead the pack," TechCrunch, January 14, 2020, https://techcrunch.com/2020/01/14/us-patents-hit-record-333530-granted-in-2019-ibm-samsung-not-the-faangs-lead-the-pack/.

158 Akhilesh Ganti, "Economic Moat," Investopedia, updated March 21, 2020, https://www.investopedia.com/terms/e/economicmoat.asp/.

159 Clayton M. Christensen, The Innovator's Dilemma: When New Technologies Cause Great Firms to Fail (Harvard, MA: Harvard Business School Press, 1997).

160 Mark Wilson, "The secret history of the Motorola Razr, the first great phone of the millennium," Fast Company, December 9, 2019, https://www.fastcompany.com/90435781/the-secret-history-of-the-motorola-razr-the-millenniums-first-great-phone.

161 "Concrete Facts," Concrete Helper, accessed August 6, 2021, http://concretehelper.com/concrete-facts/.